Step Right Up!
...I'm Gonna Scare the Pants Off America

Step Right Up!
the Pants

...I'm Gonna Scare Off America

by WILLIAM CASTLE

G. P. Putnam's Sons, New York

DEDICATED TO MY THREE GIRLS

Ellen, Georgie, Terry

and

The thousands of kids whom I
have scared the daylights out of,
who now have kids that I hope
I can continue to scare the daylights out of.

Credits for photo insert: p. 1: Photo by Leland Cheong, Honolulu Advertisers, Honolulu, Hawaii. p. 5: Top right, Castle with Price, and left, Castle with "Mr. Sardonicus," still photographs courtesy of Columbia Pictures, a Division of Columbia Pictures Industries, Inc. p. 8: Top, Castle in *Day of the Locust,* photo copyright © 1974 by Long Road Productions. All rights reserved.

SBN: 399–11470–X

Library of Congress Cataloging in Publication Data
Castle, William.
  Step right up!

  1. Castle, William. I. Title.
PN1998.A3C335   791.43'0232'0924   [B]   75-43519

Excerpts from *Rosemary's Baby* by Ira Levin © 1967 by Ira Levin. Reprinted by permission of the publisher, Random House, Inc.

PRINTED IN THE UNITED STATES OF AMERICA

CONTENTS

PART I

Adventures of the Spider Boy

Chapter I

The Spider Boy

A CLOCK was projected on the screen, its single large hand stationary on zero. As my voice came over the sound track, the hand began to move, ticking off the seconds—5 . . . 10 . . . 15 . . . 20 . . .

"Ladies and gentlemen—when the clock reaches sixty seconds, you will be insured by Lloyds of London for one thousand dollars against death by fright. Lloyds of London sincerely hopes none of you will collect. . . . But just in case, isn't it comforting to know that your loved ones are protected. You are now insured against death by fright!"

It has always amazed and baffled me that audiences will wait patiently in line and pay money to have the wits scared out of them. I once took a poll, but the answers were varied and inconsistent: "I just like to be frightened." "I want to scream." "It gives me a thrill." "I want to hang on to my boyfriend." I think the real answer lies deep within each one of us, and starts with our childhood fears. Sitting in a darkened theatre, watching a horror film, we suspend disbelief, confident that we're not screaming for our own lives. The nightmare is happening to somebody else. Alfred Hitchcock, the master, likened the suspense and horror picture to a wild ride on a roller coaster—excitement, screams, thrills, without any real danger.

I was first infected with that kind of fear when I was about

9

six. My father had taken me to my first play, a horror piece called *The Monster*. DeWolf Hopper played the madman. Sitting in the darkened theatre, I clutched my father's hand in abject terror, finally embarrassing the hell out of him by wetting myself during the second act. In consternation, he pulled me up the aisle toward the men's room, but it was too late.

As kaleidoscopic bits of my childhood slowly come into focus, I remember I was frightened most of the time, but never knew why. I was clumsy, awkward, withdrawn and unable to make friends. When I was nine years old my parents decided to send me to camp.

"Too much 'mother,'" my father declared. I resisted, but off I went, bag and baggage, to Camp Pontiac. My first night away from home was spent in tears of self-pity. Then, came rejection by my fellow campers when they found out I was too clumsy to take part in their daily sports. Unable to play baseball or basketball, even unable to swim, I was good for nothing.

My name was William Schloss, Jr., which didn't help matters any. They called me "Schlupps," "Slush," "Schlumps," and the more they kidded me, the more I hated myself.

One afternoon, the boy in bunk number two looked at me with utter disdain. "You're worth nothing, 'Slush,' absolutely nothing." The others loudly agreed. Silent, I sat on the edge of my bunk, feeling miserable. Then slowly I began to put my legs around my neck. I was double-jointed—my one claim to fame. When my feet touched behind my neck, I looked up in defiance. The boy in bunk number two gasped in awe. "Look, 'Schlupps' is a spider!"

Camp Pontiac held its annual circus on the baseball field.

"Ladies and gentlemen—step right up. Witness the marvelous feat of 'The Spider.' Unbelievable! Spine-chilling! . . ."

As the boy in the barker's outfit screamed, I waited for my cue. Dressed in black, I slowly walked out on the small stage, my heart pounding. Putting my legs around my neck, my toes touching, I felt a hush fall over the crowd, then thunderous applause. That night became an emotional breakthrough. I was no longer alone and frightened. I was special—who else in the entire camp could do what I did? I was the star performer—"The Spider Boy."

The following year, my mother suddenly died—pneumonia. I tried to cry at the funeral, but the tears wouldn't come. My mother was still alive; they were burying someone else, not my mother. A year later, my father died—a coronary. At the funeral, again I couldn't cry. I wanted to, but couldn't. I felt nothing—it wasn't really happening.

My only sister, Mildred, eleven years older, had just gotten married. I went to live with her and slept on the living-room couch. Frustrated and filled with resentment, I built a defensive covering, sealing it with a false bravado, allowing no one ner me. Constantly, I went out of my way to prove myself to someone—anyone.

Starving for recognition and applause, one night, on a dare, I stripped to the waist and decided to swim the Hudson River. A group of gawkers gathered to watch. Bowing to the spectators, I plunged into the icy waters. The other side looked a long way off, but I was determined to make it. People on the shore screamed their excitement and applauded my stupidity.

Suddenly, a cramp gripped my stomach. As I tried to make it back to safety, the pain became more intense. The people on the shore became a blur as I started to go under the icy waters. As I fought for air, portions of my twelve-year life came back to me in slow motion. My brief span on earth was coming to a close. At least I would be remembered for something and my name would be in the papers. Then total darkness enveloped me.

Blurred faces came into focus as I vomited river water onto the grass. A man was giving me artificial respiration. A passing river patrol boat had come to my rescue.

My next death-defying stunt was performed on the platform of the 116th Street subway. It was the rush hour and

11

the station was jammed. Eagerly awaiting my great moment, I noticed the lights of the oncoming subway in the distance. The timing was perfect. Dramatically throwing up my hands, I proudly announced to the waiting passengers that "The Spider" was going to his death, and leaping off the platform, I awaited destruction. That really scared the shit out of the customers. The train roared nearer—nearer. Oh, Jesus, what had I gotten myself into! I closed my eyes and prayed that the goddamn train would stop in time. The motorman must have gotten my message.

Again and again I heard the circus barker's call, "Step right up," the applause, the attention. And each time, patiently, my sister and her husband would have to pick me up at the police station.

"Sometimes you act crazy, Bill," my brother-in-law, Allan, stated.

"Why can't you live a normal life just like any other boy?" my sister chimed in.

"Because I'm different, that's why," I defiantly stated.

The following day I made plans to run away from home—destination Hollywood. That was where I belonged, among the greats. Joe, the elevator man in the apartment house, volunteered to become my manager, and we decided we'd hitchhike to California when I could get some money.

Opening my sister's purse I emptied it of all the cash—$30. In my excitement I forgot to leave a note. Joe and I hitchhiked to Albany, where he suggested we spend the night at a "friend's" house.

Dreaming about Hollywood, I eagerly awoke the next morning. My wallet with the $30 was gone, and Joe had vanished into thin air. Bewildered, I found Joe's "friend" in the next room. "Where did Joe go?"

A shrug. "Who knows?" she said. "Maybe he went to Hollywood without you."

It took two days to hitchhike back to Manhattan. Afraid to go home, I decided to spend the night on a bench in the park

12

in front of our apartment. Mildred found me sound asleep. "What's to become of you, Bill?"

I smiled sheepishly, "I'll think of something . . . I always do."

When I was thirteen years old, in 1927, I bought a balcony seat with $1.10 I had taken from my sister's purse, eager to see the play, *Dracula,* starring Bela Lugosi. Enchanted, I watched Count Dracula suck his victims' blood. Almost every night for the next two weeks, with $1.10 from my sister's purse, I sat in the balcony and listened to frightened audiences scream. Soon I was no longer watching the play; I had more fun watching the audiences.

One night after a performance I decided to go backstage and meet the great Lugosi. Opening a stage door, for the first time I entered the backstage world of make-believe. I boldly announced to the old man sitting there that I was a friend of Mr. Lugosi's and that he was expecting me. My bluff worked and the old man said Mr. Lugosi was in dressing room number one.

Hesitating outside his dressing room, I summoned courage to knock. A deep, accented voice bade me enter. For a fleeting moment I thought of escape, but it was too late—I was face to face with Count Dracula.

Luminous, piercing eyes looked into mine and I was suddenly struck dumb. "What can I do for you, young man?" the deep voice inquired. I started speak, but the words didn't come. Count Dracula smiled and waited patiently. I managed to stammer, "I've seen the play twelve times, sir . . . and I think you're wonderful."

"Please sit down, Mr. . . . . ?"

"Schloss," I said.

"Mr. Slush?" (That night I knew I had to change my name. "Castle" is the English equivalent.) "Would you like to watch the play from backstage tomorrow night?"

I couldn't believe what I was hearing.

13

Bela Lugosi was a humble, gentle man, quite unlike the roles he portrayed. Every chance I had after that, I watched the special world of horror and fear from backstage. I knew then what I wanted to do with my life—I wanted to scare the pants off audiences.

Bela Lugosi was to make it all possible. When I was fifteen, I received a call from a producer who was getting ready to do a road company tour of *Dracula*. Mr. Lugosi had suggested me as the assistant stage manager. Amazed that Lugosi had remembered me, I excitedly accepted and promptly dropped out of high school.

I suggested a few new promotional gimmicks for the play—a closed black coffin outside the theatre and Oriental incense to get the audiences in the mood. The stage manager agreed to try another of my ideas—Count Dracula would vanish on stage in a cloud of smoke, then suddenly reappear in the audience. Snarling at the frightened spectators, he would again vanish and appear back on stage. I began to learn firsthand the value of good publicity and showmanship.

Adolf Hitler was unwittingly to teach me the lesson again nine years later. Hitler was indirectly responsible for opening the doors of Hollywood for me.

CHAPTER II

Brother, Can You Spare a Dime?

ADOLF HITLER, Orson Welles, and William Castle have one thing in common—we are Taureans. It was April 24, 1939, my twenty-fifth birthday. Hitler had invaded Czechoslovakia the month before. I felt we'd eventually get into it, but I wasn't about to worry on my birthday, especially since my girlfriend, Pat, a sculptress, was giving a birthday party for me at her Greenwich Village studio.

Riding the subway to the Village, I reflected on my good fortune. Earlier that day, I had received a check for $10,000, the first of three installments from my father's estate. Little did I know that the birthday party in my honor would lead to a summer of madness and that I was to meet two emissaries that evening—one from Adolf Hitler, the other from Orson Welles—and that fate already had plans for the $10,000 check in my wallet.

An old wizened panhandler sidled up to me as I walked toward Pat's studio. "Hey mister," a voice rasped from a toothless mouth. I paused. The harsh voice continued, "Got a nickel, a dime? I'm hungry. Please, mister, I gotta eat."

I remembered the many times I'd been broke and hungry, which was most of the previous nine years. The Depression years, when prosperity was supposed to be just around the corner; somehow, until now, I could never quite find the corner.

At first the jobs had come fast. After *Dracula,* I had been stage manager for *An American Tragedy*. Then I tried my hand at acting, in the lead role opposite Marjorie Main in *Ebb Tide*. That was followed by a lead in *No More Frontier,* and then a role in Chamberlin Brown's revival of *Oliver Twist.* When I was twenty, my sister, Mildred, her husband, Allan, and their young daughter, Joan, moved to Dallas. Although they wanted me to go with them and join my brother-in-law in the dress business, I opted for the theatre and stayed in New York. Then the jobs stopped coming. The Broadway theatre was having a tough time. Almost everyone was out of work, but we all continued to make our daily rounds of theatrical offices, hoping.

I spent five years job hunting, existing mainly off summers in the Borscht Belt where I got free room and board and a couple hundred dollars for being a social director. In the winter, I gained sustenance doing impersonations of Hollywood stars on cruises aboard the SS *Statendam.* All the time I seemed to be getting further and further away from my dream of scaring audiences.

"I'm hungry. Please, mister, I gotta eat." The old man was still there. With exactly $10 in cash—a five-dollar bill and five singles, I started counting out the singles, putting them into his outstretched hands. His eyes popped. He stared at me a moment with bloodshot eyes. Gripping my hand, he started to hug me, then planted a wet, slobbery kiss on my cheek. "God bless you, mister . . . You'll have good luck tonight." And with this good omen, I headed for the party.

Pat opened the door and threw her arms around my neck. All my theatre friends were there, and Pat introduced me to a thin red-headed actor with a large nose. Recognizing the name Everett Sloane, I realized he was one of Orson Welles's elite Mercury Players, a special group of young actors that had rocked Broadway for several seasons, their productions far-out and completely original. I had tried unsuccessfully on several occasions to meet Orson Welles. The usual. "Mr. Welles is very busy." "No, the play is all cast." "Why don't you send a résumé of your work?" "I'm sorry, Mr. Welles is seeing no one."

Seizing the opportunity, I plied Everett with questions about Mr. Welles's whereabouts. I knew Welles tried out his plays at the Stony Creek Theatre in Connecticut during the summers, before bringing them to Broadway.

"Orson's leaving for Hollywood," Everett said. "he's going to start preparing *Citizen Kane*."

Excited, I inquired what was happening to Stony Creek.

"Orson's closing it," Everett informed me, and glancing at his watch, said he had to catch an early plane for the Coast the following day. He was playing a lead in *Citizen Kane*.

Some instinct made me yell as he was about to exit my life. "Everett, wait." Stopping at the front door, he hesitated. "Everett, before you go, I misplaced Orson's home telephone number. Do you happen to have it with you?"

Everett paused and looked at me quizzically, then shrugged. "I don't know if I should . . . oh, well, I'm leaving tomorrow anyway." Pulling out an address book, he gave me Welles's home phone number.

Committing it to memory, I headed for the telephone in the bedroom. It was now or never. After all, it was my birthday, and the panhandler said I would be lucky.

The deep melodious voice came on at the other end. "Hello, Mr. Welles, this is Mr. Castle. No, please, don't hang up. I'm a Broadway producer." (I had never produced a thing in my life.) Clutching my wallet, I almost screamed, "I've got lots of money! Please, Mr. Welles, let me take over Stony Creek. You won't be sorry." Either Orson Welles liked something about my voice or thought I was somebody else; in either event, he agreed to meet with me the following day.

Glancing up, heady with success, I noticed a lovely girl had entered the bedroom. She was looking for her purse. She had a fresh, wistful quality; not beautiful, but there was something lovely and youthful about her.

"You are Herr Castle," she said, with a slight German accent which made her all the more enchanting. "My name is Ellen Schwanneke."

I found out she was an actress, the star of *Mädchen in Uniform*, a very successful German film. It had just been re-

17

leased in this country, and the New York critics had given her rave reviews.

She looked right into my eyes. Melting, I whispered, "Let's get out of here."

"We can't," she said. "It's your party, you must blow out the candles."

It was a warm night, and we walked around the Village while Ellen poured out her heart to me. She wanted to act but could find no work. She had run away from Hitler, hated what he was doing to her Germany.

"Miss Schwanneke, why don't you work for me? I'll star you in a play at Stony Creek, my new theatre, this summer. You'll be great. How about it?"

Smiling, she shook her head slowly. "You are so fast, Herr Castle. You do not know me, my work, what I feel. No, I am sorry."

At about five in the morning we were still walking.

"You Americans are so quick. Herr Castle, I must see the play first before I commit myself."

"Oh, the play." (I'd completely forgotten I didn't have a play.) Suddenly an idea hit me. She reminded me of the movie star Janet Gaynor. "Have you ever heard of a play called *Seventh Heaven?* It would be a perfect vehicle for you. Janet Gaynor did it as a silent film with Charles Farrell. I'll even get Farrell as your leading man. Fräulein, I can see it now in bright lights across the marquee—'Ellen Schwanneke and Charles Farrell starring in *Seventh Heaven,* A William Castle Production.' How about it?"

"Herr Castle, it sounds very nice, but I must have more time to think about it."

Shit, I wanted to make a deal right away. Maybe if we kept on walking, she'd say yes.

CHAPTER III

The Girl Who Said No to Hitler

THE following day I was in Orson Welles's outer office. It was a madhouse of preparations for his leaving for Hollywood the following day to film *Citizen Kane*. I had been waiting an hour when a puff of smoke appeared, followed by "The Boy Wonder" himself. I rarely, if ever, have felt such incredible magnetism in a man. He grinned his boyish grin and, puffing cigar smoke, extended his hand. "Come on in."

We entered his spacious office and he waved me to a chair. Welles didn't sit, he paced. I started to sweat. Finally he spoke in his booming voice. "Why should I let you have Stony Creek?"

I stood up and began pacing with him.

"Do you smoke cigars?" he asked.

I didn't smoke cigars, but for the occasion, replied, "Of course." He handed me one of his famous Churchills, stopping long enough to light it for me. Choking, I puffed away. There was a silence while Welles stared out the window. For several moments I thought I was dismissed.

Then he abruptly turned and said, "You haven't answered my question."

Smiling, I quietly stated, "Because we're both Taurus." He laughed, and I plunged ahead. "I have money, but I know that isn't important to you. What is important is that I have talent. We're both the same age. . . . I've been in show business since I was fifteen. . . ." I rattled off my credits to him. "My love for the theatre is just as great as yours."

19

Welles turned and looked straight into my eyes. "You got a deal, Castle." Then he left the room abruptly.

Ten minutes later I was back on the street, the cigar still in my mouth and a lease for the Stony Creek Theatre in my pocket. Five hundred a week for ten weeks—5,000 bucks. I was now an impresario.

I got the rights to *Seventh Heaven,* but before the contract was signed, a call came from Actors Equity. The board had heard I had made a deal with Ellen Schwanneke and was taking over the Orson Welles playhouse that summer.

At the meeting, the board members were very polite but firm when they informed me I could not use Miss Schwanneke. My stomach did nip-ups and I must have gone white. Somebody handed me a cup of water. I complained of the heat but was really sick to my stomach. "Why can't I use Schwanneke? She's a great actress and should be allowed to work in America."

The great star Alfred Lunt, a board member, calmed me down. "Mr. Castle," he patiently explained, "no alien can play in summer stock; it's an Equity rule. You see, it takes away employment from American actors, and you wouldn't want to do that, would you, Mr. Castle?"

"Of course not," I snapped back. "But . . ."

Lunt interrupted. "If you had a play that was especially written for her, something no American actress could portray as well, then there might be a possibility."

Breathing a sigh of relief, I quickly said, "Is that all? I *have* a play written especially for Miss Schwanneke. I got it in Germany last year. No American actress could possibly do it. It was tailored especially for the great Schwanneke's talents." (I had never been to Europe in my life and had no such play, but I went on and on, hanging myself.).

"What is the name of the play, Mr. Castle?" Mr. Lunt asked.

Jesus. I thought to myself. I knew little or no German. Remembering a phrase from my childhood, one used by my parents, who were of German descent, when they wanted to

20

discuss something that was not for my childish ears, I quickly blurted out, "The name of the play is . . . *Das Ist Nicht für Kinder.*" Mr. Lunt stared at me as I continued shooting off my big mouth. "It means *Not for Children.*"

"I know," said Mr. Lunt, "I speak German."

"I guarantee it will be on Broadway in the fall, Mr. Lunt. It has forty people in the cast. Think of all the work it will mean for all our good American actors, forty! Maybe I'll write ten more in, making it an even fifty. Won't that make some American actors happy?" There was a long pause. "Come on, Mr. Lunt, give me a break."

"I'll tell you what, Mr. Castle," he said politely. "This is Friday. You bring in the play *Das Ist Nicht für Kinder* on Monday at noon, with a cast of forty, tailored especially for Miss Schwanneke, and I'll take it before the board of directors."

"Yes, sir, I'll be here with the play."

Now, all I had to do was write the goddamn thing! It was 3:00 P.M. and there was no time to lose. Racing to my one room on Riverside Drive, I tried to figure what kind of play could be written by 12:00 Monday.

Four P.M. I started to write. One hour later, the title page was completed—*Das Ist Nicht für Kinder,* written by Ludwig von Herschfeld. That name sounded as good as any. A new German playwright was born.

Six pots full of coffee and forty-eight hours later, the play was written. It had the forty characters I had promised—thirty-nine, to be exact, and a dog.

I had wanted to write a horror play, but Schwanneke had balked: "There's enough horror in the world. People want to laugh in the theatre, not be frightened." So I wrote a tour de force for Schwanneke, about a German girl coming to America for the first time, her love life and adjustment to the American scene.

Whenever I had a suit pressed or cleaned, which was rarely, I used the German-Jewish tailor around the corner. Manuscript in one hand, suit in the other, I raced to his shop.

"Hans, please have this cleaned." I handed over the suit. "Oh—and a special favor, Hans. . . . Do you think you could get your son Willie to translate this from English into German?" I showed him the play and Hans shouted for his son.

Willie agreed to translate the play for $10, but it would take him a week. That was too late, it had to be ready by Monday. For an extra $10 he promised to stay up all night and have it on Sunday.

Although international relationships were strained, there was still a German consul in New York. On Monday morning, with the translated manuscript in hand, I pleaded, cajoled, and begged a German vice-consul to stamp a swastika on the cover and to throw in some red ribbons to make it look official.

In Central Park, I threw the manuscript onto a pile of refuse and jumped up and down and stamped on it several times to make it look reasonably worn and dirty. Then I scorched the edges, just enough to make it look like it had come out of some bombed-out building in Europe. A watching policeman thought I was completely nuts, but possibly harmless, and waited to see if I would become violent.

Eleven-thirty A.M.—thirty minutes to go—I hopped into a cab and arrived at Actors Equity with five minutes to spare. Two hours later, permission was given by Actors Equity to use Miss Schwanneke in *Das Ist Nicht für Kinder* at the Stony Creek Theatre.

An easily assembled cast moved to Stony Creek in Connecticut that summer and started rehearsal. The theatre was excellent; Orson Welles had completely renovated it. We all lived in a little house about a block from the theatre, where a nice, motherly woman cooked our meals and looked after us.

Engraved announcements were sent out—"William Castle proudly presents the American debut of Ellen Schwanneke, star of German stage and screen, in Ludwig von Herschfeld's masterpiece *Das Ist Nicht für Kinder*." After the second week of rehearsal, I checked the box office and found no

22

tickets had been sold. People had been calling, but when they were told Orson Welles and the Mercury Players were not performing, they lost interest. I had bitten off more than I could chew. I was unknown, and Ellen Schwanneke was not the box-office attraction I thought she would be.

That night I woke up in a Castle sweat. I had had a very realistic nightmare about opening a play with thirty-nine actors and a dog on stage and two people in the audience. Disaster! My play was closing before it opened.

To make matters worse, a heat wave suddenly hit Connecticut. Air conditioning was unheard of, and the theatre was like a furnace. People not only weren't buying tickets, they weren't even on the streets.

Rehearsal had broken early because it was just too hot to work. Sitting in the box office paying bills, I wrote a final check on my remaining $5,000. In one month I had blown the full $10,000 and there were no customers in sight.

Looking up, I thought I saw a customer approaching and I quickly shook the ticket seller, who had dozed off in the heat. "Wake up, Joe. We've got one—sell her some of the expensive seats."

As the young lady approached, I realized it wasn't a customer after all, it was Ellen Schwanneke. What the hell did she want?

She looked deeply concerned. "Bill, I must speak to you privately. Something terrible has happened."

My heart sank as I took her to a corner of the lobby. "What's the matter Ellen? You're not ill?" Silently she opened her purse and handed me a gold-embossed card. "It's an invitation from Adolf Hitler to return to Germany."

I studied the card, which was written in German. Puzzled, I said, "Why you?"

"It's the festival. All the great German stars will be present and they have summoned me to attend, all expenses paid." There was a letter with the invitation, signed by Dr. Joseph Goebbels, the Reichsminister of Propaganda and Enlightenment. Ellen translated for me. It said in effect that the Führer would be honored if she would attend a special reception in the Führer's Wing of the Brown House in Munich and to please reply immediately to Dr. Goebbels.

Ellen explained she had left Germany because of the Nazis. They controlled the arts, and she didn't like their interference with free expression. Her father, a star comedian of the German stage for years, had recently died. He had also run "Schwanneke's," for years the most celebrated café rendezvous of artists and actors in the German capital. "Just before the Nazis came to power, he passed away," she said, "and it was a blessing. If he'd seen what they've done to Germany, seen the caliber of the German theatre falling lower and lower, he would have suffered more than I."

Moved by her words, I pressed her further. Tears freely flowing, she continued. "There is no race in art but I happen to be what the Nazis call one hundred percent Aryan. I was brought up with stage people, and whether they were Christians or Jews made no difference. Now, in Germany, I am expected to give them up and consider them the scum of the earth. It offends my two deepest loyalties: personal and artistic. That is why I'm here in your country, because I refuse to obey their rules and adhere to their principles. But we're not even going to be able to open the play here and I can get no other work. It doesn't look like I have much choice but to go back to Germany."

There was silence for a moment as she continued crying.

"Ellen, have you any family in Germany?"

"No, not anymore."

"Tell me the truth, do you ever want to go back?"

Her eyes blazed. "Not as long as Hitler is in power. He has taken my Germany. I want nothing to do with him."

It was like an oven in the theatre lobby. Ellen was still crying, and my shirt was soaking wet—not from her tears, but from sweat. I grabbed her by the arm and took her out into the fresh air. "Stop crying. I'll take care of everything. You'll never have to go back—I'll see to that."

She looked up at me with those big brown eyes. "What are you going to do, Bill?"

I couldn't help smiling at the preposterous idea that was forming in my head. "Wait and see, just wait. I think Adolf Hitler has brought us good luck . . . the dirty bastard!"

With the invitation in my hand I went to the Western Union office down the street. It was just closing. I told the pretty girl that sent the wires that it was imperative she stay open . . . an emergency! When I started to dictate, she almost fainted.

"Cable to Adolf Hitler, Munich, Germany. Dear Mr. Hitler: Ellen Schwanneke turns down your invitation. She has positively said no. She wants nothing to do with you or your politics. She will not return to Germany as long as you remain in power. Signed, William Castle, Producer/Director, Stony Creek Theatre, Connecticut. P.S. She's working for me now."

The pretty girl asked in a shaky voice, "Do you really want me to send this?"

"Of course, and send another one of the same to Dr. Joseph Goebbels . . . G-O-E-B-B-E-L-S."

Later that day, I had twenty copies each made up of the gold-embossed invitation from Hitler, the letter from Goebbels and my cable.

I went into Manhattan to see the managing editors of every large daily New York newspaper. To each one I said the same thing. "Look, I'd like your advice on this matter. Miss Schwanneke doesn't want any publicity for obvious reasons, so please don't print this. But I want you to listen to this incredible story." I played it very naïve and dumb. If the editors didn't ask for copies of the invitation and cable, I'd leave them on their desks anyway, as if I'd forgotten them.

Covering all New York this way, I hoped someone would swallow the bait. This was a good publicity story. I smelled it. But in my wildest dreams I never imagined what the full result would be.

25

The next day the absolutely incredible happened. Luck was with me. It was one of those rare days when nothing major in world affairs had happened and no really big news items had appeared to fill the daily papers. My timing had been perfect. We made the front pages. Four New York newspapers carried banner headlines:

"THE GIRL WHO SAID NO TO HITLER"
"STOOD UP HITLER, BANNED ON NAZI STAGES"
"GERMAN ACTRESS SNUBS FUEHRER"
"FUEHRER'S IDEA OF HAVING FUN ISN'T SCHWANNEKE'S"

Some papers printed the invitation and my cable. All had long articles about Ellen Schwanneke and her American debut. I jumped for joy. I had actually attracted more attention than Orson Welles. The *Daily News* said I was even more theatre-mad than Welles. Then wire services picked up the story and it hit front pages all across America—The Girl Who Said No to Hitler was playing at Stony Creek under the direction of William Castle.

I was at the box office when the papers hit the streets and the orders started pouring in. Although opening night was still a week away, we were sold out in a few hours. *Not for Children,* an obscure play written in forty-eight hours, was going to be a commercial hit.

Now that the play was an insured success, I relaxed and continued final rehearsals. But one thing I had overlooked was the German-American Bundists. Letters came in addressed to Schwanneke and me protesting her snub of Hitler. Some went as far as to threaten her life. Others said they would try to prevent the show from opening at all.

I needed one final publicity stunt to make it the biggest opening of the season—something that Orson Welles would be proud of. I must admit that I am totally ashamed at what I did.

At 4:00 A.M. the night before the play opened, the alarm

clock went off. Hurriedly, I threw on a bathrobe and in total darkness, went to the theatre. The streets were deserted. With some lumber from backstage, I smashed windows in the theatre and overturned the box office. Then, with red paint, I drew swastikas on the walls. I went back to my room and waited for the results.

At 8:00, members of the cast and crew awakened me. Panic had set in. They had already been to the theatre, and now they dragged me there to see what had happened. A small crowd was standing around. Several people asked whether we'd open that night.

"Ladies and gentlemen," I responded, "*Not for Children,* starring Miss Ellen Schwanneke, will open as scheduled even if I have to get the governor of Connecticut to give us the state militia for protection." And that's exactly what I did.

The only way I got through to the governor was by saying I was Orson Welles. I told him what happened and hysterically demanded complete protection. He promised it, and he kept his word.

On opening night soldiers with helmets and guns surrounded the theatre. Klieg lights flashed everywhere. Members of the audience arriving in formal attire were carefully inspected. It was one hell of an opening.

CHAPTER IV

The Big Time

SAMUEL MARKS, an emissary of powerful Harry Cohn's Columbia Pictures, was intrigued not only with *Not for Children,* but with the entire company. He had such delight and fun with the entire atmosphere at Stony Creek that he decided to move in with us for a few days while we began rehearsal for a second production, *This Little Piggy Had None,* a horror play. The story was about the mental breakdown of a timid man who is so taunted by his facial resemblance to a pig that he finally cracks up and becomes a murderer. At last I was going to frighten the wits out of the audience.

It was a difficult morning of rehearsal, and the leading man was becoming discouraged. He wasn't acting enough like a pig. I called lunch and we all proceeded to the beautiful lawn in back of the theatre where fried chicken, salad, and lemonade were spread out on the table.

Munching on a chicken leg, Sam Marks casually asked if I would be interested in coming to Hollywood and working for Columbia Pictures. A piece of chicken got stuck in my throat, but I managed a croak. "I thought you'd never ask."

Sam smiled and said, "I can make no promises, but I think Harry Cohn will like you. At least it's worth the gamble." I was so excited that my appetite vanished. Sam tried to calm me down. "Remember I can offer you nothing, only an introduction to Harry Cohn. But I'll tell him about the great work you've done here."

28

"Sam, I can be ready to leave in two weeks. Is that okay?"

He said it would fit in perfectly with his plans. There was some business he had to attend to in New York that would keep him busy for about a week; then we could drive out to the Coast in his car. Making sure not to get my hopes too high, he again stated that it was just a chance. But what a chance, I thought; to meet and possibly work for the great Harry Cohn at Columbia.

Time moved very slowly, but I kept busy rehearsing. Then Sam called and told me he was returning to the Coast immediately, flying back that day.

"Bill, why don't you take my car and drive out yourself?"

"That's great, but I don't drive."

"That's all right Bill, I'll put an ad in the paper for someone who wants to go to California and would be willing to drive you. See you in Hollywood, Bill; wire before you leave . . . and good luck."

During the next few days three or four people called, interested in driving Sam's car to Hollywood. I decided on Charlie, a very likable fellow about my age, who wanted to get to San Francisco. Wiring Sam, I told him we were leaving that Sunday.

Because of the trip, I canceled another scheduled production, Sidney Kingsley's play *Dead End.* Having already paid for the stage props, I took them with me, throwing them in the back of the car with my luggage.

The ride out west was an enjoyable one. Neither Charlie nor I shaved, and we wore sweatshirts and dungarees. We must have looked like bums as we drove into Cheyenne, Wyoming in the middle of the night. Looking for a place to sleep, Charlie made a U-turn in the middle of the block. A police car motioned us over to the side. A cop got out and flashing a light in our faces, studied our unshaven and grubby appearance and Sam Marks's expensive car.

"You guys made a U-turn in the middle of the block."

"Sorry," I said with great charm.

"Where you headed?" the cop asked.

29

"Hollywood."

"Well, keep on going." Without asking to see any identification papers, he walked back to his patrol car and drove off.

Being too tired to keep driving, we ignored the cop's advice and pulled up in front of a modest-looking house on a tree-lined street. As we went in to get rooms I thought I spotted a police car, but I was too damned sleepy to care.

The clerk gave us two adjoining rooms and asked for $15 in advance. I asked why it was so expensive, and he looked at me knowingly and winked. "It'll be worth every cent."

The room was dirty and sparsely furnished. I couldn't figure out why it was so expensive, but I was exhausted and so I flopped onto the bed and immediately fell asleep.

I was awakened by a knock. Opening the door, a luscious blonde entered. She whispered, "Are you ready, darling?" A red light went off in my head. I was in a whorehouse! Well, it had been paid for in advance, so why not?

Just as things were getting started, the door burst open and two cops, guns drawn, were in the room. "Put your hands on your head and don't move."

On top of the blonde, hands over my head, I felt like an idiot. Charlie, my driver, was standing outside the open door in handcuffs.

"Jesus, fellas," I said. "What the hell's the matter? Honestly, I didn't know this was a whorehouse." They suggested I get my clothes on.

Handcuffed, Charlie and I were hustled downstairs and into a patrol car. "Do they arrest you in Wyoming for getting laid?" I asked the cops. They remained silent. What I didn't know was that shortly after the police had stopped us for making a U-turn, there had been a holdup at a gas station. We answered the description of the holdup men; even the getaway car looked like Sam's.

At the police station I was fingerprinted and questioned. Denying everything, I demanded my rights as a citizen. When they asked to see the car registration, I was dismayed to find out Sam had forgotten to give it to us, and when they opened my luggage and saw the theatre props I was carrying—counterfeit money, handcuffs, a blackjack and stage guns, including several sawed-off shotguns—they knew they had another John Dillinger. I was allowed to make one telephone call. Shit! Sam Marks wasn't home.

I tried to convince the police I was working for Harry Cohn at Columbia Pictures in Hollywood. They listened silently, their stony faces occasionally nodding, then promptly tossed us into a barred cell and locked it. They probably threw away the key. After all, they had two desperadoes—I had finally hit the big time!

Chapter V

Get Your Ass in Here!

GRASPING the bars with both hands, I shouted at the top of my voice, "H-E-L-L-L-P!"

Angry voices came out of the night, "Shut up . . . go to sleep."

Turning to Charlie, I said meekly, "That's a good idea. Let's go to sleep."

He gave me a disgusted look, then stretched out on the dirty mattress that was on the floor and immediately fell asleep. Maybe he'd been in jail before.

I was in a strange city and accused of robbing a gas station. Concealed "weapons" were found in my suitcase, and even though they had only fired blanks, they were real and might have taken live bullets. Why in the hell did I take those stage props with me, and why didn't I ask Sam Marks for his car registration?

It was almost morning, and I was sure the police would find out it was all a mistake and would release us in a matter of hours. I decided to get some sleep. A thin mattress, almost black from dirt, lay on the floor. I looked at it and gingerly eased myself onto it. Closing my eyes, I tried to sleep.

Something was crawling on me. "Charlie," I whispered, "there's something on me." But Charlie was snoring. I lay perfectly still, not daring to move. Whatever was crawling was now on my neck, slowly moving upward. My hand went to my mouth. A big black tarantula was trying to be friends. I

32

snatched the monster off, and I watched him scoot through the bars.

The rest of the night was uneventful—snores from Charlie and the prisoners in adjoining cells. I must have dozed off because the next thing I knew it was daylight and breakfast was being served—some slop they called cereal, and lousy coffee in a tin cup.

I started to itch. I found my body covered with large red welts. Charlie, covered with the same red welts, said they were bedbug bites.

It was impossible to eat what they called "breakfast" but I did manage to get the coffee down and, asking myself what Humphrey Bogart would do in a situation like this, I took the tin cup and sharply rattled it across the bars. I'd once seen Bogart do this in a movie, and he got plenty of attention. I continued rattling until a guard came up, told me to keep quiet, and took away my cup. Bogart would have roared, "You lousy stinking screw, I want out." All I managed was a meek "Yes, sir."

Later that afternoon two other men were thrown in with us. One of them said he was in for rape and the other for robbing a liquor store. The big ugly one (the rapist) looked me over and asked, "What are you in for, Mac?"

Looking him straight in the eye, I lowered my voice, "Holding up a gas station, Mac . . . but I'm innocent."

He just laughed. "They all say that, Mac." Then he lowered his voice and whispered, "Do you want a goofball?"

Still whispering, he said, "An upper, Mac . . . it'll make you fly." He had smuggled some in—of all places—in his rectum. I was really getting frightened. This was no movie of terror; this was for real.

We spent all that night and the following day in our cell.

On the third night another man was thrown in with us. He had been accused of killing his wife. His eyes were crazed and wild. He kept on ranting about his wife's being unfaithful and how he had strangled her. Why he picked me for his confidant I'll never know. Maybe he thought we had something in common. Anyway, it wasn't a total loss. There was some great material for a horror picture. I only hoped I'd be alive to use it.

I paced the cell that night with my friend the killer. Lips parched, unshaven, dirty, weak from lack of food and unable to sleep, I started to sob uncontrollably. "The Wyoming Strangler" tried to comfort me, but suddenly everything went black and I lost consciousness.

I found out later that the police had called Harry Cohn when I was first arrested. Cohn's secretary buzzed him in his private dining room at Columbia Studio in Hollywood. "Mr. Cohn, the Cheyenne police are calling you . . . do you wish me to put the call through?"

Cohn, probably chewing on a piece of steak, barked, "Yeah, put 'em on."

"Sorry to bother you, Mr. Cohn, but we have a man in jail here. He claims he's working for you . . . name of William Castle."

Still chewing, Harry Cohn barked, "Never heard of the bum," and hung up.

As I was lying unconscious in my cell, Sam Marks was talking with Harry Cohn, who was being shaved by the Columbia barber. "I wonder what happened to my car and Bill Castle. It's been two weeks since I heard from him."

There was a silence as the barber continued shaving. Just as Sam was about to leave, Harry's bark stopped him. "What'd you say the guy's name was?"

"William Castle."

From underneath the hot towel Harry Cohn muttered, "The bum's in jail in Cheyenne, Wyoming." From that point on I got the model prisoner's VIP treatment. Everybody from the police chief to the DA and the mayor came to apologize and to inquire about the state of my health. I dined on steaks, french fries, and apple pie. My real buddy, the smiling DA, even invited me home to meet his family. He had a lovely daughter and hoped I would put her in the movies. Shoving an official paper under my nose, he asked me to sign. It was a release stating that the city of Cheyenne could not be held responsible for my false arrest. I signed it. Charlie, my driver, signed too. We would have signed anything to get out of there. Later, Harry Cohn called me a jerk for forfeiting my rights and said I could have sued the city of Cheyenne for a fortune.

I arrived in Hollywood three days later, September 20, 1939. Charlie delivered the car to Sam Marks and took a bus for San Francisco. Checking into a cheap hotel near the studio, I waited for Sam to call and let me know when I was to meet Harry Cohn. I checked every half hour with the switchboard operator to make sure she knew my name and room number, but nobody called.

I didn't leave the hotel all day, but that evening I wandered down Hollywood Boulevard, fascinated by the tall palm trees. I found myself in front of Grauman's Chinese Theatre. A pretty red-headed girl was putting her foot in Jean Harlow's footprint, so I decided to put mine in Lon Chaney's.

"Someday I'll be a superstar," she said.

Smiling, I replied, "And I'll frighten audiences."

Over a soda, she told me she came from Brooklyn and her name was Susan Hayward. She confided in me that it was really Edythe Marrner before it was changed. She had made a screen test and was supposed to play opposite Gary Cooper in *Beau Geste.* I told her I was under contract to Columbia and was a good friend of Harry Cohn's. We toasted each other with sodas and hoped we both would get our wishes.

When I got back to my hotel there was a message from Sam Marks that I was to meet Harry Cohn the following morning at 11:00.

At 10:30 I walked through the portals of Columbia for the first time. Standing in awe at the reception desk waiting to be announced, I saw Loretta Young and Melvyn Douglas walk in. Miss Young actually smiled at me and said good morning. I was about to reply when the guard gave me a pass and directed me upstairs.

An office with three secretaries in attendance was followed

by a reception room in which an executive secretary personally guarded The Great Man.

I must have been visibly nervous because Margaret Lee, Mr. Cohn's executive secretary, smiled and said, "Sit down and relax; Mr. Cohn's running late." She added as an afterthought, "Frank Capra's in there."

I began thinking about the great films Capra had made—*It Happened One Night, Mr. Deeds Goes to Town, Lost Horizon, Mr. Smith Goes to Washington, You Can't Take It with You* — and of all of his Oscars. I must have been in a trance because the next thing I heard was, "How do you want it?"

Looking up, I replied, "Huh? Want what?"

"Coffee—how do you want it?"

I mumbled "black," and the next thing I knew, a cup of black coffee was in my hand.

At that moment, the door opened and Frank Capra walked out. Standing up abruptly, I spilled the whole goddamn cup of coffee all over myself.

Mr. Capra smiled at my predicament. "Seems you had a little accident. Don't worry, we'll dry you out. Has someone got a towel for this gentleman?"

"Mr. Capra," I said, "My name is William Castle, I've always admired . . . "

At that point a voice barked from the other room. "Get your ass in here!"

CHAPTER VI

The Dream Factory

I ENTERED The Great Man's private domain soaked with coffee. It was the longest walk I'd ever had. Breathless, I stopped in front of Harry Cohn's massive desk. Behind him, dozens of featureless golden Oscars stared down at me with unseeing eyes.

I stood speechless for what seemed an eternity. Finally The Great Man spoke. "You're a goddamn mess, Castle."

"I spilled my coffee, sir."

"I can see that," he snapped. "For chrissake, sit down." I sank into a nearby chair and stared at him. Turning in his swivel chair, he faced the window and looked out on Gower Street, then swiveled back toward me and sadly shook his head. "What a mess."

"Mr. Cohn," I stammered.

He shot back, "Yeah."

I wanted to tell him how much I wanted to work for him and of all the wonderful things I had done in the theatre, but all that came out was a weak "I . . ." followed by a dismal "Nothing, sir."

Cohn was the most dynamic, magnetic, and frightening human being I had ever seen. "Sam Marks tells me you might be Columbia contract material." There was a pause, followed by a sharp crack on his desk with the riding crop he always carried. "Why do you want to work for Columbia?"

I finally found my voice. "Because I want to learn every-

37

thing there is about the picture business. . . . I have talent, I'm . . ."

"Bullshit," he interrupted, "I'll tell *you* when you have talent. Don't you ever tell me how good you are again." Then he smiled for the first time, and for a brief second his eyes softened and I smiled back. "Columbia's a tough studio, and I demand the impossible from my people. I think that eventually *young people* will control the picture business. We must open our doors to them, not only actors and actresses, but writers, directors, producers. . . ."

I was put under contract to Columbia Pictures for a trial period of six months, with further options for seven years if I survived. Harry Cohn saw to it that my exposure would encompass every phase of picture making. When he told me he would teach me the picture business he wasn't kidding. It was a seven-way contract, the only one of its kind in Hollywood—writer, director, producer, dialogue director, production assistant, film editor, and actor. Cohn's pet theory was that to be a good director you had to start by acting. If you were eventually to get behind the camera, you had to begin in front of it. I was to receive the bountiful sum of $50 a week.

The first thing I did was to become familiar with the studio. In the good hands of Margaret Lee, Cohn's secretary, I was introduced to everyone.

"Have you ever been on a stage before and seen a picture being shot?" she asked.

I shook my head no, as the heavy doors of Stage Two opened and I entered "The Dream Factory" for the first time.

They were making Clifford Odets's *Golden Boy* and I watched as Rouben Mamoulian directed a scene with Barbara Stanwyck and Adolphe Menjou. I was amazed at how many men and women it took to make a movie. There must have been sixty people milling around. I couldn't figure out what in the hell they all did.

Standing next to me was a young man about my age, with curly black hair. He seemed ill at ease, nervous, and frightened. Whispering, I tried to reassure him in Harry Cohn fashion. "Relax, kid. It's my first day, too." He was very good-looking, and I wondered whether he was one of the young hopefuls Mr. Cohn had spoken about and if he'd be competition to me. "I'm Bill Castle, I have a seven-way contract. What do you do?"

"I'm William Holden," he said "and I'm supposed to be an actor, but at the present moment I have grave doubts." Just then he was called and he nervously began rehearsing a scene with Barbara Stanwyck. It was his first picture, and it was heartwarming to see Stanwyck give him confidence. Her patience and understanding completely relaxed Holden, and as a result he gave a strong performance. Barbara Stanwyck is not only a superstar, but a great lady.

Within the first month, I began to get impatient. I had not seen Harry Cohn again, and I was tired of just watching. I wanted to do something—anything.

Brittingham's Restaurant across the street from Columbia was a convenient place to eat. After sitting on my ass all day, I decided to get some dinner. The restaurant was completely deserted except for one other man who was sitting alone at an adjoining table. Wanting company, I looked over and smiled. "Why sit by yourself, come on over and join me." Looking up from his soup, the man silently nodded and moved, soup and all, to my table.

I ordered the blue-plate dinner and leaned back to appraise my guest. He was youngish, and had a strong but pleasant face and eyes that were full of mischief.

"My name is Bill Castle. I work for Harry Cohn."

There was a brief silence before my friend, preoccupied with his soup, quietly asked, "Do you really know Harry Cohn?"

"Do I know Harry Cohn! I'm one of his best friends." There was another pause in the conversation as the waiter served my dinner. I continued. "By the way, what do you do, Mr. —er—"

He spoke quietly. "I'm sort of in the picture business, too."

"Maybe I can help you," I boasted. "Youth is what we need in our business. I'll introduce you to my pal Harry Cohn."

Again, a long pause. "I'm afraid I haven't introduced myself. My name is George Stevens."

After picking myself up from the floor, I managed, "Sorry, sir." My dinner didn't land in my lap, but the egg certainly landed right on my face. I did everything except stand up and salute.

George Stevens, one of the great producer/directors in the motion-picture industry, had already created *Alice Adams*, *Quality Street*, *Woman of the Year*, *Talk of the Town*, and *The More the Merrier*. He was to go on to win two Academy Awards for *A Place in the Sun* and *Giant* and to bring to audiences his brilliant production of *Shane*.

At this time he was preparing *Penny Serenade*, starring Cary Grant and Irene Dunne, for Columbia. They were two of the biggest stars on the Hollywood scene, having recently completed *The Awful Truth* for Columbia.

Trying to cover up my blunder, I looked at Stevens and became Mr. Humble. "Mr. Stevens, sir, I'm really just an apprentice learning the picture business."

George Stevens laughed. "Your performance was delightful, totally refreshing. Do you really work at Columbia?" I raised my hand and took an oath. He continued. "And are you a friend of Harry Cohn's?"

Blushing, I looked down at my pot roast. "I did see him *once.*"

Stevens smiled. "Maybe I should speak to him about *you!*"

"Please don't," I stammered. "I'd rather he didn't hear about this."

Stevens signaled the waiter for our checks and started to leave.

"Sir, when are you starting *Penny Serenade?*"

"Next Friday," he replied.

"I've always wanted to work for you. Do you think it's possible . . . I mean, sir, you're the greatest . . . and—oh, the hell with it—I want to be your dialogue director."

"No chance," he replied. "I never use dialogue directors; don't believe in them."

"Well," I said brightly, "can I at least come on the set and watch you shoot?"

He smiled and shook my hand. "Of course, anytime you'd like. Well, good night, Bill, and thanks for a *most* entertaining evening." And with that he was gone, and so was I, as I cursed my pot roast.

For the next few days I stayed in hibernation. Nobody knew or seemed to care that I was the bright young fresh talent that Harry Cohn had been looking for. Misery set in as I lay on my bed and counted the cracks in the ceiling. Suddenly the telephone rang. Who in the hell could be calling this late? Picking it up I growled, "Yeah?"

A disembodied voice echoed, "Bill Castle?"

Sarcastically, I muttered, "I'll see if he's in. Who's calling?"

The voice replied, "George."

"George who?" I snapped.

"Stevens—George Stevens," the voice replied.

"That's a lousy joke, especially at this hour," and I promptly hung up. The phone rang again. I picked it up. "Come on, you jerk, stop bothering me."

As I started to hang up again, the voice stopped me cold. "Bill, don't hang up, this is *really* George Stevens. I hope I'm not disturbing you. I spoke to Harry about you, and if you want to be my dialogue director, report for work, Stage One, tomorrow at eight. And Bill . . . don't *ever* hang up on me again!"

What a kind, considerate, thoughtful man George Stevens was. He had actually kept his promise and spoken to Harry Cohn about me. Little did I know that the following day this kind, considerate, thoughtful man would almost choke me to death.

41

Chapter VII

God, the Stars, and the Flea

THE sensitive antennas of Hollywood were all waving in anticipation. *Penny Serenade,* the biggest and most important production at Columbia, would start in December 1939.

News, good or bad, travels fast within a studio and as I briskly walked toward Stage One, colleagues congratulated me on my good fortune. I felt great, except for one thing: I had no idea what a dialogue director was or did. Of course I could ask Mr. Stevens, but I didn't want to bother him. He must have assumed that I knew what the hell I was supposed to do when I asked for the job.

The title "dialogue director" had a nice sound to it. It probably had to do with instructing the actors on how to get the best values out of their lines. But if I were to direct the dialogue of the actors, what exactly did George Stevens do?

A big sign was hanging outside the stage door—"CLOSED SET—NO ADMITTANCE"—and a red light was flashing. At least I knew what the red light meant; a scene was in progress and absolutely no one could go in. After what seemed an eternity, the red light went off.

There were about eighty people inside. George Stevens was perched on a crane high in the air, looking down. I don't think I've ever been closer to God. I was just about to greet him with a "Hi, George," when someone clapped his hand over my mouth and whispered, "Don't talk, it bothers him." When I started to walk toward Stevens, the man whispered, "Don't walk, it bothers him."

"Can I breathe?" I inquired.

Sam Nelson, the assistant director, grinned. "Not too loudly." He explained that George Stevens demanded absolute silence at all times, and that anybody interrupting his concentration was quickly thrown off the set. When he rehearsed a sequence, the entire crew was asked to leave and he worked alone with the actors. Stevens originally started in silent films and still used music to get his actors into the mood of a scene.

I was given a pair of booties, a felt covering that fits over your shoes so they don't squeak when you're walking.

God finally came down from the sky and I tiptoed over. Stevens briefly glanced at me and then turned away, still concentrating. I wondered if he even remembered me.

The set, consisting of a small living room, kitchen, bedroom and bath, was being lit. Everyone ignored me, so I found a seat on a nice comfortable canvas chair. Just as my rear touched the canvas, a stern voice whispered, "You can't sit there—that's George Stevens's chair." I stood up quickly.

A young, deeply tanned man approached and peered quizzically into my face. "You're Bill Castle?" He was the only nonwhisperer in the group, and his voice sounded vaguely familiar. "I'm Cary Grant . . . welcome."

Six hours later, Grant and Irene Dunne, his co-star, were still rehearsing the same difficult three-page scene. The many complicated camera moves took hours of rehearsal. Finally Stevens was satisfied and wanted to try a take. Immediately the makeup men and hairdressers came in and busied themselves around the two stars.

Grant and Dunne got into their positions and a bell sounded. George Stevens heard someone tiptoeing in the background and angrily turned around.

Sam Nelson shouted "Quiet!" It was like a tomb. Sam quietly said, "Roll 'em."

Then a buzz, and the soundman quietly said, "Speed."

George Stevens softly said, "Action."

Camera rolling, the scene started. Irene walked to the window and looked out. Cary, seated in a chair, got up and walked over to her, camera following, and put his arms

43

around her. Holding her close, he kissed her. She started to cry. George Stevens was watching the scene with fierce intensity. Cary Grant, trying to cheer her up, read his first line.

I heard a voice yell, "Cut!" and was surprised to find it was my own. I said, "Cary, you read the line all wrong. Your timing was off. Let me show you how to get your laugh. Now watch *me*."

If it is possible to vanish into thin air, that's what eighty people tried to do. Breaths were held to bursting point. Looking at George Stevens, I smiled and waited for his nod of approval. Stevens walked toward me slowly.

"Cary read it wrong, George."

George didn't answer—instead he put his hands around my neck and started to choke me. Murder was written in his eyes. Finally deciding I wasn't worth killing, he shouted, "You're fired! Get off my set."

Cary Grant came to my rescue. "Wait a minute, George. Bill's perfectly right. I read the line wrong, missed my laugh. The way Bill read it was much funnier."

Stevens glared, then motioned me into a corner. "Cary saved your ass. But if you ever open your mouth again during a rehearsal or a take, you're finished. Now sit down and shut up—forever."

It is an unpardonable sin to call "cut" on a scene. It is solely the director's privilege, not only for George Stevens but for *any director*. I learned that principle the hard way.

I found out later that day exactly what a dialogue director does. He is strictly an apprentice director. He cues the actors, but he makes no suggestions whatsoever. He keeps out of the director's hair, goes for coffee and sandwiches, and generally remains as invisible as possible.

Production on *Penny Serenade* was slow, with endless rehearsals. Stevens never seemed satisfied. Days stretched into weeks, then months; the end was nowhere in sight.

George Stevens eventually forgave me, and when he wasn't pacing or concentrating he would let me look through the camera while he patiently explained what he was trying

44

to accomplish. What had originally been totally confusing began to form a definite design.

I had moved to a small apartment on the Sunset Strip around the corner from the famous Schwab's Drugstore, where young hopefuls waited to be discovered; actors, writers, and directors gathered there for morning coffee. I usually had breakfast there before taking a bus down to Gower Street, where Columbia was located.

One morning as I waited for my bus, Cary Grant's white Rolls-Royce pulled up. Sticking his head out the window, he insisted I ride to the studio with him. This became a daily habit. Every morning I would sit on the bench and patiently wait for Cary's white Rolls to take me to Columbia.

One beautiful California day, an equally beautiful California girl sat down on the bench next to me. She had long blond hair, green eyes, and a body that never stopped. Never one to be excessively shy, I smiled, and with all the charm I could muster, started what I hoped would be a romance with a brilliant line: "Are you waiting for the bus?"

She looked at me with inviting green eyes, and sexily responded, "I wish the bus would hurry. I'm late for work."

Trying to think of something else clever to say, I countered with, "Oh, that's too bad." Our relationship was growing by leaps and bounds. "I'm Bill Castle." The name didn't bowl her over, as I had hoped.

As I tried valiantly to keep the conversation going, she moved close and purred, "Bill, are you waiting for a bus, too?"

Never at a loss for words, I quickly answered, "No . . . I'm waiting for Cary Grant to pick me up."

Without hesitation, she made her point. "You're full of shit!"

I was about to protest when the white chauffeured Rolls pulled up and Cary Grant actually appeared before her very eyes. She turned red and stammered, "Oh, my God!"

I seized the opportunity to introduce my good friend Cary Grant to my good friend—what the hell was her name? She sweetly said, "Sally." Cary gallantly suggested she ride with us. She almost fainted as he stepped out and helped her into the car.

One Saturday, George Stevens called me at home and asked if I would come to the studio immediately and meet him on the stage. Saturday wasn't a workday and I was puzzled by the strange request, but dressed in my best suit because I felt something important was about to happen.

Arriving at the deserted studio, I headed for Stage One. There were about fifteen people assembled. Stevens looked up, thanked me for coming, and said he wanted to test the earthquake scene that they were shooting on Monday.

"I certainly am most interested in watching," I said.

"You're not watching," he snapped back. "You're testing. I want you to stand in the middle of the set, and no matter what happens, don't leave." I looked at Stevens, my eyes wide. He saw my concern and reassured me. "I just want to see if it works. You don't get hurt . . . if you don't move."

Stevens sat down at a huge console table and studied a series of numbered buttons. The technicians spread out on the set.

A realistic Japanese courtyard, that led to a street outside, had been built on the huge stage. The street was entirely deserted, except for me and several lampposts.

"Ready, Castle?" Stevens shouted. Then all hell broke loose as Stevens pushed button #1 and the sidewalk started to tremble. Button #2 set the houses to shaking. The goddamn lamppost fell at the touch of button #3, and at #4 the water main broke and I was getting soaked.

The ground was splitting in front of me, and I was on my ass and holding on for dear life. Buildings collapsed in front and in back of me at the touch of buttons #7 and #8, and I began trying to get the hell off the set.

The entire street was split wide open now, and as Stevens pressed tenth button, fires started all around me. I was saying my prayers, waiting for the earthquake to be over. Oh, *God!* It was real.

Chapter VIII

My Uncle Samuel

COLUMBIA was a beehive of activity and I found myself working on as many as five different films at the same time. I would bicycle from one set to another, playing a French gendarme on one picture, a doctor in another, dialogue directing on still another, and working in the cutting room in my spare time.

I forgot my previous complaint of inactivity and cursed Harry Cohn for making me work so hard. I was homesick for New York and the theatre. It was useless asking Cohn for permission to take a vacation. The answer would probably be "Go on . . . take a vacation . . . permanently. You're fired!" So I decided just to disappear. Cohn would never know I was gone. I had only seen him once, a year ago, and he had probably forgotten what I looked like. Besides, it would only be for a week.

I packed my bag and sneaked out of the studio, heading for The Big City.

It was great to see New York again. It was alive—the hustle and bustle of the crowds, the museums, the theatres, the restaurants—all the wonderful things I missed in the crazy land of make-believe they call Hollywood.

Jack Cohn, Harry's brother, headed Columbia's New York office, and I had heard that, unlike Harry, he was a gentle man, generous and considerate. There was a hit show on Broadway that I desperately wanted to see. Tickets were impossible to get, so I called Jack and asked if he could possibly

47

get me a single ticket for that night. Jack Cohn was as nice as I'd heard, and he provided me with one of the house seats usually held for VIPs—fifth row center, on the aisle.

I arrived early so I could study the program, and as the theatre began to fill, I noticed the seat next to me remained vacant. Perhaps a beautiful girl would occupy the seat. With great anticipation I hoped and waited. Then suddenly the occupant appeared and sat down next to me. It was Harry Cohn! Of course! The seat was another of his brother Jack's VIP reservations. If only I had known that Harry was in New York.

Opening my program, I tried to hide myself inside it. Harry pulled it out of my hand and barked, "What in the hell are you doing here, Castle?"

"Seeing the play," I politely answered.

"Who gave you permission?"

"No one, sir, but I hear it's a very good play," I earnestly replied.

"Get the hell out of here . . . and go back," he snapped. "Now!"

"Back where?" I asked.

"Hollywood, goddammit," he thundered. People around us were beginning to pay attention, thinking perhaps the play had already begun in the fifth row.

The house lights dimmed and the curtain started to rise. I whispered, "Please sir, Mr. Cohn, at least let me stay for the first act." He grunted something I didn't understand and finally he shut up.

At intermission he asked if I had enjoyed the first act, and when I said yes, gave me permission to stay for the second.

At the end of the play, we filed out of the theatre onto the sidewalk. I thanked Cohn for letting me see the entire play and promised to leave immediately on the next bus.

"Goddammit, Castle, you're a character. Where the hell are you staying in New York?" I told him I was living in a cheap hotel in the West Forties. He snorted in disgust. "You've got no class."

48

The truth was, I had no money, but I wasn't about to admit that. As if reading my mind, he plunged his hand into his pocket and came out with three hundred-dollar bills which he shoved into my hand. "Check in at the Warwick Hotel. We put our people from Columbia there. Tell 'em Harry Cohn sent you and sign the bill. I'll okay it. And for chrissake, buy a new suit and comb your hair. . . . you're a mess!" I think he noticed the original coffee stains.

As he started to leave, he turned back. "You have two weeks, Castle, and if you ever tell anybody about this, I'll fire you on the spot." And with that, he disappeared into the night. Rough, tough, unpredictable, wonderful Harry Cohn.

I stood in front of the theatre for a while after Cohn left, watching as the audience streamed out. I had just a few days for New York and its theatres, my home, before returning to Hollywood, the city where my fate and my ambitions had led me. There is a finality when the bright lights on a theatre marquee go out. The name of the play and performers are erased until the next performance. Some strange urge propelled me to reenter the theatre.

Ticket stubs and theatre programs lay everywhere on the orchestra floor. It was dark inside, and eerie, the time for ghosts of the past to haunt the theatre. The curtain was raised, the stage bare, the living actors long gone. My eyes went to the single naked light bulb fiercely burning on center stage, keeping constant vigil through the night. The theatre! It was familiar. Ten years before, when I was sixteen, I had stared into a similar light bulb on another stage—the morning that producer Jules Leventhal had informed me I was to be stage manager of *An American Tragedy*, the youngest stage manager in Broadway's history.

That was in 1930, and the Depression was killing us. I had hunted for a job desperately, along with hundreds of other out-of-work actors. I had talked my way into a dishwasher's job at the automat on Forty-second Street. Hating every minute away from show business, I took my hostility out on the dirty dishes. A couple of bucks a week and free food—I was

49

barely existing. The one day I had off was spent searching for a job in the theatre. Everybody was out of work, and the competition for even the smallest part was unbelievable.

Actors Equity had a list of several new shows being cast. I noticed that Jules Leventhal was casting for a revival of *An American Tragedy.* An unemployed actor next to me turned and asked, "Are you going over to the Leventhal office?"

"No," I lied.

"Neither am I," he lied. And each of us trying to lose the other, we both headed in the same direction.

Searching through my pockets, I found two dimes and several pennies. At a corner drugstore, I headed for a telephone booth and searched the directory for Jules Leventhal Productions.

I dialed the number and waited. A secretary's voice answered, "Leventhal Productions." She sounded harried.

With authority, I demanded to speak to Jules Leventhal.

"That's quite impossible," she answered. "Mr. Leventhal's very busy casting and will take no calls."

Desperately, I tried to keep her from hanging up. I couldn't tolerate any more dirty dishes. My mind racing, I glanced outside the phone booth and noticed a huge billboard advertising Samuel Goldwyn's newest film, *Arrowsmith,* starring Ronald Colman and Helen Hayes. What seemed an eternity was actually a second. "Tell Mr. Leventhal that it's Samuel Goldwyn's nephew calling," I barked into the telephone.

There was awe in the secretary's voice as she said, "Just a minute, sir," and immediately connected me.

A deep voice answered, "Sam? Is this Samuel Goldwyn?"

"No, sir," I hastily replied, "This is his nephew William. My uncle, Samuel Goldwyn, suggested I call you. He thought you could use me in your new play."

"What did you say your name was?" the voice asked.

"William Goldwyn, sir, but I changed it to Castle because I didn't want to trade on the Goldwyn name."

"How soon can you get over here?"

"I'm around the corner," I answered.

"Fine—oh, by the way, how is your uncle? I've been meaning to call him."

"Just fine," I said, "and he sends his warm regards." And with that, I hung up and rushed off to meet my uncle Samuel Goldwyn's good friend.

The Leventhal office was jammed with actors—at least 150 of them lined up, wall to wall, in the outer office. The secretary was frantically trying to restore some order in the bedlam when I entered. Pushing my way through the crowd, I managed to attract her attention. She briefly glanced in my direction and then completely ignored me. I inched my way toward Jules Leventhal's private office and had just managed to get my hand on the doorknob when the secretary's scream stopped me cold. "Don't you dare do that . . . do you hear? You wait your turn."

I yelled at the top of my lungs in order to be heard, "I'm Samuel Goldwyn's nephew. Mr. Leventhal's expecting me."

In thirty seconds flat, she put on lipstick, powdered her nose and fluffed her hair and, giving me a radiant smile, personally escorted me in to meet Jules Leventhal. She was obviously expecting to be discovered by my uncle Samuel.

Sitting behind the desk was a balding, short, stocky man who looked like a butcher. Another youngish man, the director, was also present. Leventhal greeted me warmly and introduced me. "This is Sam Goldwyn's nephew. Charlie, have we got something in the play for him? His uncle says he's quite good."

The director looked me over and asked if I had ever done any acting. Not that it made the slightest difference, since he too was impressed by my family background and clearly hoped someday to work for my uncle Samuel. He said he was sure he could find a part for me.

Jules Leventhal then suggested we call Sam Goldwyn immediately and tell him the good news—and perhaps, as a personal favor, I would put in a good word and persuade my uncle to invest in another Leventhal production which was to go into rehearsal right after *An American Tragedy* opened.

Playing Russian roulette with my career, I pulled the trigger: "Mr. Leventhal, when did you last see my uncle?"

"Call me Jules," he answered sweetly, molasses dripping from his lips. "William, the truth is we've never really met, but personally, I've always been a great admirer . . . as a matter of fact, come to think of it, you look a little like him." The trigger clicked—the fatal shot had not been fired.

"Everybody says I look like him," I said. "Personally, I don't see the resemblance." Leventhal instructed his secretary to place a call to Mr. Samuel Goldwyn in Hollywood, immediately. Back to Russian roulette. I had to stop that phone call. If Samuel Goldwyn ever found out that I was impersonating his nephew—if he even had a goddamn nephew—I would be in real trouble.

I pulled the trigger again. "Wait, Mr. Leventhal—I mean Jules—Uncle Samuel is away on a fishing trip and can't be reached for several weeks; but I promise you, as soon as he returns, I'll personally ask him if he'll invest in your new production." Leventhal bought it. Another reassuring click of the trigger.

The fatal bullet was never fired, because that afternoon, thanks to Samuel Goldwyn, I got not only *one* part, but *five*. Of course I had practically committed Samuel Goldwyn to backing Jules Leventhal's next play, but I'd cross that bridge when I came to it. What was important was that I'd finally made it to Broadway. I would have been ecstatic with just one part, but *five!*

But fate was about to play an even stranger trick than my own—a tragic occurrence was about to change the course of my life.

Chapter IX

It's Bigger Than I Thought

I KEPT Samuel Goldwyn fishing, but Jules Leventhal never mentioned him again. Obviously he had gotten backing for his new play from some other source. *An American Tragedy* opened to mixed reviews. The name "William Castle" appeared three separate places in the program; for the other two parts I was "George Spelvin"—a fictitious theatrical name which is used when for any reason the producer doesn't want to use the actor's actual name. In various makeups, I played an old man, a middle-aged man, a young man, a prison guard, and a bailiff in the trial scene.

The art of makeup had always fascinated me and now, after each performance, I spent hours at the dressing-room mirror re-creating the grotesque images of the immortal Lon Chaney, the man of a hundred faces: *The Hunchback of Notre Dame, The Phantom of the Opera, The Unholy Three, The Blackbird, West of Zanzibar, The Road to Mandalay.* I had photographs taken of each new face and I began to fantasize that I was now Lon Chaney.

Several months later, the opportunity presented itself when the great artist died. Newspapers filled with the tragic occurrence revealed that Tod Browning, Chaney's director, would be arriving in New York. I called MGM's office daily, and was at last informed that Tod Browning was in New York.

After a matinee, not bothering to take off my old-man

53

makeup, I headed for MGM. Browning's secretary looked at the old man shaking in front of her and informed me Browning wasn't in, nor was he expected back.

As I started to leave, a tall, lean man came toward me. On a hunch, I stopped him. "Mr. Browning?" He nodded. "I'm William Castle, sir . . . may I see you for just a moment?"

Browning, his face impassive, looked at the old man standing in front of him. "What about, son?"

I proudly opened my portfolio and showed him my various makeups and disguises. He gave them a quick glance; then turned away. "I'm another Lon Chaney," I pleaded. "I *know* I am. . . . If you'll just give me a chance, I'll prove I can be just as good."

Tod Browning looked at me coldly. Shivers ran down my spine. After what seemed like an eternity he said something I shall never forget. "There is only *one Lon Chaney* and he has gone, *forever*. No one can ever take his place." And with that he angrily walked away and slammed his office door right in my old-man face. I felt that my lifelong desire to scare audiences was never going to be fulfilled in front of cameras.

Eight performances a week became my life. I couldn't wait for the curtain to rise. When I wasn't changing makeup and costumes for my five parts, I was watching the play from the wings. Soon I learned how smoothly a Broadway play can be run. Stagehands, electricians, property men, actors—all followed the guidance of the stage manager, the man responsible for the smooth running of a Broadway play. As important and responsible as his job was, the stage manager of *An American Tragedy* seemed constantly unhappy about imaginary injustices toward him. He bitterly complained to me that Leventhal didn't like him and was trying to find some excuse to fire him. During most of the performances he let his assistant take charge. And the assistant allowed me to help him. "Let me check the props for you, Al," I would suggest. "I'll hold the script, just in case an actor forgets his lines." "You want me to announce the half hour, fifteen min-

54

utes, five minutes, so the cast will be ready for curtain?" Backstage is very much like the intricate movement inside a perfect Swiss watch, and I was slowly becoming a small part of it.

One night, after concentrating too long on helping the assistant stage manager, I almost missed my own first-act cue, and in a panic, dashed on stage in my dinner jacket. The scene was a very lavish dinner party and when I said my one and only line to the hostess, "It's really much bigger than I thought" (the party), the audience suddenly burst into hysterics. Never having gotten a laugh on the line before, I was puzzled. Glancing down, I discovered my fly was wide open. In my haste I had forgotten to button it.

The stage presence of a beautiful young actress named Dorothy Watson saved me. She quickly stepped in front of me and, smiling, gazed into my eyes as she ad libbed, "The music is so divine. Shall we dance on the terrace?" I accepted, and on the offstage terrace I was able to adjust my error. After a few moments we returned to center stage as I thanked her for the delightful dance.

After Dorothy Watson came to my rescue that zipperless night, I began to watch her from the wings with complete fascination. She was not only beautiful, but had a rare talent.

The raising and lowering of the heavy theatre curtain during a performance was controlled with old-fashioned sandbags—heavy sacks strung up on the side of the theatre which regulated the force and speed of the curtain. The stage manager usually gave the signal to a stagehand who pushed a lever to raise and lower the sandbags. The heavy ropes which pulled the weight of the curtain were held firmly in place by four knifelike prongs. The entire cast was repeatedly warned not to put their hands on the ropes.

During a curtain call one night, the audience continued applauding, and the curtain was raised and lowered several times. The three principals then took their individual bows. Finally Dorothy Watson was ready for her solo curtain call. In the warm, heady glow of anticipation while waiting for the curtain to rise, she forgot the warning and put her hand on the ropes.

When the stage manager gave his signal, the force and pull of the ropes carried her hand into the knifelike prongs. She managed to get her hand free and took what was to be her final curtain call, valiantly bowing and smiling to the audience while concealing the spurting blood.

Pandemonium broke out backstage as the curtain dropped. Cast and crew were hysterical. The stage manager, sobbing, blamed himself for causing the accident and rushed around the stage, accomplishing nothing.

Riding to the hospital with Dorothy, I held her in my arms and tried to comfort her. She was sobbing uncontrollably. I tried to reassure her that everything would be all right, but my words sounded false even to my own ears.

At eight o'clock the next morning I awakened Jules Leventhal and told him the agonizing news—the doctors had amputated several of Dorothy's fingers. He told me to come to the theatre immediately.

Standing in the theatre, both of us gazing into the naked light bulb on the deserted stage, Leventhal told me that the stage manager was badly shaken and had quit. He looked at me a long moment and then made a quiet decision. "Bill, you are the new stage manager. Get Dorothy's understudy ready—we have a matinee this afternoon." The horror of reality had pushed me further into the cardboard world of make-believe. Hollywood and Broadway had that much in common—behind the lights were real people, buffeted by our own luck and tragedies.

Now, ten years later, I idly picked up a discarded program of the play I had just seen with Harry Cohn. He had said, "You've got two weeks in New York," and there was so much I wanted to see and to do.

The first order of business was to check into the Warwick Hotel and tell them Harry Cohn had sent me. I was given the VIP treatment and ushered into a suite on the top floor.

It was two in the morning and I was famished. Room service was closed for the night. Opening the door of my suite, I peered into the deserted hallway. A tray with some leftover food sat waiting a few doors away. In pajamas, and barefooted, I padded hungrily toward my goal. As I wolfed down half-eaten shrimp, cold chunks of uneaten steak and a remaining bite of cherry pie, I, a VIP, was caught red-handed by the hotel detective.

With my mouth full, I tried to explain I was a guest, that, as a matter of fact, Harry Cohn had sent me. The detective yanked me downstairs, bare feet and all. It wasn't until the night manager identified me that the hotel detective, still suspicious, let me have my VIP stripes back.

I tossed and turned for the rest of the night. Something was bothering me. I couldn't figure what. Some unfinished business, some long-forgotten incident eluded me. But what?

I awakened early, still famished, and ordered a huge breakfast from room service. The nagging feeling that occurred during the night persisted—some unfinished business, but what?

The second order of business was to keep my promise to Harry Cohn and buy a new suit. In front of the Warwick, I jumped into a waiting cab and instinctively said, "Bloomingdale's." Sitting back in the cab, I pondered why I had picked Bloomingdale's. As a matter of fact, I liked Macy's better . . . even Gimbels.

The meter read thirty-five cents when I got out of the cab. I handed the driver one of Harry's hundred-dollar bills, my only cash in hand, and awaited my change. He looked at me incredulously. "You must be kidding."

I searched through my pockets and assured him it was the smallest bill I had. The cabdriver, whose name I noticed was Louie Schwartzwald, glared at me. To get change for a hundred-dollar bill in New York City is next to impossible, especially during the rush hour. I told Mr. Schwartzwald meekly that I was going to make some purchases at Bloomingdale's and if he would be kind enough to wait, I would soon be out with the exact change. Mr. Schwartzwald shook his head and insisted on coming into the store with me.

I made my purchases in Bloomingdale's, and as I handed

over the hundred-bill and waited for the change, the nagging "what" I had been searching for suddenly surfaced with the clang of the cash register. Now I knew what the elusive, nagging, unfinished business was—I had to pay back the man in the Black Derby Hat the money that I had owed him for over six years.

Together, Louie Schwartzwald and I raced to the cab with my new wardrobe and I gave instructions to drive to Greenwich Village as fast as possible. My honor was at stake.

CHAPTER X

The Man in the Black Derby Hat

LONG hair, beards, bald heads, berets, knitted wool caps, but no Black Derby. The cab moved slowly along Macdougal Street as I leaned out the window and continued to search. The meter was now $4.80 and ticking away.

Suddenly I spotted the Black Derby Hat. "That's him . . . over there!" The cab abruptly pulled to a stop. I stood on the curb and watched. He was dressed exactly as I remembered—a shiny blue suit, collarless shirt, wire-rimmed glasses with a slight crack in the right lens and, of course, the ever-present Black Derby Hat. I often wondered if he slept with it on. Legs spread apart, head proudly raised toward the sky, he seemed to be surveying the entire row of brownstones that lined the block. As I approached, he sensed my presence and turned around. For a moment he just stared. Then his moon-shaped face broke into a smile of recognition. Without a word, he grabbed me in a bear hug and squeezed until I could hardly breathe. Squat, short, and chunky, he was made of iron. Albert Strunsky—his empire, Greenwich Village. The brownstones he was surveying all belonged to him, as did many other sections of the Village.

Legend had it that Strunsky escaped a Russian pogrom against the Jews and, killing a few Cossacks along the way, fled to America when he was seventeen. Settling in Greenwich Village, he found work as an apprentice to a blacksmith, shoeing horses. When cars came in and horses went out, he purchased a small grocery store in the Village. He worked long, tedious hours and the little store prospered. Albert Strunsky managed to save enough to acquire a small portion of land. Every Sunday he would spend hours on his land. Kneeling, he would sift the rich brown soil through his calloused fingers, and dream of the future. Land was cheap then, and Strunsky continued buying more and more of his "precious earth"—all in Greenwich Village. In the 1920s he started to build apartment houses, blocks of them. Albert Strunsky became known as "The Village Landlord."

Trying to catch my breath after he released me from the bear hug, I managed a weak grin. "Papa Strunsky . . . you remember me." Everyone in the Village called him "Papa."

"Of course, I remember 'Simple Simon.' Forget, I don't . . . Money, you owe me."

I pointed to a broken window on the top floor of one of the brownstones. "I lived in that room, Papa, remember? Six years ago."

Strunsky's face, creased and lined with the years, looked like parchment stretched in the sun. "So, you want to move back again? It'll cost you more. The rent, I've raised." Surveying me carefully as he surveyed his empire, he hesitated, trying not to embarrass me. "But if you're broke . . . you'll stay rent-free. You can owe me."

I already owed him $500 worth of food, loans and back rent. I shoved my hand in my pocket and pulled out a hundred-dollar bill and handed it to him. "On account, Papa. I'll pay the rest as quickly as possible."

He looked at the money, his eyes twinkling. "A bank robber you've become?"

"No, Papa, I'm in the motion-picture business. I live in Hollywood."

Strunsky pounded my back. "Congratulations, 'Simple Simon.' So, maybe a movie star . . . a Jewish Robert Taylor?"

Trying to explain my duties at Columbia wasn't easy. He plied me with questions. I managed to sidestep how I got the hundred dollars.

Arms around my shoulder, he again hugged me roughly,

60

then glanced at the corner where a little girl was playing hop-scotch. He shouted, "Sarah, come over quick," and grinning, he pointed to me.

When the little girl joined us, he started to chant,

> Simple Simon met a Pieman
> Going to the fair.
> Said Simple Simon to the Pieman
> Let me taste your wares. . . ."

The little girl stared at me, her eyes wide with amazement.

I was "Simple Simon," but that had been in 1934, and it didn't seem quite as funny to me then. I was still very young, only twenty, but my "success" in *American Tragedy* was already four years in the past.

Papa Strunsky had invited me to celebrate Christmas Eve at one of his favorite restaurants, and after dinner, he pulled a package out of his pocket. "Happy Hanukkah, Simple Simon." Opening it, I discovered a wristwatch. His eyes danced with merriment as he enjoyed my excitement. "So, now on time you'll be."

Proudly, I presented him with a gift—a necktie I had purchased the day before.

Greenwich Village was alive with Christmas lights and decorations and as we walked it began to snow. Noticing my unhappy silence, Papa Strunsky tried to cheer me up. "In the theatre you'll make it. I know. For artists, I'm lucky." We passed a window covered with holly, and Papa pointed to it. "He was down on his luck," Papa began, knowing I knew who he was talking about. "But such a talent he had, I told him." Pulling his velvet collar up against the now heavily falling snow, Papa gazed at the window. "A long time he lived there, writing." Strunsky was referring to the famous American playwright Eugene O'Neill. "They're all my children—writers, painters, sculptors, musicians, actors, poets—and which of my children will become successful, I know."

We walked on down Macdougal Street that night and

stopped in front of the building where I lived. Papa contemplated for a moment, then looked at me. "During the lifetime of a man, he should fall on his *tokus* many times. But if he's worth anything, always he picks himself up. So now, 'Simple Simon,' get up. And harder you should try. . . . because money you owe me, and forget, I don't."

I climbed the five flights to my room wondering how I could ever repay the money I owed. I switched on the light in my one room (bath privileges two floors down) and noticed a package lying on the bed. It was a bottle of brandy, with a card attached. "Drink in good health."

The definition of bohemian is a vagabond—a writer or artist living an unconventional life. During the 1930s, Greenwich Village was the artists' commune, and Papa Strunsky was their saint and savior, a patron of the arts. The Village was colorful and carefree, and I lived in a beehive of activity, with poet Maxwell Bodenheim as a next door neighbor and sculptor Ernest Gutman, creator of futuristic masterpieces, living two floors down. It was a lean, hungry time for almost all the artists in the Village, and Papa Strunsky sponsored many of them for weeks, months, even years. It made no difference to him. Someday they would pay him back. Many great works of art were dedicated to him by the artists he helped. Whenever anyone sold a painting, sculpture, book, or poem, the celebration would begin and last for several days. Back rent would be paid by the lucky artist; and bottles would open and the wine begin to flow.

Every day I made the rounds of the Broadway agents and theatrical managers' offices in search of work, but there was none. Back in the Village, I would try to join in the happiness of others. An artist can paint, can even create a masterpiece when he is alone. A book can be written alone, a poem created, music composed, sculpture shaped. But try to act by yourself—it's an impossibility. Somehow I got by. Every weekend at a little club called The Village Vanguard I would do impersonations of the Hollywood stars—Lionel Barrymore, Frank Morgan, Jean Hersholt, Ronald Colman, Edward G. Robinson. Some nights I would stand on the little stage in clown makeup and recite Chekhov's "The Swan Song." Audiences would throw pennies, nickels and dimes, and when I took my final bow, I would hurriedly gather the loose change. As a bonus, I got free suppers.

I continued owing back rent, and constantly borrowed money while I struggled to find work in the theatre. Then one day it appeared my luck might have changed.

It was a cold, bleak December day and having spent my last nickel on the subway, I shivered against the cold as I made my daily rounds. "Don't call us, we'll call you. . . . No casting today. . . . Sorry, Mr. Belasco is out of town. . . . Sorry, Mr. Frohman is not seeing any actors." Theatrical doors were shut and bolted.

On impulse, I walked toward the Belasco Theatre where Sidney Kingsley's play *Dead End* had opened to rave reviews. The possibilities of an actor's dropping out of a hit play were a million to one. It was a crazy hunch, but I had nothing to lose and at least it would get me out of the cold.

It was deserted backstage, and as I was about to leave, the stage door opened and a youngish man with horn-rimmed glasses appeared. Introducing myself, I asked if anyone had given notice.

He shook his head. "In a hit show? Actors don't dare even get sick. We expect to run for two years!" He tried to cheer me up. "Why don't you leave your phone number . . . just in case?"

I shook my head. "I don't have a phone, thanks anyway. Sorry to have bothered you, Merry Christmas."

A "Merry Christmas and good luck," came back.

I opened the stage door and discovered it had begun to snow. Suddenly I wanted to stay in the warm, comfortable womb of the theatre. In an attempt to delay leaving, I cried out, "I was a stage manager once, and . . ." Then, unable to stop, rattled off my small list of credits.

The stage manager, sensing my desperation, quietly asked, "Would you like tickets for the show?"

"No, thank you. I'll be on my way." I paused at the door.

"I'll leave a telephone number, just in case." And giving Papa Strunsky's number, I said good-bye.

It was snowing heavily as I started trudging back to the Village, flat broke as usual. The streets were almost deserted, traffic barely moving. On Thirty-fourth Street, a hot-dog vendor was just closing his stand. My stomach, trying to inform me I hadn't eaten since the night before, growled angrily. I attempted to engage the vendor in conversation. "The snow hurts business, doesn't it?"

"Who buys hots in lousy weather like this?" he snorted.

I agreed sympathetically and politely inquired what plans he had for the frankfurters he couldn't sell.

"Eat 'em myself—it'll probably snow all weekend."

Eagerly I offered to help. I could almost taste the sauerkraut. The stand, now closed, was being wheeled away. Watching my precious hot dogs disappear and up to my ankles in snow, I raced after him. "Wait . . . please, I'm hungry."

He continued wheeling, muttering, "You wanna eat, buy. No free hots today. Get lost!"

A Papa Strunsky he wasn't. And so, trying to make peace with my stomach, I continued my trek into nothingness.

The New York University clock announced it was five. It had taken me two hours to walk from the Belasco Theatre. In front of Washington Square, I noticed some children had made a large snowman. My empty stomach was playing tricks with my imagination—the snowman was walking toward me.

Standing in shock, I felt the abominable snowman throw his arms around me. It was Papa Strunsky, white derby and all, completely encased in snow. "For hours I have been waiting. Good news I've got. A man called. Be at the Belasco Theatre, ten o'clock tomorrow morning he said." Excited, jubilant, elated; it was the first time I had ever danced with a snowman.

That night Papa Strunsky invited me to celebrate with dinner at his home. I ate until I was ready to burst. When I finally got back to my room and started putting my trousers under the mattress to press them, I discovered that Papa Strunsky had slipped a ten-dollar bill into one of the pockets. That made an even $500 I owed him.

Lying in bed trying to sleep, my mind raced with excitement. *Dead End* was a hit play. The stage manager had said it would last two years. My luck *had* changed.

I jumped in a cab the following morning and proudly announced, "The Belasco Theatre, please."

Upon arriving, I immediately searched for the stage manager. He was talking to a young man, approximately my age, and motioned me over. "Just after you left yesterday, an actor gave notice . . . illness. It's not much—just a bit—but important enough for Mr. Kingsley to want to meet you . . . personally." With that, he excused himself and disappeared into one of the dressing rooms.

Looking at the young man, I smiled. We were alike in appearance, and he too had the lean, hungry look of an out-of-work actor. He seemed uneasy and, with a sinking sensation, I knew we were both up for the same part.

"Did they call you, too?" I asked.

He nodded. "Last night."

"Me too," I replied. Hearing my name called, I saw the stage manager waving me toward the dressing room. As I turned to leave, the young man whispered, "Good luck."

"Mr. Kingsley," the stage manager said, "this is William Castle, I thought perhaps he might be right for the part."

Sidney Kingsley shook hands warmly and invited me to sit down. "Just a few lines, Castle, but very important to the play. Do you mind reading them for me? The part of the intern."

"Of course not, Mr. Kingsley," I answered nervously. He handed me a typewritten sheet and settled back to listen.

When I finished, Kingsley smiled encouragingly. "Thank you, and now will you please wait onstage."

My competition studied me. "How'd it go?"

Before I could answer my shadow's name was called, and he nervously walked into the dressing room.

65

I paced the stage and counted the minutes, and after what seemed an eternity, my shadow returned. "Kingsley asked me to wait."

"Me too," I said.

We were two shadows, desperate for the job, each trying not to let the other one know. Suddenly my name was called—the part was mine. Putting my arm around him, I tried to say how sorry I was, but the words wouldn't come. He wished me luck, and I walked into the dressing room with my heart pounding.

Sidney Kingsley stood up. He seemed ill-at-ease and slightly embarrassed. "I'm sorry, Castle, but I decided to use the other actor. Thank you for auditioning and I hope . . ." The rest of the sentence was muffled as I left the dressing room blindly.

Choking back tears, I informed the other actor that the part was his. Together we wept, but for different reasons. (The young man's name was Philip Bourneuf, a brilliant actor, who later became well-known both in the theatre and motion pictures.)

Standing in the alley outside the theatre, I despised myself. For almost a year, I had been a freeloader—how could I go back to the Village and face Papa Strunsky? I had to find work—any kind of work—and start paying him back.

On Fifty-ninth Street and Third Avenue, I watched throngs of Christmas shoppers going into Bloomingdale's. Pushing my way through, I asked for the personnel director.

Mrs. Atwell was as cold and businesslike as the name plate on her desk. She scanned my application. "I see you've worked in department stores before, Mr. Castle."

"Oh, yes, Mrs. Atwell, many . . . Baltimore, Philadelphia, Washington."

"And what did you sell, Mr. Castle?"

"Everything!"

Mrs. Atwell nodded her approval. "We have a temporary position in men's furnishings. Report to Mr. Goodrich tomorrow at nine."

Having never worked in a department store before, I stammered, "How . . . how much will it pay?"

"Twelve dollars a week." And handing me my employment slip, Mrs. Atwell methodically went back to her work.

The following morning I reported to Mr. Goodrich, the floorwalker in men's furnishings, and was put in charge of shirts and ties. "You know how to fill out a sales slip?"

"Of course!" I said.

Confident, he handed me a sales book and disappeared. I looked around for my first customer. Suddenly six of them descended, demanding to see my merchandise—all in a hurry.

That afternoon the shirt and tie department was in such utter chaos that I hid in the men's room. When I returned, Mr. Goodrich was waiting for me.

"You've completely disrupted Bloomingdale's." His blue suit bursting with indignation, he pulled my sales book away and thumbed through it. "Good heavens, you're selling shirts at half price!" Scowling, he branded me a misfit and ordered me from his department.

I went back to personnel. Mrs. Atwell was waiting for me, Mr. Goodrich had spread the news. Clucking, she reexamined my application. "You've been in the theatre, Mr. Castle? Or is that, too, a lie?"

"No—I mean yes, Mrs. Atwell."

"Well, perhaps we have something you're better suited for. Go up to the toy department, fourth floor, and ask for Mr. Timothy."

After giving me a brief once-over, Mr. Timothy announced, "You'll do . . . you'll do quite well."

"What will I do quite well, Mr. Timothy . . . play Santa Claus?"

"Oh, dear, no!" He giggled. "You're *much* too thin." And snapping his fingers and motioning "Come with me," he quickly deposited me with a birdlike lady. "Fit him, Miss Hastings. He'll be on 'Page Seven.'"

I asked Miss Hastings what I would be on "Page Seven," but she merely cooed, "You'll see, you'll see."

67

As she continued cooing, Little Jack Horner came over, whining that his shoes didn't fit. Little Miss Muffet fretted about her wig, and Jack and Jill bitterly complained that they both wouldn't fit on the same page. Miss Hastings continued her incessant chirping as she took care of their problems efficiently. Then, beaming, she handed me a costume—pointed shoes with bells, knee breeches, a crazy rainbow-colored shirt, the hat of a dunce, the nose of a fool and an empty bucket.

It was for Bloomingdale's "Living Nursery Book," and on each page, a different character appeared—Little Bo-Peep, Jack and Jill, Little Miss Muffet, Peter Piper, Old Mother Hubbard, Little Boy Blue, and on "Page Seven"—Simple Simon! Me!

For twenty-five cents, the entire family could walk through the pages. It was the big attraction in the toy department, and each day hundreds of children screamed with delight.

It was on "Page Seven" that Papa Strunsky saw me fishing with an imaginary pole out of an empty bucket, and, laughing until tears came to his eyes, he kept shouting with glee like the other children:

> Simple Simon met a Pieman
> Going to the fair.
> Said Simple Simon to the Pieman
> Let me taste your wares. . . .

I was still starving for recognition, applause—trying to prove myself to someone, anyone.

Now, after only a relatively short time and still heady with my "successes" in Stony Creek and Hollywood, I turned and gave Papa Strunsky one of his own great bear hugs as the memories came rushing back.

Barely two years later, on January 2, 1942, *The New York Times* ran the following notice:

FRIEND OF ARTISTS IN VILLAGE DIES

Albert Strunsky—"Papa Strunsky" to a generation of Greenwich Village artists whose doings he so much admired that he refused at times to charge them rent—died Wednesday.

Struggling aspirants of the arts, writers, sculptors, and the rest learned that Mr. Strunsky's soft Russian heart abhorred evictions as they themselves abhorred the thought of paying rent. Mr. Strunsky shunned reporters in those days for, as he explained, each mention of his name and charities brought fresh waves of hopeful squatters to his door.

Papa Strunsky died at the Beth Israel Hospital, seventy-five years old. He had been ill for some time at his home, 44 Washington Square South. . . ."

I had managed to pay him back all but $50.

CHAPTER XI

The Chance of a Lifetime

HARRY COHN'S private dining room, the domain of his exclusive chef, Andy, was located on the third floor of Columbia's administration building. It was a symbol of one's status to be invited to lunch there. The "chosen," personally selected by Mr. Cohn, dined each day at the long table. "King Cohn" sat at the head, flanked on either side by motion-picture royalty—producers, directors, writers, top stars, visiting dignitaries from other studios and, of course, the ever-present studio executives that comprised Harry Cohn's team.

The menu in 1942 was opulent—caviar, smoked salmon, three-inch steaks, large tomatoes halved with slices of onion in between, bagels and lox, assorted fruits, cakes, pies, beverages—and all free. Cohn figured that if Columbia picked up the tab, he could limit the lunch hour to *exactly* an hour and thus save money. Every day, executives, top producers, and directors assembled at noon and were finished by 1:00 P.M. Cohn would rise, throw down his napkin, and stride out of the dining room, ordering, "Back to work."

I had never had the fortune to be invited to sip nectar with the Gods, but I had peeked in once and had seen a group of blue suits doubled over with laughter. While I couldn't hear what was being said, I watched Cohn point a finger at some unfortunate who was cast in the role of court jester that day.

One morning I spotted Andy struggling with several cartons of groceries. Taking a few of the heavy boxes, I carried them to the dining room, set the boxes down, and sank into

Harry Cohn's chair. I was daydreaming, and I didn't notice Margaret Lee, Cohn's secretary, enter. In her cultured voice, she inquired why I was sitting in Harry's chair and what the hell I was doing in the dining room anyway. Andy came to my rescue saying I had helped him with the groceries. Satisfied, she informed Andy that Cohn wanted chocolate cake for lunch, and vanished.

The aroma of grilled steaks filtered in from the kitchen, making my saliva dance. Andy's voice rang out, "I'm making a steak for myself . . . do you want one?"

"Medium-rare," I yelled back. "Do you think it's safe?"

"If you're out of here before twelve," he shouted. There was a pause before he continued. "When is Mr. Cohn going to give you a picture to direct?"

"Who the hell knows?" I said dejectedly.

"How long have you been at Columbia, Bill?"

"Three years . . . and I'm farther away from directing a picture than I was when I started," I complained bitterly. "I'm ready to direct. I know I am."

Andy appeared at the doorway. "Come and get it, Castle. Chow's ready."

"Can't I eat at the table, Andy?"

"You want to get me fired? You eat in the kitchen with me."

On Tuesday, October 7, 1942, Andy and I were carrying the usual cartons of groceries to the third floor when he informed me the dining room would be closed that day for repainting. Carrying the food into the kitchen, he asked what I wanted for lunch.

"Double lamb chops, french fries, and mint jelly, please, Andy."

"Why don't you sit at Mr. Cohn's place today? . . . You've always wanted to."

"Do you think it's all right?" I asked.

"Why not? The room's closed, but if it will make you feel safer, I'll lock the door."

71

It was noon when he brought my lunch, putting it at Cohn's place, which I now occupied. He proceeded to the kitchen to get his own lunch, but never returned.

Suddenly the door crashed open and in stalked Harry Cohn with his entire entourage. He stopped short, seeing me sitting in his chair. There was a brief pause. Then the bomb exploded.

My face was red. Getting up, I stammered, "They're painting the dining room this afternoon, Mr. Cohn. . . . I'm . . . I'm going to help them."

"Who told you that shit?" he barked.

"Andy did, sir."

I looked toward Andy for acknowledgment, but all he did was grin. The double-crossing sonofabitch! Cohn, glaring at me, took my plate and slammed it down in the next place. Sitting down, he motioned to the other executives.

"I hope you won't mind if we join you," he snapped, biting on a piece of celery. "Or do you want to eat in private?"

"No . . . yes, sir . . . I mean no, sir. . . . You stay, I'll leave."

As I turned to go, Cohn put his hand on my shoulder and pushed me into a chair. "Andy tells me you think you're ready to direct a picture. . . . He says every time he feeds you, you complain to him."

"Mr. Cohn," I said, "that's not true."

Cohn glanced at Andy.

"Isn't that correct, Andy? Doesn't Castle complain about my not giving him a picture?"

"Yes, sir," Andy said, smiling. "He certainly does, and man, can he eat. I never saw such an appetite."

Sinking deeper and deeper into my chair, I tried to lose myself under the table. Why was Andy doing this to me?

Still smiling, Andy broke the silence. "Don't you think you should give him the chance, Mr. Cohn? Then he won't eat in my kitchen anymore."

Cohn looked at Andy, his eyes twinkling. "You think he's ready, Andy?" Andy nodded.

Cohn now addressed the members of his staff as Andy re-

72

treated into the kitchen. "What do you think?" he asked. To a man, they agreed that to give me a picture to direct would be the end of Columbia Pictures, Inc.

Harry turned to Irving Briskin, the head of production (the "Briskin Unit" that made inexpensive B pictures for Columbia.) "Irving," Cohn said, "how about that new picture you're starting."

"I hope you're not thinking of Castle," Briskin said, trying to hide his smile.

Cohn snapped back, "Let's find out if he's as great a director as he told Andy he was." Handing me a script, ironically named *The Chance of a Lifetime,* Cohn told me to start reading.

Later I found out that Harry Cohn had known for weeks that I was eating in his kitchen. He had instructed Andy to feed me as long as I continued to help him, and not to let on that he knew. That morning Cohn had called Andy and told him he was going to let me direct. "Get him at the table, in my chair, eating. Use any excuse . . . I want to scare the ass off him."

Two hours later, I finished reading *The Chance of a Lifetime.* It was a lousy, dull, contrived, miserable script; the characters wooden, and the dialogue unbelievably bad. My first picture, and I had won a turkey!

Depressed, I tried to decide what to do. I could see Harry Cohn and tell him how bad the script really was. But he would probably throw me off the picture, and I would have to wait three more years for another chance. On the other hand, if I made it and the picture was as lousy as it read, Cohn would fire me anyway.

Later that afternoon I was in Irving Briskin's office. "Mr. Briskin," I said, "let me be honest. The script is rather good; it has some interesting possibilities. With a good cast and a minor rewrite, I think we might have something."

Briskin glowered at me. "What's wrong with the script?"

"Nothing, Mr. Briskin, sir," I said. "I just think it needs a little clarification."

73

"Bullshit! You shoot that script exactly as it's written, and I don't want you changing one lousy word."

"But sir, maybe a little . . ."

"No, goddammit! No rewrite! Now get out of here—I'm busy."

Realizing any further conversation was futile I departed, then on impulse, went to Harry Cohn's office.

"Whadda' ya want, Castle? . . . Be quick—I'm in a hurry."

"Mr. Cohn, sir, I want to talk to you about my new picture."

"Yeah, what about it?"

"I feel . . . sir . . . that *The Chance of a Lifetime* is. . . ." Cohn looked at me impatiently. I hesitated, then continued. ". . . a marvelous opportunity, and I just wanted to come in personally and thank you for giving me the chance . . . of a lifetime." Nervously laughing at my little joke, I quickly walked out, leaving him staring and shaking his head in dismay.

The next two weeks were hectic—meetings, casting, finding locations, costumes, special effects, more meetings, selecting a cameraman, still more meetings—and trying not to rewrite a single word.

I tried to work up some enthusiasm for the project, and finally, on the opening day of shooting, I walked on the set with head high, as though I were going to direct *Gone with the Wind.*

Chester Morris, a fine actor, played the lead. He tried to breathe some life into a part that had died at birth. Jeanne Bates hopelessly tried to play the femme fatale. Every day I viewed the rushes, and my assistants told me what a great job I was doing. Irving Briskin remained silent as long as I didn't change a word of dialogue. Finally I started to believe I was getting a good picture, and I plowed ahead, completing the picture in twelve days.

I saw the final cut with Irving Briskin. When the lights came up he turned to me and uttered the not unexpected. "It's a piece of shit!"

To help me correct the "piece of shit," Briskin took the end of the picture and put it at the beginning, then spliced a section of Reel Four into Reel Two, a section of Two into Four and some of Five into Six. Reel Seven he took out entirely. Eight, he trimmed, and Nine, he left alone. After his glowing contribution, *The Chance of a Lifetime* became even more muddled and screwed up than it had been originally, if that was possible.

I waited for the reviews with trepidation. When they finally came out, I hid in the men's room at Columbia. The Hollywood trade papers, which inform the motion-picture industry what they were doing daily, were totally unanimous. *Variety* said, "*The Chance of a Lifetime* has one claim to fame—it's probably the *worst* directed picture in the history of motion pictures." The *Hollywood Reporter* went on where *Variety* left off: "William Castle, in his directorial debut, proves he is totally unfit to handle a motion picture—any picture. Why Harry Cohn, who is usually pretty shrewd, gave Castle a chance to direct, is beyond this reporter's belief."

Several hours later, stunned and shaky, I tried to leave the studio without anyone seeing me. Heads turned the other way as I passed, and little groups broke their conversation as they stared after my departing figure. I guess everybody in the whole industry had read my goddamn reviews.

I reached the front door, but the guard stopped me just as I was sneaking through and informed me that Harry Cohn wanted to see me immediately.

Cohn was furious, his eyes ablaze. "Where the hell have ya been?" I didn't answer. He stormed up to me, his chin jutting. "Didja read your reviews, Castle?"

"Yes, sir," I managed.

"And whadja think of 'em?"

"They weren't very good," I stammered.

"Christ, I've read some bad ones, but these are probably the worst!" Noticing I was ready to cry, he stopped. "Sit down, for chrissake." I did as he told, and I waited for him to continue. "Those half-assed guys who call themselves critics—what the hell do they know? Have any of them ever writ-

ten, produced, or directed a picture? If they had any goddamn talent, they wouldn't be lousy critics." He continued to
storm as he paced around the room. "How dare they question my judgment? If I say you're a good director, then goddammit, you're a good director, and nobody's going to
change my mind, except me! The script was a piece of shit. I
told Briskin not to make it. Why in the hell you didn't come
to me at the start and tell me what garbage it was, I'll never
know. Why, for chrissake?" He paused and waited impatiently for my answer.

"I didn't want to bother you, Mr. Cohn. . . . You were
very busy. . . ."

"I'll tell you when I'm busy—you don't tell me," he
snapped. Without taking a breath, he continued. "Look at
Capra, Stevens, Cukor, Mamoulian, LaCava, Hawks, Lu-
bitsch. . . . You don't think they've had flops?" He paused.
"And DeMille—I don't think he ever got a good review, but
audiences love his pictures . . . they make millions. Remember one thing, Castle—if a script is bad, no director, no
matter how brilliant, can make it into a good picture."

Cohn paused, then walked to his desk and returned with a
script which he handed me. I looked up at him.

"Your next picture," he announced.

I glanced at the cover. *The Whistler.*

"Read it, and when you've finished, call me at home and let
me know how you like it. The switchboard'll put you
through." As I started to leave the office, he called after me.
"And for chrissake, Castle, this time be honest."

I read *The Whistler* three times before I called Cohn. It was
one of the most terrifying screenplays I'd ever read.

A little after midnight, I called Cohn at home. "It's horrific, Mr. Cohn. . . . Exactly what I've been waiting for.
. . . I'll scare the shit out of audiences."

CHAPTER XII

Three Kings and an Ace

AT first I was worried that my age, twenty-nine, would be a hindrance in directing the two stars of *The Whistler*. But Richard Dix and J. Carrol Naish, veterans of many fine movies, liked my originality and fresh approach and encouraged me to try out any new idea I came up with. I tried every effect I could dream up to create a mood of terror: low-key lighting, wide-angle lenses to give an eerie feeling and a hand-held camera in many of the important scenes to give a sense of reality to the horror. To achieve a mood of desperation, I insisted that Dix give up smoking and go on a diet. This made him nervous and irritable, particularly when I gave him early-morning calls and kept him waiting on the set—sometimes for an entire day before using him in a scene. He was constantly off-center, restless, fidgety, and nervous as a cat. When I finally used him in a scene, I'd make him do it over and over until he was ready to explode. It achieved the desired effect—that of a man haunted by fear and trying to keep from being murdered.

The story involved a mentally tortured man (Richard Dix), who thinks his friends believe him responsible for his wife's death. Driven by desperation to seek death himself, and lacking nerve to commit suicide, he hires a murderer through a "booking agent" to do the job. The agent gets in touch with a professional killer (J. Carrol Naish) and turns him loose. Then Dix receives word that his wife is alive. Panic-stricken

77

at the thought of the killer on his trail, he tries to call off the deal, but the "booking agent" has been shot to death by the police, and Dix doesn't know who his murderer is—or when he is to be killed.

When I had finished cutting the picture, I showed it to Harry Cohn in his projection room. He didn't say a word throughout the entire running, and when the lights came up, he turned to me.

"Whadja think, Castle?"

I started to answer, then, smiling, said, "Oh, no, Mr. Cohn. . . . I'm not going to fall into that trap again."

"What do you mean?" he grunted.

I hesitated, then said, "I want you to tell *me* what I think."

Cohn chuckled. "You're learning. It's goddamn frightening . . . but it needs work." He made several suggestions, and each time I knew he was right. Harry Cohn was a master in manipulating film.

That evening I suggested having some sort of gimmick at the audience level. We could have an actor dressed like the character Richard Dix played, run up the aisle of the theatre screaming and have several plants in the audience faint. I had used gimmicks in the theatre; why not for a movie? Sure that it would let audiences participate and add to the enjoyment, I pleaded with Cohn. He turned me down cold, saying my idea was ridiculous and wouldn't work. Someday I'd use a gimmick for a picture. I knew audiences were ready for something different.

Three days later, I was called to Cohn's office. "I'm loaning you out for your next picture, Castle."

My face fell. "Why, Mr. Cohn? You said you liked *The Whistler.*"

Ignoring me, he went on. "Report to the King brothers at Monogram tomorrow morning at nine."

"But, Mr. Cohn, that's minor league. I want to stay at Columbia. If you liked *The Whistler,* why would . . ."

Cohn started to yell. "Sometimes you're a goddamn idiot. I screened *The Whistler* for the King brothers the other night.

78

They loved your direction, begged me to let you make a film for them, paid me five times what I'm paying you—and you're complaining?"

"Do I get to keep the difference?" I inquired.

"Get the hell out of here while you're still ahead!" he barked.

In every contract, the studio has the right to loan the services of an artist to another studio or producer. The salary is usually much larger than the artist is receiving, and the studio pockets the difference. As the contractee, ordinarily getting $100 a week, I was being loaned out by Columbia at $500 a week. The extra $400 was probably used to repaint Cohn's dining room and to defray the cost of the free lunches.

The following morning I awakened at 7:00 and looked outside. It was raining like hell. Wondering how I was going to get a cab in that weather, I began to shower and shave and to think about my new assignment. Pondering what the King brothers might be like, I didn't hear the doorbell ring. When I heard the pounding on the door, I opened it and discovering a young man about my age, with an umbrella.

He wiped his feet and introduced himself. "My name's Hymie."

"Hymie who?" I questioned.

"Hymie King—I'm the youngest." Sitting down in the chair, he patiently waited while I continued to dress. "Frank said I should pick you up and take you to the studio. It's raining," he added.

"Yeah," I said, "It was very thoughtful, but I haven't had breakfast yet."

"That's all right," he said. "You can eat at the office."

At Monogram, I soon found myself in a big office where a fat, balding man sat chomping a cigar. He introduced himself as Frank King. He pointed to a wiry, dark man who was chewing gum and smoking a cigarette at the same time and who looked like the prizefighter he once was. "This is my brother, Maurie King, and of course you know Hymie."

The King brothers had recently left Chicago after selling out their vending machine business and had come to Hollywood to become movie moguls. At the time, they looked and seemed ill-fitted for their new roles, though later they were to become proficient in turning out motion pictures. Frank King was a very sensitive and perceptive showman. In my opinion, he could have headed any major studio.

There was another lean, bespectacled man seated across the room, but nobody bothered to introduce him.

"You want some danish and coffee?" Frank offered.

Nodding, I accepted and waited for the meeting to begin.

"Harry Cohn showed us *The Whistler* the other night," Frank said, taking a bite of danish. "It's a great picture. Isn't that right, Maurie?"

Maurie nodded.

"Hymie?" said Frank.

Hymie nodded.

"We think your direction is great. Isn't that right, Maurie?"

Maurie nodded.

"Hymie?"

Hymie nodded.

"We're paying Cohn *ten* times what he's paying you . . . too bad you can't keep some of the gravy. But if you make us a good picture, we'll give you an extra thou' as sort of a bonus. You put it in your pocket and don't tell Cohn nothin' about it."

"Frank, tell Bill about our new picture," said Maurie.

"In a minute, Maurie," said Frank. "First of all, I want Bill to get to know us and relax completely. Why don't you stretch and walk around? You seem nervous. One thing you don't want to be is nervous."

I assured them I wasn't nervous, but they insisted I was, and so I got up, stretched and walked around. After I got my morning exercise, I asked if I could see the script.

"We want your honest opinion," Frank said. "Why don't you go into the next office—it's empty—and read it? When you've finished, come back and tell us what you think of it.

Hymie, take Bill into Phil's office and make him comfortable."

Hymie silently escorted me into Phil's office and, just as silently, departed.

The script was miserable. It was even worse than *The Chance of a Lifetime*. It seemed to be about a gangster who is shot and dies and goes to heaven. They won't accept him up there and send him back to earth. It was a ridiculous premise, and the dialogue was so bad an eight-year-old child could have done better.

There was a knock on the door. Hymie poked his head in. "Frank wants to know if you've finished yet."

I lied. "No." I needed more time to think about what to tell the Kings.

"Frank says please hurry." And with that, Hymie closed the door.

Taking a piece of paper from a pile on the desk, I drew a line down the middle. On one side I wrote "Tell the Truth," and on the other, "Lie." Under each heading, I listed the possible results:

Tell the Truth	*Lie and Say It's Great*
1. Harry Cohn furious—has to return money on deal.	1. Kings and Cohn very happy.
2. King brothers furious.	2. $1,000 bonus.
3. King brothers spread word—Castle difficult.	3. Chance to direct another picture.
4. Possible suspension, no salary.	
5. Maybe I'm wrong—it's a good picture?	

I walked into the other office and announced I had finished reading it. The three Kings were grinning with anticipation.

"Well, what do you think?" Frank asked. There was a

pause as they waited for my answer. The room was deadly still, except for the sound of rain from outside.

Clearing my throat, I proceeded, "Frank . . . Maurie . . . Hymie. . . ." All eyes were riveted on me. "I think the script is terrible."

The rain cut through the silence as Frank turned in his seat to watch it fall. Maurie lit a cigarette and popped a fresh piece of gum into his mouth. Hymie went to the bathroom. The bespectacled stranger, still sitting in the corner, was asleep.

I waited until Hymie returned and then continued. "I know you're angry, but I don't think you should make this picture."

Frank bounced up from his seat. I thought he was going to hit me, but instead he shook my hand. "You hear that, Maurie? Bill doesn't like the script. And he's right . . . absolutely right. It's terrible." Chomping on his cigar, he sat down again.

"We knew it was lousy," Frank announced. "If you'da said you liked it, we would've sent you right back to Cohn. I said to the boys, when you were inside reading, 'I hope he hates it because I like him, and I think he's right for the picture.' Isn't that so, Maurie?"

Frank signaled to Hymie, who shook the sleeping man. Yawning, the man opened his eyes. "This is Phil Yordan, Bill. He's a writer."

It was still raining when we arrived at Phil Yordan's house in Coldwater Canyon. He ushered me into his study, slouched into a leather chair and peered at me.

"They're characters, aren't they? But they're great. Don't ever sell them short; they know exactly what they're doing." Phil Yordan had just moved to Hollywood from Chicago and was soon to become a internationally famous as a screenwriter, producer and playwright— *Anna Lucasta.*

Stretching, Yordan asked, "You think we can save any of the script?"

"I doubt it," I said.

"Then let's throw it away and make up a new story."

"Frank said it had to be finished in two weeks."

"We can do it," Phil said. "But first, we have to have a good idea . . . you have any notions?"

"Let's do a murder mystery—something frightening," I said.

"That's a good idea." There was a long pause as we both thought about frightening ideas. "How about a guy that wakes up and finds his wife murdered in bed?"

"I saw that picture last night," I said.

"I must have, too." Phil smiled.

Suddenly I had an idea. "How about a girl from a small town . . . she's a waitress, and she marries this guy after her first date with him . . . let's make him a glove salesman. . . ."

Phil picked up the story from there. "And the police find a body strangled to death by a killer wearing gloves."

"The girl is supposed to meet him in New York at a certain cheap hotel, but he doesn't show and leaves no message. . . ."

"That's great." Phil said. "Then what happens?"

"She meets another guy at a bar and finds out several women have been strangled by a man with gloves. She starts to suspect her husband, and when he finally shows up, she thinks he's the killer and tries to hide him from the police."

"He didn't really do it?" asked Phil.

"Nah," I said. "We gotta have a switch at the end."

"What switch?"

"How the hell do I know?"

"It's pretty good," Phil said. "Let's go over it once more. . . ."

Two weeks later, the script was finished and we gave it to the King brothers. They loved it, and this time they weren't kidding.

"We gotta make this picture for fifty thousand dollars, and you have seven days to shoot it," announced Frank.

"That's impossible," I said.

"Nothin's impossible," said Frank, "and besides, you have a thousand-dollar bonus if you pull it off."

We started casting. We had titled the picture *When Strangers Marry,* and, to give it a fresh look, we decided to use comparative unknowns who didn't look like actors.

One afternoon, coming back from lunch, I found a young man waiting in my outer office. As I entered, he awkwardly stood up and I motioned him into my office. He seemed nervous and ill-at-ease.

"Relax," I said. "What's your name?"

"Robert Mitchum."

The cast was complete—Dean Jagger played the husband, Kim Hunter the girl, Robert Mitchum, the murderer, Neil Hamilton the police lieutenant and, for a bit at the end, we chose a complete unknown. Rhonda Fleming.

I wanted the film to express the melancholia of being troubled and lonely in a strange city. Using dull, flat gray light throughout I managed to make the film stark and unrelenting, projecting the story as an actuality rather than something being enacted for a camera or audience. The terror was accentuated by the use of irritation sounds and quick cuts of grotesque and surprising images. But the miracle was that I managed to finish it in seven days, for $50,000. I got my $1,000 bonus.

I was in the cutting room one morning when the operator said there was a call from New York. Irritated, I picked up the telephone. It was a girl I knew in New York.

"Have you heard about the reviews?"

"What reviews?" I asked.

"*The Whistler* . . . they were fantastic! Every paper in New York gave it a rave. They came out this morning. The *Daily News* gave you four stars. Kate Cameron said, 'Under William Castle's brilliant direction, the audience's attention is riveted to the screen throughout.' The New York *Post*'s Archer Winsten: 'A note should be added in praise of the director, William Castle. Realizing he had charge of the story in which atmospheric and psychological overtones could be used to advantage, he made the most of his opportunity.' Otis L. Guernsey, Jr., *Herald Tribune*: 'I bow from the waist. Director William Castle has taken this material and molded it coolly and deliberately into many shapes of suspense. He has cut the dialogue down to a minimum and, à la Hitchcock, substitutes meaningful action and props. . . . Throughout the entire picture it is Mr. Castle's expert touch that has brought sizable drama to the film.' Alton Cook, New York *World Telegram*: 'William Castle, a new name among directors, has assembled a good cast and drawn the most from them in a picture full of his dexterous skill. This is one of the year's most compact and movingly narrated manhunts.' "

"Wow!" I said. "I don't believe it!"

There was a pause, then she hurriedly went on. "There's another reason I called. A friend of mine is producing a play on Broadway—we saw the picture together. Wait a minute . . . let me put him on."

A deep, pleasant voice came on. "Hello, Bill, this is Clay Blaney. My congratulations—you made a fine film. I have a new play that I'm bringing to Broadway in the fall . . . a suspense mystery . . . and I'd like you to direct it. Would you be interested?"

I caught my breath. "I don't know, Mr. Blaney. I'm under contract to Columbia, and I'm scheduled to do another picture for the King brothers, *John Dillinger*. I don't know if I'll have the time."

"I wish you'd consider, Bill. It's a great play and perfect material for you . . . just up your alley. Why don't you think about it? I'll send you the script."

I promised I would.

The play, *Meet a Body*, arrived. I sat up half the night reading it. It had a tremendously exciting first act. The second and third acts needed work, but I felt it was a damn good play. And Blaney was correct, it *was* right up my alley. I had promised the King brothers I would direct their new picture, but this was a great opportunity. Of course, I'd have to get permission from Harry Cohn.

* * *

Cohn was yelling at somebody over the phone when I entered his office. Angrily slamming down the phone, he turned to me. "I guess you heard about it already, huh? Well, the answer is no."

I stared at him puzzled.

"David Selznick tried to buy your contract from me this morning."

I was nonplussed. "I didn't know about Selznick, Harry," I said.

"Well, you do now, and the answer is still no. You're staying right here at Columbia."

I plunged. "Selznick will give me the chance to make bigger and better pictures . . . not lousy Bs. Are you ready to do that?"

"Goddammit, Castle!" he screamed. "You've made three lousy pictures, and already you're a genius! I'll tell you when you're ready to make bigger pictures."

"Please, Harry" —I dared use of his first name— "let me go with David Selznick."

"*No! No! No!* You're staying *here.* And that's the *end* of the conversation."

"Harry," I said, "a producer in New York called. He wants me to direct a play. A murder mystery. It's called *Meet a Body.*"

"Have you read the play?" he growled.

"It's great," I answered.

"Well." He paused. "Well . . . I guess I owe ya somethin'. How long will you be gone?"

"About six weeks."

"How much you gettin' paid?"

"About six thousand dollars and royalties."

"I'll take you off salary while you're gone," he muttered. "While you're in New York, look around for a story for the next *Whistler.* When ya leaving?"

"As soon as possible," I answered.

"G'wan, get outta here . . . and fall on your ass on Broadway."

CHAPTER XIII

Two Can Be Buried as Cheaply as One

THE *Super Chief* left Los Angeles for Chicago on Tuesdays and Saturdays; there was a change of trains and then an overnight run to New York. The sleek, luxurious train was outfitted to make the fast journey the utmost in comfort—handsomely appointed sleeping cars, special drawing rooms, a game room, bar, observation car, and the gaily furnished dining car. Motion picture personalities loved the Chief because it allowed them to sleep, relax or work with their pretty secretaries in complete privacy. The train was completely staffed and the service impeccable.

Having never traveled on the *Super Chief,* I looked forward to the journey. Sam, the porter, ushered me into my drawing room. "I'll have your luggage in a jiffy, Mr. Castle, and if there's anything you need, just push that button."

"Anybody in the picture business on the train, Sam?"

"Judy Garland got aboard at Pasadena with Marjorie Main and some publicity people from MGM."

Judy Garland had graduated from the popular Andy Hardy series with Mickey Rooney and was zooming to stardom. I had read in the trade papers she was going on tour for *Meet Me in St. Louis,* a musical she had just completed.

As I entered the dining car the following morning the steward wished me a cheery good-morning and, motioning me to follow, seated me at a table and left me with the breakfast menu.

Glancing up, I saw Judy Garland, Marjorie Main, and several other people being escorted to a table. I smiled and bid them good morning. Just then the train lurched and Judy Garland almost fell into my orange juice. She laughingly apologized as Marjorie Main exclaimed, "What in the hell are *you* doing here?"

An old friend, Marjorie had co-starred with me in a Broadway play called *Ebb Tide* fourteen years before. She was now becoming well known in motion pictures. (It was later that she became Ma Kettle in the *Ma and Pa Kettle* series.)

Miss Garland and entourage proceeded to a table at the far end of the car, and Marjorie excused herself, saying she'd like to have breakfast with an old friend. She sat down and ordered breakfast and then leaned back and laughed aloud. "Golly, William, it's been years. . . . You were just a green kid when we did *Ebb Tide* together. You were double-jointed . . . I'll never forget. . . . "

The soft rhythmic clacking of the wheels riding the tracks helped me to remember 1930. I had heard they were casting *Ebb Tide* and wandered into Louis Isquith's theatrical office on Forty-fourth Street. I was sixteen years old, and my horoscope had said I would be lucky that day. I tried to get in to see Isquith, but as usual was turned away—this time by the office boy, a young man about my own age.

"Sorry, the play's all cast except for *one* part and you're not right for it," he said, instantaneously promoting himself to high potentate.

"A dollar says I'm right for the part," I gambled.

"Make it two, and you can read the script," he said. Handing him the two dollars, I waited. "You'll have to read it here," he said. "And be fast—before Mr. Isquith comes back from lunch."

Sitting in the office, I read *Ebb Tide*. The part was *exactly* right for me—a young clamdigger named Sim Carter, barefoot, dirty, overalls, and straw hat . . . a grown-up Huckleberry Finn.

Holding up an extra two dollars, I suggested to the office

boy that he wasn't feeling well—an instant stomach ache.

"Make it an even five dollars for the whole deal—reading the script, my stomach ache, and taking the afternoon off." I gave him the three dollars. He moaned aloud and, clutching his stomach, gave an Academy Award performance as he staggered out. I was in complete charge of the office for the rest of the afternoon.

Louis Isquith, the producer, a tall, lean, balding man came back from lunch and saw me sitting there. "Where the hell's Ben?" he demanded.

"He didn't feel well, complained of stomach cramps . . . I'm taking his place."

Isquith, too busy to question me further, entered his office and slammed the door. For the remainder of the afternoon, I interviewed actors, turning them down for the part. One had an appointment at three to read for Mr. Isquith, and I gave him a friendly tip: "Read it with a lisp, that's what he wants." Isquith thought he was a fairy and turned him down cold.

By 4:00 I had completely memorized the part. I knocked on Mr. Isquith's door and announced that I was ready to read. Bewildered, Isquith thought he had an appointment with me and told me to proceed. When I had finished, he called in the director, J. Kent Thurber, and asked me to read again. They doubled up with laughter and offered me the part.

We began rehearsals at the New Yorker Theatre on April 2, 1930. A good actor will start off very slowly during rehearsals and read his part, referred to as "sides." Improving at each rehearsal, he continues to build his character until he is finally able to give a polished performance. I was the only one who knew my lines at the first rehearsal—but there it stopped and, like a broken record, I remained the same.

Several days before opening, Thurber took me aside and informed me that I was monotonous and lifeless. He tried to help, but I rigidly stuck to my one-level performance. Watching Marjorie Main, I saw how expertly she molded and shaped her part. Most of my scenes were with her and she tried to help me, but I still remained flat and dull. It was my first big part, and I sounded like a rank amateur.

Opening night there was a knock on my dressing-room door. Marjorie Main stuck her head in. "Break a leg," she yelled. (Actors wish each other just the opposite of "good luck" on opening night, so as not to jinx them.)

"Break a leg," I thought. Maybe I should do just that—at least the audience would know I was onstage.

"Fifteen minutes!" yelled the stage manager.

Continuing my makeup, which consisted of making myself as dirty as possible, I slipped into my overalls, mussed my hair, and took off my shoes and socks. In bare feet, I surveyed myself in the mirror. My feet were too clean. Dirtying them like the rest of myself, I heard the call, "Curtain going up," and soon I was standing in the wings, nervously awaiting my cue.

Marjorie Main was onstage as Cove Carrie. She looked just as dirty and unkempt as I. Humming to herself, she peered out the window on stage left. "That no-good Sim Carter is always late . . . probably off someplace asleepin' in the mud." My cue to enter.

Shaking with fear, I shambled on stage. Before I could say my first line, I felt a sharp pain shoot through my foot. One of the stagehands hadn't swept the stage properly, and several loose nails were on the floor, one of them lodged in my foot. Forgetting there was an audience out front, I dropped to the floor and proceeded to pull the nail out, grimacing with pain. Blood began seeping through, and being double-jointed, I crossed my legs and began to lick my foot, trying to stop the blood.

The audience thought I was washing my feet with my tongue. They howled with laughter and began applauding. Suddenly realizing where I was, I jumped to my feet and tried to remember my first line. Panic-stricken, I began to stutter while the audience continued laughing. The stage manager threw me the line, but I couldn't stop stuttering. I finished the scene, and still stuttering, walked off to applause.

The following day, the critics all commented on "the stuttering clamdigger," saying: "An utterly convincing performance by William Castle, as the young clamdigger who sat on the floor and washed his feet with his tongue." "William Castle's performance, one of the most original to come along in quite a while, was the highlight of an otherwise dull evening." J. Kent Thurber kept the accidental washing of my foot in the play and suggested I stutter at every performance. To my delight, I received applause every time I finished the scene.

One evening I came to the theatre and saw my name in lights opposite Marjorie Main. Being double-jointed had finally paid off.

"Chicago . . . Chicago . . . thirty minutes . . . Chicago." The conductor's voice rang out. The forty-four hours had passed quickly and now, back to 1944, I prepared to change trains. The next day I arrived in New York.

Seeing no cabs, I had started to walk toward the subway when suddenly I noticed a solitary, unoccupied cab at the far end of the street. Dragging my luggage, I rushed toward it.

"Busy?" I asked. Immersed in a book, the driver didn't answer. I repeated the question—still no response. Impatiently putting my luggage in the cab, I climbed into the back seat and waited. The driver wet his thumb and turned a page of his book.

Finally, he casually closed the book and turned. "Where to, mister? I haven't got all day." Then the face creased into a smile. "You're the guy with the hundred-dollar bill . . . Bloomingdale's! What the hell are you doing here?"

Meeting Louis Schwartzwald at Penn Station was one chance in a million, but to find him reading what eventually was to become one of the most expensive pictures in Hollywood . . . the odds are too great to calculate.

"Whaddaya doin' in New York?" he repeated.

"I'm going to direct a Broadway play."

"Well, whaddaya know?" was Louie's sage reply. "Where you stayin'?"

"The Plaza," I answered.

"The Waldorf's better."

"The Plaza," I insisted.

"Well, if you're gonna be stubborn," he said.

"Please, Louie, let's just go to the Plaza."

Arriving in front of the hotel, Louie handed me his book. "Why don't you read this? . . . It'll make a helluva movie. It's about this lawyer, see? He's crippled, see? And he's hitched to this beautiful dame. . . ."

The name of the book Louie Schwartzwald gave me was *If I Die Before I Wake,* an Inner Sanctum novel written by Sherwood King. Out of the mouths of babes and cabdrivers. Louie was right. It was perfect for my next *Whistler.*

The following morning I made an appointment to see Clay Blaney. It was the first time I had ever walked into a theatrical office and found the red carpet laid out for me. The office was filled with actors, and Blaney's pretty secretary said they were all waiting to see me. Smiling and waving at the crowded office, I walked smack into a closed door.

The entire afternoon proved a waste, and after interviewing fifty actors, I asked Clay Blaney to carry on and got the hell out. Casting is not easy.

Word spread that I was casting, and it seemed every actor in New York was there the following day. In one hectic week, I finally managed to assemble the whole cast.

The three acts of *Meet a Body* took place in a Lower East Side funeral parlor. During the first act, a strange-looking man comes into the funeral parlor to make arrangements for a funeral. Picking out a lush coffin, he inquires about prices. When asked who he is making funeral arrangements for, he says himself. He writes a check, opens the door, and leaves. A shot is heard offstage and, staggering back, he drops dead. At the end, the audience finds out who the murderer really is and there is a shoot-out.

Rehearsals began at 10:00 A.M. the following Monday. It felt great to be back in the theatre. We were scheduled to open at the Forrest Theatre on October 2, 1944. Clay Blaney wanted to try out the play in Boston before bringing it into New York.

Rehearsals finished early one day, and I called the publishers of *If I Die Before I Wake,* the book Louie Schwartzwald had given me. I was told the motion picture rights were controlled by the agent, T. W. Murray.

Murray was an old friend, nicknamed "The Commodore," because he always wore a yachting cap. On several occasions he had tried to get me parts on Broadway.

"The book's six years old, and nobody's bought it for a movie. How about two thousand dollars?"

"How about one hundred dollars down," I said, "and four hundred when I make the picture?"

"I'll take two hundred dollars down," said the Commodore, "and pay me the rest when you start shooting."

"Suppose I never make the picture?"

"Let's worry about that when the time comes. . . . We'll think of something."

Now having acquired the story of my new *Whistler,* I went back to the hotel and started packing for our opening in Boston.

Opening night was "nervous time," and I think I was the most worried. Going backstage, I reassured the cast they'd be great, and went out front to watch.

The theatre was filled, and I stood in the back and waited apprehensively. The house lights dimmed and the curtain went up. I crossed my fingers and prayed. The first laugh came, right on cue—Ruth McDevitt's line to Al Shean, and his reply. The audience howled. Sighing with relief, I waited for the "strange-looking man" to get shot and stagger onstage, a bullet hole through his head—that should get a scream. It did.

When the curtain came down on the first act, there was a buzz of excitement throughout the audience. Standing in the lobby, I strained to hear comments but most of the audience

93

talked about other things. One young couple said they couldn't wait for the second act.

The rest of the play worked like a charm. In the last act, I had tried something rather daring. The killer, on the run, jumps from the stage and flees through the audience. Six cops, with guns drawn, follow him, shooting as he tries to escape. Landing in the loge, he gets shot and does a spectacular fall over the rail, almost into the audience. It was a great gimmick for the spectators, making them part of the play. The reaction was more than I had hoped for.

As the final curtain came down, there was instantaneous applause. The cast took twelve curtain calls.

The next two weeks were sellouts, and the audience loved the play. I calculated that we'd run for at least two years on Broadway. I couldn't wait for our New York opening.

A New York opening is unlike any opening night in the world. Word had gotten around that *Meet a Body* was a hit, and cosmopolites, dressed in dinner jackets and evening gowns, haughtily filed in. Casually scanning their programs, they looked bored already, seeming to dare the play to be a success. The six members of the Royal Family (the critics) sat in the fifth and sixth row, center. Usually late, they knew they controlled the destiny of a play.

The reviews came out the following morning. As great as they had been in Boston, they were unanimously lousy. Most critics said it was a good first act, but then *Meet a Body* in New York went nowhere. John Chapman, critic for the *Daily News*, questioned my judgment in "undertaking" *Meet a Body*. He continued: "After Castle's auspicious debut in *The Whistler*, it's too bad he was unable to follow it." The New York *Times* said *Meet a Body* died at the funeral parlor and was waiting to be buried.

Six critics had buried the play, but the body had not died—as yet. Angry and frustrated, I decided to fight back. Audiences would attend the play despite bad reviews, but I needed a gimmick—something special to bring them in.

I placed a large ad in the obituary pages of the New York papers:

YOU ARE CORDIALLY INVITED TO ATTEND A FUNERAL AT THE
FORREST THEATRE. TWO CAN BE BURIED AS CHEAPLY AS ONE.
BRING A DATE AND GET HER BURIED FREE WHILE YOU ATTEND
Meet a Body

Tickets were engraved in black and each lady who had free admission was given a small funeral wreath. The play stayed open, and *Meet a Body* lived, in spite of the critics.

Before I returned to Hollywood, I decided to hang around and attend the opening of *When Strangers Marry,* the picture I had done for the King brothers.

At the opening, the Brooklyn Strand Theatre was packed, and the New York reviews were fabulous. The critics had done a 360-degree angle, each one personally singling me out, and praising my direction.

Orson Welles had a column in the New York *Graphic,* called "Orson Welles's Almanac," in which he wrote:

> Plant things that grow above the ground today, and go immediately to the Strand Theatre in Brooklyn and see a "B" minus picture called *When Strangers Marry.* It's A plus entertainment but because it's a quickie without any names on it, *When Strangers Marry* hasn't had much of a play. Making allowances for its bargain-price budget, I think you'll agree with me that it's one of the most gripping and effective pictures of the year. It isn't as slick as *Double Indemnity* or as glossy as *Laura,* but it's better acted and better directed by William Castle than either.

The low-budget B picture in the 1940s, before the advent of television, was a training ground for talented young directors who were forced to use their imagination in lieu of money. Many famous producers and directors graduated from this school (Robert Wise, Charles Vidor, Mark Robson, Val Lewton). Now I felt my schooling was over and I was ready to graduate into bigger and more expensive motion pictures.

I called Welles at his office in Hollywood. Immediately his booming voice came on the line. I wondered if he remembered me. We hadn't spoken in six years, since the fateful day in his office when I had gotten the Stony Creek Theatre. But the warmth of his greeting closed the gap.

"Congratulations. By the way, did you read James Agee's review on *When Strangers Marry* in *Time* magazine?" There was a pause as I heard him puff on his perennial cigar. "Let's do a picture together, Bill. You direct and I'll produce—or I'll direct and you produce."

I caught my breath and quietly said, "I'd love to, Orson."

I told him I was still under contract to Columbia, but Welles assured me he could handle Harry Cohn and told me he would send along some books and scripts that he thought would make great movies. If I had anything, I was to send it to him.

I bought a *Time* magazine, and read the review by James Agee (the dean of critics):

> I want to add to Orson Welles and Manny Farber my own respect for the Monogram melodrama, *When Strangers Marry*. I have seldom for years now seen one hour so energetically and sensibly used in a film. Bits of it indeed gave me a heart lifted sense of delight in real performance and ambition which I have rarely known in any film context since my own mind and that of moving-picture making were sufficiently young. Thanks to that I can no longer feel by any means so hopeless as I have lately that it is possible to make pictures in Hollywood that are worth making. When I think even no further than William Castle who made this and of the Val Lewton contingent, I know there are enough people out there of real ability to turn the whole place upside-down.

On a pink cloud at Welles's offer, I now decided to turn Hollywood upside-down. The harsh ring of the telephone jarred me back into reality. The operator announced that Harry Cohn was on the line.

"When the hell are you coming back to the studio, Castle?" the voice barked over three thousand miles. "You're going to direct another *Whistler* in three weeks."

CHAPTER XIV

Mutiny on the *Zaca*

THE girl was beautiful, married to a cripple who was a famous criminal lawyer. She plans his murder. Choosing a sailor as her lover, she manipulates him into the act of murder. *If I Die Before I Wake* had the potential of a great motion picture—shocking, provocative, filled with suspense. Although I knew I would have to make it on a low budget, it was a challenge that I felt sure would finally propel me into more expensive A pictures.

I had written a ten-page treatment (a short screen version) of *If I Die* but when I called Harry Cohn's office I found out he was on holiday and wouldn't return for several weeks. Impatient and wanting to put a screenwriter to work immediately, I made an appointment with the story editor at Columbia.

At my insistence, he read the treatment immediately. I was stunned by his reaction. He rejected the material and informed me that Harry Cohn would hate it.

"Why?" I asked.

"The leading lady is a murderess. Mr. Cohn likes his heroines good, sweet, and pure."

"Bullshit!" I yelled and, grabbing my treatment, stalked out of the office and slammed the door.

My contract with Columbia was exclusive, and any material I owned was their property. The story editor had officially turned it down, and Harry Cohn was out of town.

Frustrated and angry, I impulsively sent the book and my

97

treatment to Orson Welles, informing him that if he was serious about working with me, I'd like him to consider *If I Die Before I Wake*. A month later, he wrote:

Dear Bill,

About *If I Should Die*—I love it. It occurs to me that maybe by saying I had ideas for it, you'd think my ideas are creative. Nothing of the sort. What I'm thinking of is a practical use Mercury could find for the property. I have been searching for an idea for a film, but none presented itself until *If I Should Die* and I could play the lead and Rita Hayworth could play the girl. I won't present it to anybody without your O.K. The script should be written immediately. Can you start working on it nights?

Give Rita a big hug and kiss and say it's from somebody who loves her very much. The same guy is crazy about you and you won't ever get away from him.

ORSON

(Rita Hayworth was the reigning superstar at the time, and Orson married her some months later.)

I was preparing another low-budget epic, *The Crime Doctor's Warning*, starring Warner Baxter, when Bill Graf, Harry Cohn's new executive secretary, called and said that Mr. Cohn wanted to see me immediately.

In an unusually expansive mood, Cohn announced he was taking me off *The Crime Doctor's Warning*. He told his secretary to hold all calls and, all charm and smiles, called me by my first name. I started to worry.

Cohn crossed the room and sat down beside me. "I just made a deal with Orson Welles to do a picture for us at Columbia. That boy's a genius." He handed me a treatment and asked me to read it immediately.

Glancing at the cover, I read, *If I Die Before I Wake*.

"You know, Bill," Cohn continued, "it takes a genius like Orson Welles to find material like this. The dame being a murderess is a brilliant and original idea."

Shocked, I sat frozen while Cohn informed me that he had

given Orson the choice of anybody in Hollywood to be his associate producer and he had picked me. Furious, I reached Orson in New York. He excitedly told me how he had sold *If I Die Before I Wake* to Harry Cohn for $150,000. It was a package deal—Orson would produce, direct, write and co-star. I had paid $200 and Columbia had turned it down.

"We'll be working together, Bill. Isn't that what we planned? Get to New York as quickly as possible so we can begin preparations."

Trying to rationalize that working with Orson in any capacity would be a great learning experience, I tried to push aside my disappointment in not being able to direct. Orson had said that Cohn agreed to let Rita Hayworth play the girl and that *If I Die* was to be one of the big pictures of the year. If I had directed, it would have been an inexpensive $70,000-budget *Whistler*. After a sleepless night, I decided to see what would become of *If I Die Before I Wake* in the talented hands of Orson Welles, the boy genius.

It was only the first of many sleepless nights. Orson, an insomniac, refused to believe that anyone required sleep and picked the wee hours of the morning to call with any new idea he had at the moment.

"This is Orson," his voice would boom. "I hope I didn't wake you."

"No, Orson." I yawned. "I'm always up at four A.M."

"You're leaving for Mexico," he said. "Acapulco, at noon today." I was now wide awake. He continued, "I want the *Zaca*."

"What's a zaca?" I asked.

"Not a . . . *the Zaca*," he replied, "Errol Flynn's yacht. I want you to make a deal with him."

"Yes, Orson, but how do I find the *Zaca* and Errol Flynn?"

"That's your worry."

I arrived in Mexico City the following day where I changed planes—a one-propeller crackerbox that flew between the mountains, in the roughest, bumpiest ride I ever had. For the first time ever, I saw a pilot get airsick. As the

99

stewardess held a cold towel to his forehead, he tried to keep the crackerbox up in the downdraft.

Landing in Acapulco, I checked in at a hotel and ate a delicious Mexican salad laced with fresh fruits. During the night, I had "Montezuma's Revenge," more popularly known as "the Mexican trots."

The following morning, I headed for the good ship *Zaca*, "trotting" all the way. I hired a motor launch, and soon headed directly for a sleek, magnificent yacht anchored in the calm Acapulco waters. As the launch grew nearer, I read the proud name: *Zaca*.

The "hero man," Errol Flynn, bronzed, stripped to the waist and looking exactly as he did in his swashbucklers, lounged on the aft deck with a glass in his hand. (He always had a glass in his hand.) Introducing myself, I inquired where the men's room was. He corrected me laughingly. "The head is down below."

When I finally reappeared on deck, he charmingly told me he had a concoction that would fix me up immediately. Quickly mixing the ingredients, he handed me a glass filled with an amber liquid. "Drink it down fast," he said.

My stomach caught fire and suddenly I felt immediate relief.

"What was that, Mr. Flynn?" I gasped.

"Secret brew. . . . Someday I'll patent it, sell it to American tourists and call it 'Old Dad's Brew.' "

"Mr. Flynn, I want to start negotiations."

"Call me 'Old Dad,' " he said, taking a swig of his drink. "What can I do for you?"

"Orson Welles would like to use the *Zaca* in his new picture."

"Good old Orson. . . . We've had some great times together. . . . How is the 'boy wonder'?"

"Fine, Mr. . . . I mean, 'Old Dad,' " I replied. "Now, about the *Zaca*."

"How long would you need her for?" he asked.

"About a month," I replied.

"Fifteen hundred a day, including lunches for the crew."

"That's a little steep, isn't it?" I said. "I thought perhaps a thous—"

"Take it or leave it," he snapped back.

"I'll take it," I reassured him. "We'll have to change the name of the boat. . . ."

"Ship," he corrected.

"Ship, I mean . . . from *Zaca* to *Circe.*"

"For fifteen hundred a day, you can put Harry Cohn's name on it for all I care. But one thing I insist—and I want it written in the contract—I'm the only one that navigates the *Zaca* . . . or *Circe*, or whatever it's called—understood?"

"Agreed," I said and on that we shook hands.

(It is interesting to note an item in the *Hollywood Reporter,* June 20, 1974—"A novelty shop in St. Tropez has now chalked up at least one hundred customers, all women, who eagerly pay $65, American, for a little box of rotted wood, guaranteed to come from the late Errol Flynn's yacht, *Zaca.*")

I called Orson and told him the deal I made with Flynn. He seemed satisfied, and before hanging up, informed me that he had changed the title of the film. It was now *The Lady from Shanghai.*

If I Die had already come a long way from the $70,000 *Whistler* I had originally planned. It was now budgeted at $2,300,000, and the budget was to spiral upward like a thermometer left in the hot Mexican sun.

Orson and Rita Hayworth (now Mrs. Welles), followed by their entourage, were the first to arrive. Meeting them at the small airport, I managed a few Mexican mariachis to serenade their arrival. I was surprised at Rita Hayworth's local popularity. Half of Acapulco was on hand to greet her. Gay Mexicans screamed "Olé," and bestowed flowers. Orson, wearing a white ice-cream suit and wide panama hat, puffed his cigar as he escorted his radiant wife.

Rita looked different. Her beautiful long red hair had vanished. Now blond, her hair was closely cropped and clung to her lovely face. (Orson later explained that he gave Hayworth a completely new look by personally engineering the shearing of her locks. Harry Cohn, seeing Orson's creation, went home ill.)

The encyclopedia quotes a phrase by James Froude: "A man of genius is a spring in which there is always more behind than flows from it." Orson Welles was such a man.

Since we were to spend a great deal of time aboard the *Zaca*, I decided to keep a ship's log of my own.

November 2, 1946:

Hot and sunny. Met with Errol Flynn aboard the *Zaca*. Welles, accompanied by Dick Wilson [his assistant since the origin of the Mercury Theatre], will share credit with me as associate producer. Orson delighted with the yacht. He and Flynn went swimming.

November 3:

Hot and sunny. Dick Wilson and Sam Nelson, the assistant director [who I had worked with on *Penny Serenade*], went to the Mexican union to try to integrate Mexican crews with the Hollywood crew. The language barrier is going to be quite a problem, also everything seems to be "mañana time."

Everett Sloan, cast as the brilliant crippled criminal lawyer, Albert Bannister, tried on his leg braces for the first time. He complained bitterly that they hurt and refused to use them. I finally convinced him that he'd get used to them.

November 4:

Cloudy and rain. Orson, Dick and myself looked for locations. Orson picked several.

November 5:

Hot and sunny. Orson changed his mind. His whims and demands many, he has spent the first week picking locations, then changing his mind and picking others.

November 12:

Orson started rehearsing. Actors, memorizing their lines, arrive on set to find Welles smoking his perennial cigar and doing a complete rewrite.

November 17:

Cloudy and the heat oppressive. First day of shooting on *Lady from Shanghai.* The dark clouds seemed like an evil omen. Orson was rehearsing a scene with Rita Hayworth on the aft deck. We were twenty miles out, in rough waters.

Errol Flynn was at the wheel trying to keep the *Zaca* on a straight course. Charles Lawton, Jr., the cameraman, a filter to his eye, was waiting for a break in the clouds. Orson was ready to make his first take. Sam Nelson yelled for quiet as Orson took his place next to Rita. The sun had now come out. I was standing next to one of the camera assistants. He was working bareheaded, and the sun was beating down with fierce intensity. The mixer yelled, "Speed . . . Take One," and waiting a beat, Orson said his first line. The camera assistant started to stagger. Reaching out, I tried to help him.

Horrified, I watched him turn blue, as fighting for breath and clutching his chest, he dropped to the deck. Orson and crew members rushed to his aid but it was too late. The assistant cameraman was dead—a fatal coronary.

Errol Flynn, as captain, took instant command. Pouring himself a stiff drink, he took a hefty swig. "Bring me a dufful bag," he ordered, and swaying against the pitching *Zaca,* announced, "We'll bury him at sea." Opening the duffel bag, he staggered toward the dead camera assistant. "Put him in the bag and sew it up."

Orson ordered me to get ashore as fast as possible and notify the Mexican authorities.

November 20:

Temperature rising; so was the budget. Shooting resumed. Entire day's work ruined because reflections from the water's surface kicked up more intensity than the light meter recorded, causing over-exposure. Insects made

103

shooting a nightmare as thousands of them swarmed over arc lights, blocking them out.

November 22:

Tropical night, a velvet sky, alive with stars. I had been invited to dine aboard the *Zaca*. After a gourmet feast, we lay on deck chairs drinking brandy and appreciating the soft, caressing breeze under the full moon. Nora Eddington, Errol Flynn's wife, pregnant and leaving tomorrow for Los Angeles to have their baby, was seated next to her husband.

Flynn, finished with his brandy, cleared his throat and started to philosophize. "If a wife is no longer able to service her husband because of her pregnancy, the husband should be allowed to bed down with another woman until his wife is able to assume her full responsibility." Pouring another drink, he glanced at his wife. "Don't you agree, darling?" Mrs. Flynn, her eyes blazing, remained silent. Errol Flynn looked toward Orson. "How about you, Orson, don't *you* agree?"

Orson quickly glanced at Rita and in his booming voice declared, "No comment."

"Rita, don't you agree?" inquired Flynn.

Looking him straight in the eye, Rita spoke softly. "Well, Errol . . . I never thought you'd ask me. . . . If a male were unable to function . . . for various reasons, a female should have the same right. . . . Don't you agree, Errol?"

Flynn quickly poured another drink and turning to me, the only bachelor, asked, "What do you think, Bill?"

I thought for a long moment. "Errol . . ." All eyes were on me. "May I have a little more brandy?"

November 23:

Hot and muggy. Nora Flynn left for Los Angeles. Errol saw her off and didn't return to the *Zaca*, telling none of us where he was going. A search party was sent, to no avail. He had disappeared. Again, we were forced to stop shooting aboard the *Zaca* until we could find him. The contract clearly stated the *Zaca* could not be used without him.

November 27:

Errol Flynn finally returned. He brought a playmate with him—an Amazonian from the surrounding hills who looks like a Ubangi savage without the plate in her mouth. She has the brawn of several football players and the height of a giraffe. Her skin is the color of the dark amber liquid Flynn gave me to ease my stomach. She understands no English and speaks in a high-pitched voice in a jibberish even the Mexicans can't understand. The romance of the century began when Flynn stowed her aboard the *Zaca*.

November 30:

Cool and beautiful. We have the day off and are lounging on the *Zaca's* deck. Mexico's president, Valdez Miguel Aleman, accompanied by Nicholas Schenck, president of MGM and several other Mexican dignitaries, all dressed in immaculate white, pulled alongside the *Zaca* in their motor launch. Errol Flynn welcomed them with great "hero gallantry" and lavishly began the introductions.

"President Aleman, Mr. Schenck, I would like you to meet my guests . . . Rita Hayworth . . ." The president bowed and kissed Rita's hand. Errol continued introductions. "And, of course, you know Orson Welles." Again the bows and handshakes. Errol paused for breath and then went on. "And this is William Castle . . ."

Flynn, with great charm, then gestured to the huge Amazonian savage seated next to me, saying, "And this, gentlemen . . . is Mrs. Castle."

The president of Mexico glanced imperceptibly at "Mrs. Castle," then back at me, as Nicholas Schenck did a triple-take. Turning scarlet, I decided to jump overboard.

For the rest of the picture, the only English words the Amazon learned were "Me Missy Castle." Skipping along the deck of the *Zaca*, she'd point at me and in her shrill voice give me nightmares as she kept repeating, "Me Missy Castle."

Even today, thirty years later, some of the old-timers who worked on *The Lady from Shanghai*—grips and electricians—will ask whenever I walk on a set, "How is Missy Castle?"

December 5:

2:00 A.M. Temperature down, budget rising. Orson called me from his room. He sounded breathless as he croaked, "Get over here fast." Rushing to his bungalow, I found him stretched out on the bed acting out Hamlet's death scene, as Rita, frantic, grabbed my arm and led me to the groaning Orson. One of his eyes was about three times its normal size, red and ugly. He had been bitten by an insect. Moaning, Orson grasped my arm, pulled me closer, and croaked, "My eye, where's my eye?"

I assured him it was still in its socket and that he'd be all right. Pulling me still closer, he whispered, "You'll direct the picnic scene tomorrow, Castle."

"The hell I will, Orson." Getting a doctor in Acapulco quickly was like everything else—"mañana." Shooting suspended again.

December 10:

At a downtown theatre in Acapulco, we viewed the film Orson had shot so far. The remarkable footage again proved his brilliance. After the showing, Orson took me aside and told me he had finished filming in Acapulco, and wanted to get the cast and crew back to Hollywood where he would resume shooting. I was delighted, until he informed me I was to remain and shoot additional footage. "Close shots of insects, snakes, iguanas—any reptile you can find in the jungles."

I am now a reptile director—teaching snakes and iguanas to act.

December 12:

Everybody's gone. I'm alone except for a Mexican cameraman and two helpers who don't speak English. Heat unbearable. I search for talented reptiles. "Anyone seen a photogenic iguana who wants to be in pictures?" I am constantly thirsty, my lips parched, I drink heavily from a nearby stream—cool and inviting. The thought of food makes me nauseous. I am losing weight.

December 20:

Dense jungle. This morning I coughed up specks of blood. I feel light-headed, but I keep reassuring myself—two more days, then home. I am completely dehydrated—keep drinking the delicious water. The heat is intense but I feel cold—no, I'm burning up.

With fascination I stared at a huge iguana. "Hello, Señor Iguana. How about a nice close-up? . . . Look right into the camera." The iguana looked at me and with one of its big, revolving eyes, winked—then slowly put its legs around its neck. My God! The iguana was double-jointed! Suddenly the evil iguana started to grow. It was now forty feet. A double-jointed, forty-foot iguana taking over the world, on top of the Empire State Building.

I heard myself screaming, but the Mexicans didn't understand.

"Llame el médico." "El tiene fiebre y es loco."

The greatest horror picture ever made. Thousands of police and soldiers trying to destroy the monstrous iguana. The world was in flames and I was burning. Suddenly everything went black.

Cedars of Lebanon Hospital in Hollywood was to be my new home for many weeks. A nice lady in a surgical gown and mask over her face told me I had been flown in and was in quarantine—but not to worry. I asked her what in the hell I was not supposed to worry about. "Doctor will tell you," she purred.

Doctor, wearing a mask and gown, told me I had amebic dysentery, but not to worry. (You can be dying, and they'll tell you not to worry.) I caught the bug while drinking the delightful Mexican waters. My stomach was being eaten away. I found out later that they hadn't expected me to live.

Some days later, they moved me from quarantine to the VIP fifth-floor apartments at Cedars. If you're going to be

107

sick, that's the place to be. My first visitor was Harry Cohn. As usual he was most complimentary. "God, Castle, you look like hell. . . . How much weight you lost?"

"Thirty-five pounds," I announced weakly.

"You were too heavy anyway."

"Harry—" I paused. "These rooms are terribly expensive and doctors and nurses and . . ."

Interrupting, he comforted me with his usual bark. "I'm paying for everything—so goddammit, don't worry; just get well." I must have dozed off because Cohn was gone when I awakened.

Rita Hayworth paid me a visit and brought flowers. That evening Orson arrived. Sitting down on the chair next to my bed, he gently took my hand and held it for a moment as he gazed into my eyes. "Bill," he said, "my dear friend . . . I deeply feel your suffering. . . ." Suddenly I noticed he was wearing *black!* That was the moment I knew I'd get well just to spite "the boy wonder."

Charles Higham's *The Films of Orson Welles* says of *The Lady from Shanghai:*

> Of all his films, I find this one the most ravishing: a masterpiece of evocative imagery, conjuring up as no other film has done, the feeling of the tropics, of the lazy movement of a yacht at sea, of the beauty of marshes and palms, and the misty calm of remote ports of call. For all its somber comic characteristic sniping at the rich—at the symbolic little party of faded-liberal sailor, wicked lawyer, murderous wife, and voyeur partner sailing from the Caribbean to San Francisco—the film is essentially a romantic work.

The Lady from Shanghai was a box-office failure. Today it is considered a masterpiece.

CHAPTER XV

The Twin Syndrome

AFTER a long convalescence, I finally reported back to work with great expectations. These soon vanished when I was handed a script called *Boston Blackie's Return.* That film was followed by *The Lone Wolf's Revenge.* I was in debt to Columbia due to my illness, and I was forced to direct films that I could do with my eyes shut. Finally, I rebelled over a script called *The Crime Doctor's Secret,* which was a sequel to *The Crime Doctor's Warning,* the film I'd been directing before my adventure in Acapulco.

Refusing to accept the assignment, I had a meeting with Cohn. Coldly and unequivocally, he stated that I was to do any picture assigned to me.

Coldly and unequivocally, I refused. The silence hung heavy in the room. Cohn broke it, speaking like dry ice. "You know what your refusal means."

Probably the firing squad, I thought, and wondered when the execution would take place. A registered letter came the next day:

COLUMBIA PICTURES CORPORATION
November 30, 1947

Dear Mr. Castle,

You have heretofore advised us that you will not render your required services under and pursuant to your employment agreement with us in connection with our motion picture photoplay now entitled *The Crime Doctor's Secret* to which you have heretofore been assigned.

Please take notice that because of your said refusal we have suspended payment of any salary payable to you under said employment agreement effective as of close November 28, 1947.
Very truly yours,
Columbia Pictures

by Duncan Cassel
Asst. Secretary

The goddamn letter with all the legal gibberish meant one thing—*I was suspended!* Out of work, and unable to work anywhere in the picture business until I sank to my knees and begged Harry Cohn to forgive me. (Every contract had a suspension clause the studio could exercise if they felt you were difficult. The contract was still valid, but you weren't paid, and you couldn't work anywhere in the industry.)

One reverse rule of psychology that I've always followed is that when I'm in trouble and fall on my behind, I usually celebrate either by giving myself a party, eating a scrumptious dinner, or getting drunk.

I didn't feel like getting drunk, and it was too late to have a party, so I decided to shave and dress in my finest and to feast in the dining room. At least I had credit for another week. And so, with elaborate preparation, wearing my dark blue suit, I entered what was to be the experience of my lifetime.

The dining room was almost full, and as the headwaiter ushered me to a table in the corner, I noticed one of the most beautiful women I had ever seen, sitting at a table with an actor, Lowell Gilmore. She was breathtaking—a cross between Marlene Dietrich and Ingrid Bergman—high cheekbones, chiseled aristocratic features. I held my breath as my heart started to pump. My adrenalin was working overtime.

I knew Lowell Gilmore slightly, but as I reached the table, he suddenly became my dearest and closest friend. "Hello, Lowell, how good it is to see you. I was just thinking of you today and hoping we could have dinner." Hovering over the table, I waited for an introduction. Lowell didn't respond as warmly as he should, but he vaguely remembered my name and standing up, gallantly mumbled, "Miss Ruth Falck, this is William Castle. He's a director."

Anxiously, I awaited Lowell's invitation to join him, which for obvious reasons, he didn't offer. However, in the intervening thirty seconds, I came up with the corniest line in history: "You are indeed beautiful, Miss Falck. . . . I wish you had a twin at home like you."

Miss Falck purred and bathed me with the sexiest smile I had ever felt. She had a slight foreign accent. "Mr. Castle, I *do* have a twin at home . . . who looks *exactly* like me."

Stuttering, I mumbled, "How about double-dating tomorrow, Lowell? You take Ruth and I'll take her sister. . . . By the way, what's your sister's name?"

"Ellen," Ruth purred.

"Ellen." I liked the sound. "A blind date?" I continued.

"It won't be exactly a blind date, Mr. Castle. You'll know what *you're getting*. The only problem is, she won't know what she's getting."

Arriving at the Falck residence an hour early, I paced the block trying to figure out witty things to say. At last the distant clock tolled eight—the appointed hour. I raced to the door and pushed the doorbell. There was a pause. Slowly the door opened and there in front of me was—which one was it? Ellen or Ruth?

A ripple of soft laughter filled the air. "Which one am I, Bill?"

Suddenly there was no doubt. "You're *Ellen!*" I stated quietly. I know it sounds corny, but if it is possible to fall in love at first sight, that night I did.

I managed to keep the hotel from evicting me for another month and also managed a lot of free meals with Ellen's family. I was still on suspension, but now that I had fallen in love and wanted to get married, I was ready to capitulate to the formidable Harry Cohn.

Dinner was being served at Ellen's house when the telephone rang. Ruth answered and told me Harry Cohn wished to speak to me. Choking on a piece of chicken fricassee, I wondered how in the hell he had tracked me down. Grabbing the phone, I waited for the inevitable bark.

111

"Castle! Where the hell are you?"

"On suspension," I replied humbly.

"I know that, stupid! . . . Where are you now?"

"At a friend's house for dinner." What the hell business was it of Cohn's? I resented his Gestapo methods in tracking me down. "How'd you find me?"

There was a pause and his rasping voice lowered conspiratorially. "I have my own ways." There was another pause as I waited for him to tell me what in the hell he wanted. "I hear you're getting married—is it true?"

How did he find out? I had just proposed. I wondered if he had Ellen's apartment tapped.

"Well, goddammit," he thundered, "is it true?"

"Yes!" I defiantly yelled back.

"So when am I going to meet her?"

"Never." I managed to swallow the word.

"What?"

"Nothing." A pause.

He caught the pause and read my thought and then snapped, "If I don't meet her, you'll stay on suspension forever, goddammit!" I gulped as he continued. "I want the both of you in my office tomorrow at eleven o'clock—and that's an order!"

As I walked back to the table, I sat silently, the chicken fricassee dry in my mouth. Ellen could see I was troubled. "What happened, Bill?" she asked.

"Harry Cohn wants to pass judgment on you . . . the sonofabitch. Well, the hell with him! . . . You don't have to meet him. . . . I'm on suspension."

"Bill, I'd be delighted to meet Mr. Cohn."

"Why?"

She smiled, then quietly said, "He sounds fascinating."

Ellen and I were seated in Cohn's office the following morning at eleven. After the introductions, he sat for a moment and then suddenly I saw a Cohn that I had never seen before—radiant, charming, gallant. It was an amazing thing to see my future bride and Cohn charm each other. It was positively nauseating.

112

After about fifteen minutes, he scribbled something on a piece of paper, folded it, and handed it to me. Taking a quick look at the message on the way out of the studio, I smiled and handed it to Ellen. We fell into each other's arms in fits of laughter. Scribbled on the piece of paper was:

Marry her quick before she changes her mind.
She's got real class . . . too much for you.
                                              Harry

Several days before the ceremony, Harry Cohn asked to see Ellen again. This time he wanted her to come in alone. Sitting on pins and needles, I waited until she came back and reported what had taken place.

Harry Cohn had wanted Ellen to make a screen test to play opposite Humphrey Bogart. A costarring role in a forthcoming Columbia picture. Flattered at the thought of playing opposite Bogart, she asked my advice. I was all for it, but decided that Ellen must make her own decision. She finally opted for one career in the family—mine.

Two days later, March 21, 1948, we were married. As a wedding present, Harry Cohn took me off suspension.

In his office the following day, Cohn announced, "I'm sending you and Ellen on a trip to Europe—all expenses paid."

I couldn't quite believe my ears. Remaining silent, I waited for his next move.

"Well," he continued, "what do you think of that? Have you ever been to Europe?"

"No," I answered, "I couldn't afford it."

Putting his arm around me, he continued. "You'll leave next week for Paris and then . . . anywhere else you want to go. . . . Take a month's vacation. It's on Columbia, for you and your bride." The clinker wasn't long in coming. "While you're in Paris," he continued, "I want you to do me a small favor. . . ."

I waited.

CHAPTER XVI

The Little Monster

THE "small favor" Cohn wanted during my honeymoon was to direct a second unit—background shots and scenes with actors' doubles—that needed authentic French backgrounds. Ellen and I winged to Paris, I with great anticipation, Ellen with a strange foreboding.

It rained incessantly for the next two weeks, and what was to be just two days of work turned into a nightmare. Each day the French promised the sun would shine, and each day turned out to be rainy, dark, and gloomy.

When the sun did eventually come out, I managed to shoot the second unit shots.

On the last evening, after climbing five flights to our garret apartment, Ellen and I toasted each other on our good fortune in leaving the "City of Light" and I reassured her that at our next stop, Rome, the honeymoon would really begin.

In Rome we checked into the Excelsior Hotel. I was thrilled; Ellen was still disturbed. At the reception desk, the concierge handed me a cablegram with our key. Turning to Ellen, I showed her the small, square envelope. "I wonder who that's from!"

"Probably Harry Cohn, asking you to come back to the studio immediately," Ellen said.

IF YOU ARE NEEDED IMMEDIATELY FOR TOP COLUMBIA PICTURE WOULD YOU FLY RIGHT BACK. STOP. REGARDS. HARRY COHN.

"What do you think, darling?" As I watched her eyes blaze, I knew the answer. The honeymoon was over. "It won't hurt to find out what the picture is. . . . He did say it was a big one. . . . I'm not suggesting we go back, but it won't hurt to find out—will it? After all, it is my career."

We were sitting in our room when Ellen, in tears, ran to the bathroom and slammed the door. I sent the following cable to Harry Cohn.

I AM VERY INTERESTED IN KNOWING NAME OF TOP PICTURE AND STAR. STOP. CANNOT PROMISE ANYTHING UNTIL I FIND OUT. STOP. BILL CASTLE.

Ellen wanted to go shopping, and I wanted to stick around the hotel to wait for Cohn's answer. We went shopping. Every ten minutes I called the hotel to find out if a cable had come from America. On the fourth try, the operator said the cable was there.

Rushing back to the Excelsior, I tore open Cohn's answer.

WON'T KNOW UNTIL BEGINNING WEEK IF I NEED YOU. IF YOU LEAVE ROME ADVISE. STOP. HARRY COHN.

Goddammit, he didn't answer my question. What was the picture and who was the star?

Ellen and I had our first argument that night. It started quite simply and got right to the point. Eyes afire, she flatly announced in a tone I'd never heard before. "We're leaving for Capri . . . now!" She began packing her things angrily. "I've had it. I'm going to Capri, and if you don't come with me, I'm going alone— *period!* "

I was furious. She didn't understand the motion-picture business. "My career's at stake," I yelled.

"Bullshit!" she screamed back. Suddenly she stopped packing and studied me for a long time before speaking. "You know, Bill, you sell yourself short. I know very little about the picture business, but how can Harry Cohn respect you when you don't respect yourself?"

115

"I don't know what you're talking about." I knew damn well what she was talking about. I've always sold myself short.

"You're too available," she continued. "He thinks he can snap his fingers and you'll come running. Let him see that you're independent. And for God's sake, don't crumble every time you hear his name."

"Well, at least I can let him know where we're going," I suggested apologetically.

"Have you ever thought of leaving a forwarding address at the hotel?"

Ellen has amazing wisdom as well as strength. She not only has been a perfect wife for me throughout the years, but my partner as well.

Capri is probably one of the most beautiful spots in the world. They say, "See Naples and die," but one should see Capri and live.

We had an idyllic twenty-four hours basking in the warm sun and swimming together before Cohn's next cable arrived.

Opening the small, square telegram, I read the following message:

WHILE DON'T LIKE INTERFERING WITH VACATION WANT YOU FOR MARGARET SULLAVAN/ JIMMY STEWART PICTURE IF YOU'LL FLY BACK IMMEDIATELY. STOP. ADVISE. STOP. HARRY COHN.

"Jesus, Ellen, that will be the biggest and most important picture of the year. Margaret Sullavan and Jimmy Stewart are two of the biggest stars in Hollywood. What a break . . . at last."

Rushing to our room, I started to pack. "Ellen, please send a cable to Harry Cohn immediately. Tell him I accept, thank him, and inform him we're flying back immediately."

Ellen left the room silently. She sent a cable, all right, but not exactly the one I had dictated. Later that afternoon she showed me a copy of what she had sent to Cohn.

IMPOSSIBLE TO LEAVE CAPRI. STOP. ALL
PLANES BOOKED. STOP. EARLIEST ONE ON JULY
3. STOP. BILL CASTLE.

"Oh, God, Ellen," I moaned. "You've ruined my career."
"Just wait and see what happens," she purred.
The following morning Cohn's answer came.

JULY 3 TOO LATE. STOP. HAVE BOOKED YOU ON
PAN AMER LEAVING JULY 1. STOP. GET BACK.
STOP. HARRY COHN.

"That's today," I informed Ellen. "Now let's really start
packing."
When we arrived in New York, I wanted to go straight
through to L.A. It was a long flight, and Ellen, always looking
after my health, insisted we stop over and get some rest, then
fly in the following day.
At about 2:00 A.M. I awakened with a sharp pain in my
right side. I groaned out loud and awakened Ellen, who is a
light sleeper. Turning on the light, she stared at me. My face
was white and I was writhing in agony.
"Shit!" I mumbled. "Of all times to have an appendix attack."
The pain increased with such intensity that I had trouble
breathing. Ellen quickly called the hotel doctor. A few minutes later he arrived. I had to be hospitalized immediately.
"I'm not going to any hospital!" I screamed. "I have to get
back to start my new picture!" Then I collapsed on the floor.
The next thing I knew, it was morning, and another doctor was checking me over. "Does it hurt here?" he said, poking my right side with his goddamn thumb.
"Yes!" I screamed. After about ten minutes of poking, he
announced it wasn't an appendix attack, but a kidney stone
that was the little monster. I would have to go to the hospital
immediately. They hadn't taken me the night before because
there were no beds available.
Stubbornly, I refused to go. The pain was still intense, but

I was getting used to it. I had to get back to Hollywood at any cost.

The doctor reluctantly approved, but flatly stated that if I didn't pass the stone by 2:00 that afternoon, I was headed for the hospital.

I couldn't let one lousy little kidney stone louse up my career. My temperature was 103°. The doctor said he would be back at 2:00 P.M. He would reserve a room in the hospital—just in case.

Over my protests, Ellen put a call through to Harry Cohn at the studio in Hollywood. Dona Holloway, his executive secretary (a good friend who later became my partner), answered the call. Ellen explained I was in tremendous pain and obviously wouldn't be able to keep the meeting with Harry Cohn. Dona, terribly concerned, assured Ellen she'd take care of everything, including Cohn.

I started to argue, but Ellen just looked at me and I shut up and went back to my pain. About twenty minutes later, the telephone rang. It was Harry Cohn calling, personally!

He instructed Ellen to get me back to the Coast immediately and he'd have an ambulance at the airport, with his personal physician in attendance. Ellen informed him I was in no condition to travel.

"What did he say, Ellen?" I moaned.

"Nothing." she said. "And now, dammit, pass that stone!"

Since that morning I have often used the element of time to build suspense in my pictures. Whether it's a ticking bomb, or minutes ticking by on a clock during an emergency, the device has always worked. The passing of my kidney stone was a similar experience.

"What time is it, Ellen?" I said weakly.

"One o'clock. You have an hour."

I peed. No stone.

"What time is it now," I gasped.

"One-thirty," Ellen replied.

I again tried. Nothing. The pain was building. Minutes ticked by. I drank more and more water to flush out the stone. "How much more time do I have?"

118

"Fifteen minutes."

Go, boy, go, I repeated to myself. You can do it, I know you can. Your career's at stake. No more lousy quickies. Goddammit, pass that stone!

Four minutes to two . . . three minutes. One last try before the doctor came. It worked—plop went the stone. It was the size of a lemon seed. Saved three minutes before the hour! Exhausted, I sank back into bed. The pain disappeared miraculously, and my fever dropped. I felt weak, but suddenly I was famished.

At precisely 2:00 the doctor arrived. The hospital room was canceled and, weak as a kitten, I headed back to Hollywood and my big chance.

Dona Holloway's face was as ashen as mine had been when I greeted her in Cohn's outer office.

"Bill, bad news," she said.

My heart sank. "What is it, Dona?"

"Let Mr. Cohn tell you," she replied as she turned away, hiding her tears.

Harry Cohn's face reflected gloom as I entered his office. "Sit down, Castle. . . . How do you feel?"

It was the first time Harry Cohn seemed at a loss for words. I sat dumbly, staring at him. "We—I—tried to reach you, but you'd already left," he stammered.

I remained silent.

"We canceled the Sullavan/Stewart picture. . . . Decided it was too downbeat. . . . I'm sorry." Cohn seemed again at a loss for words. Then he smiled. "Strange, but sometimes things happen for the best." He then told me he had gotten a phone call from William Goetz, who had recently formed a new company with his partner Leo Spitz. The name of the company was to become Universal-International.

"Bill Goetz said he wanted you over there and asked me if I'd let you go." Cohn walked to his window and gazed out. "What do you want me to do, Bill? . . . It's up to you."

Tears came to my eyes. "I think I'd like to try another studio, Harry, . . . If it's okay with you."

119

Chapter XVII

Do Indians Wear Bathing Caps?

THE day before reporting to Universal-International, I had a strange dream—Harry Cohn had died and I was at his funeral. Only it wasn't Cohn's, it was my father's. I tried to cry, but the tears wouldn't come. I felt nothing. It wasn't really happening. I was going to live with my sister now—I wasn't sure I'd be happy in my new home.

In 1949 Universal-International looked like a huge country club. Rows of bungalows surrounded by flowers and manicured lawns gave the feeling of peace and tranquillity, completely different from the factory look at Columbia. William Goetz, in charge of production, was a soft-spoken, gentle man quite the opposite of the volatile Harry Cohn. At our first meeting, Goetz told me Harry Cohn had negotiated my deal with him. "Harry insisted that we pay you almost double before he agreed to let you go."

My first assignment was a big disappointment, *Johnny Stool Pigeon*, a pedestrian thriller. Its only claim to fame was that I cast a young actor named Tony Curtis in a minor role. Shelley Winters, then a comparative unknown, was also in the cast.

Universal-International, in trying to compete with the other majors, had a succession of failures. Critically acclaimed, the pictures did poorly at the box office. Their policy changed from art to action, and from expensive, imaginative films to low-budgets. Again I was caught in the trap.

The screen version of a popular radio series, *The Fat Man*, was my second directorial assignment. It was a potboiler of little merit, except that I was able to cast Rock Hudson in his first picture and convinced Goetz to use Emmett Kelly, the Ringling Brothers clown, as the villain in the piece.

The Cave of the Outlaws, starring Alexis Smith and MacDonald Carey, was my next epic. Filmed mostly in the Carlsbad Caverns where we lived underground like moles, there was little excitement about the whole project.

Frustrated and angry, I asked for a meeting with William Goetz. "Mr. Goetz, I have a gimmick that'll make millions at the box office."

Goetz smiled as he patiently listened to my multimillion-dollar idea. Encouraged by his smile, I went all the way into my pitch. I wanted to do a modern adaptation of Jules Verne's *From the Earth to the Moon*. I had read the book many times. I handed Goetz my twenty-page treatment. "It's a great piece of showmanship, Mr. Goetz. Audiences are ready for science fiction, and I have a gimmick that's fantastic."

I remembered going to the movies when I was a kid and witnessing an astounding feat of magic. It was a Pete Smith MGM short, and audiences were given cardboard eyeglasses made up of red and green cellophane lenses. They were instructed to wear them during the short subject. Objects seemed to leave the screen and fly out at the audience. I remembered ducking a baseball that seemed to come right at me, and water that seemed to douse the audience.

"Mr. Goetz, for *From Earth to the Moon*, I want to use the same technique . . . more sophisticated, perhaps. Audiences will feel they're landing on the moon." Without pausing for breath, I continued selling. "We can call the new process, SEE-A-VISION, The New Sensation Where You're Part of the Picture. It'll revolutionize the industry and make millions."

Goetz thought for a moment, then handed back my treatment. Shaking his head, he quickly concluded our interview. "It won't work, Bill. Audiences won't wear glasses. It'll be too uncomfortable, and the cost to manufacture them would be prohibitive."

I tried to convince him that audiences would buy the glasses at the theatres, but he still disagreed and, walking me to the door, told me that Universal just wasn't interested in science fiction.

My three-year tenure at Universal was drawing to a close. I had one more picture to do under the contract, and then I was free. *Hollywood Story* was the picture, and at last I had an excellent script and a chance to direct an exciting, provocative murder mystery. It dealt with the William Desmond Taylor murder. Taylor was a director in the silent era, who was murdered in 1921. Mabel Normand, queen of the Mack Sennett bathing beauties, was the last to see him alive. The scandal ruined her career, and the mysterious killing was never solved.

Deciding to re-create the silent era of motion pictures in juxtaposition with the present day by going from black and white to color and from subtitles to sound, I managed to create an eerie effect. For the silent era, picture stars of yesteryear were cast—Francis X. Bushman, Chester Conklin, Charlie Chase, and as many of the Keystone Kops as I could locate. To be sure that *Hollywood Story* had a feeling of the past, many sequences were shot at the old Charlie Chaplin Studio.

Universal-International was pleased with the final results and wanted to renegotiate my contract for another three years. I asked for time to think it over, and called Dona Holloway and asked if she could get Harry Cohn to look at the picture immediately. She called back to say that Cohn would see *Hollywood Story* that night and he insisted I be there.

"THE END" flashed on the screen and the lights in Cohn's private projection room went on. "Great title, *Hollywood Story* —I wish we had it." Three years older than when I had last

122

seen him, Cohn looked drawn and tired. He stood up and stretched. "You know, I should never have let you leave Columbia."

I was on my guard, and Cohn sensed that. "I want you back, Bill. Sign with Columbia again and I promise you two things—money, lots of it—and you'll direct more pictures than you ever dreamed of.

Harry Cohn kept his promise—on both counts. I was back home.

Sam Katzman was a smallish man with a round cherubic face and twinkling eyes. Few people in the motion-picture industry took him seriously as a producer of quality films, but to me, Sam was a great showman.

Sitting in his office, he greeted me warmly and handed me a script. "*Serpent of the Nile* is my most ambitious project to date. All about that Cleopatra broad, Mark Antony, and that Julius Caesar guy."

Rhonda Fleming, who had worked for me in a one-line bit in *When Strangers Marry,* played Cleopatra. Raymond Burr played Caesar.

Serpent of the Nile was promoted and sold to the public as follows:

GIGANTIC! FANTASTIC!
2 YEARS IN THE MAKING!

Actually, Katzman had been *talking* about making the picture for two years. The ad should have read:

2 YEARS IN THE TALKING,
12 DAYS IN THE SHOOTING!

One night while walking along Hollywood Boulevard, I noticed a mob scene in front of the Hollywood Theatre. Police were trying to control the crowds buying tickets for Arch Oboler's *Bwana Devil.* On the marquee in blazing red letters:

"3-D—THE NEW SENSATION." A special box office was set up to sell the 3-D glasses to the public. Two years after Universal had turned me down, my prediction came true. America was 3-D happy. *Bwana Devil* made a fortune.

"It's a new process. . . . You wear glasses. . . . It's making a fortune." Katzman was excited; I was depressed. "You're going to direct *Fort Ti* in 3-D."

I decided to throw every goddamn thing I could think of at the camera. Every evening I took a large pot from our kitchen and practiced throwing things into it—knives, forks, spoons—anything I could lay my hands on. Ellen thought I was crazy, but my aim was becoming perfect.

I attended the preview of *Fort Ti*. The audience, with glasses perched on their noses, ducked constantly. Tomahawks, balls of fire, arrows, and cannonballs seemed to fly out of the screen. Smiling, I said to Ellen, "I'm not a director, I'm a great pitcher."

Slaves of Babylon was my next low-budget extravaganza. Sam had invaded C.B. DeMille's territory—the Bible. Maurice Schwartz, the famous star of the Yiddish theatre, was cast as Daniel. One noon at lunch break, he asked to see me in his dressing room.

Dressed in rags and with a flowing beard, Schwartz did indeed look like the biblical character, but he sounded like a frightened rabbit. His rich, accented sonorous tones filled his dressing room as he paced. "Kessel, at what time am I thrown into the lions' den?" he asked nervously.

"After lunch," I answered, smiling. It was the wrong choice of words.

"It's dangerous, huh?"

"Perfectly safe," I reassured him.

"How many lions will be present?"

"Twelve."

Schwartz continued to pace. I again tried to reassure him. "There's absolutely no danger, Maurice. Come on, let's have lunch."

"Who can eat?" he replied sadly.

124

As I left his dressing room he called out, "Kessel . . . be sure the lions have lunch."

Daniel was thrown into the lions' den at 2:00 P.M. A huge sheet of glass separated the lions from Daniel. Maurice carefully inspected the glass. Still unsure, he pounded the glass with his fist, making sure it was safe. The lions growled at him as they moved around restlessly.

"Kessel, how many lions did you say there were?" He started to count.

"Twelve," I answered.

"There are *thirteen* . . . Oh, my God!"

"Relax, Maurice. The lions couldn't possibly break through that glass."

"Mr. Kessel. . . . You know it. . . . And I know it. . . . But do those *meshuganah* lions know it?"

"Take One, Action!" Schwartz fell to his knees and prayed. I think he really meant it.

An amazing phenomenon occurred during the first take. As Daniel prayed to God for deliverance from bondage, he slowly lifted his head upward toward the heavens. At the precise moment that he looked upward, the thirteen lions simultaneously looked upward toward heaven, too. It was an astonishing scene—thirteen lions and Maurice Schwartz praying together.

No one could quite figure out how I achieved this feat. Actually, a high arc light had burned out. The lions, distracted by the noise, just happened to look up at the same time as Schwartz.

I was now on another treadmill, turning out a full-length feature every month.

"Sam, it won't work. The whole idea is absolutely ridiculous."

"Please . . . just try it. It's a great idea, and besides, it'll save me a lot of money."

Katzman and I were having lunch together at the Brown Derby. Our next film was to be *Conquest of Cochise.*

"Sam," I pleaded, "why can't we get the Indians to shave their heads? It'll be added realism."

Sam was appalled. "You realize what it'll cost me to get the Indians to *really* shave their heads? A small fortune!"

"But why?" I insisted.

"They won't be able to work in any more pictures for months, until their hair grows back—or unless the right tribe comes along, one with shaven heads."

"How many Indians are we using, Sam?"

"About fifty."

"That's not enough. We'll have to have at least a hundred."

Katzman moaned. "That's another reason why my idea will work."

"How about getting makeup to create some tight skull-caps? That usually works."

Sam pleaded, "Why won't you at least try my idea?"

"Sam, for chrissake, how in the hell can I go into Woolworth's and buy a hundred bathing caps?"

"So *I'll* buy them. Bathing caps are only twenty-five cents apiece. We can paint them brown. . . . Put them over the Indians' hair. . . . They'll look bald. Nobody'll know the difference. I promise you, Bill."

Several days later, Harry Cohn called and thundered, "Who in the hell authorized the scene where one hundred fucking Indians go swimming—and with bathing caps!"

I was living in a kaleidoscope. My eyes were becoming two mirrors, and every movement I made now reflected continually changing patterns.

> *Charge of the Lancers*
> *Drums of Tahiti*
> *Jesse James vs. the Daltons*
> *The Iron Glove*
> *Battle of Rogue River*
> *Bat Masterson of Kansas*
> *The Law vs. Billy the Kid*
> *The Gun That Won the West*

126

New Orleans Uncensored
Ride on Pier Six
Duel on the Mississippi
Uranium Boom
The Houston Story

Houston, Texas is unbearable in August—especially if you're going to make a picture in the oil fields. The humidity was oppressive. I waited for Lee J. Cobb to arrive; he was to star in *The Houston Story*. Lee and I had been close friends for years, and I've always felt that he was one of the most talented of the American actors. I was thrilled with the prospect of working with him.

As the plane from New York landed, I remembered we had one thing in common—we were look-alikes. People constantly asked for my autograph thinking I was Lee Cobb, and he promised many actors who thought he was Bill Castle work in pictures. We often kidded each other about this.

Filming a fight sequence in the oil fields at night was tough enough without having an exhausted star. Cobb was pale and haggard. Something was wrong. Watching him rehearse a scene where he was supposed to lift a man bodily and throw him to the ground, worried me.

"Lee." I approached him. "Are you all right? This is a tough scene to do. We can schedule it some other night."

"Nah, I feel great—just a little indigestion. Let's do the scene and get it over with."

There was a pause as I made my decision. "Let's wrap for tonight."

I was sound asleep in my room at the Shamrock Hotel when the phone awakened me. "Mr. Castle?" The operator's voice sounded tense. "Mr. Cobb needs help. He seems to be ill. You'd better get to the room right away."

Throwing a robe over my pajamas, I rushed to Lee's suite. He was on the floor, clutching his chest, writhing in pain. "My chest!" he moaned. "Call my father."

Instead, I called the hotel doctor and got Lee to a hospital right away. The best cardiologist in Houston informed me that Cobb would have to remain in the hospital and would be unable to work for several months.

That meant *The Houston Story* would have to shut down until Lee was ready to work again. We had three more days of location work in Houston, but the insurance would cover that.

Still in my bathrobe, I left Lee's hospital room. As I appeared in the corridor, a frantic nurse rushed up to me and grabbed my arm. "Mr. Cobb—you should be back in bed!" The nurse started to pull me back into the room.

Realizing that if I could fool a nurse, I could fool the camera, I played all of Lee Cobb's long shots and medium shots for the three days until we finished the location. I would get the added close-ups of Lee when he was able to work.

Ten weeks passed and Lee was back in Hollywood, feeling fine. One week before we started, he had another attack, and it was decided to recast his part. But who could follow Lee J. Cobb?

Sam Katzman insisted on a relatively new actor in pictures—Gene Barry, a fine actor, but as unlike Lee J. Cobb as anyone could be.

Looking at *The Houston Story* when it was completed, I shook my head in dismay. Three of us were playing the same part. I could be seen running down a street in Houston in a long shot; a medium shot of Lee J. Cobb as he continues running and rushes through a door; a close shot of Gene Barry entering and being hit; medium shot of me staggering, and a long shot of Lee J. Cobb falling to the floor.

The picture is occasionally released on the late-late movies. My friends have a lot of fun watching the three of us perform in one part.

An epic, *The Saracen Blade*, went into production. It was a herculean task for me to adhere to the schedule. Carolyn Jones played the queen, Ricardo Montalban the king. For three years I had been up to my ass in queens, kings, and jokers.

The author demonstrates proper film audience reaction.

clockwise, this page: In 1940, with Tony Martin and Rita Hayworth; the making of a publicity coup; Castle, on left, rehearsing Ellen Schwanneke at Stony Creek, 1939; with Cary Grant in younger days; on board the *Zaca* with Errol Flynn.

left: With Harry Cohn in Hawaii.

below left: "My best wishes to Sir Castle," from the other king of chills, Alfred Hitchcock.

below right: With Cary Grant and Joan Crawford in more recent days.

next page, top to bottom: *Macabre* fans line up to risk their lives; the famous Lloyds of London's insurance policy; Castle's dramatic "departure" for another *Macabre* opening.

best wishes
Sir Castle

MACABRE

The Producers of the film MACABRE, undertake to pay the sum of ONE THOUSAND DOLLARS in the event of the death by fright of any member of the audience during the performance.

BENEFICIARY AGREEMENT

In the event of my decease by fright during the performance of the motion picture "MACABRE", I hereby instruct the producers to pay ONE THOUSAND DOLLARS ($1,000) Life Benefit to my beneficiary named below.

_____   _____
BENEFICIARY'S NAME   RELATIONSHIP

I understand that if I have a known heart or nervous condition the One Thousand Dollars ($1,000) is not payable.

_____
NAME

The above agreement is insured by Lloyd's of London.

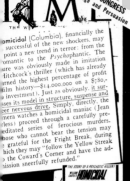

THE TINGLER

top left: *Time* likes *Homicidal* better than *Psycho*.

top right: Vincent Price and a friend "give Castle a hand" at *Tingler* opening.

left: Smiles all around with "Mr. Sardonicus."

below: At opening with one of "13 Frightened Girls."

above, left: Castle's Thanksgiving "gift" to Hitchcock, attended by Jean Arliss (*Homicidal*).

above, right: A fan samples "Percepto" at *Tingler* opening.

below: Fan club members welcome Castle to a *Tingler* opening.

above: Castle on the *other* side of the camera portrays Harry Cohn-like producer in *The Sex Symbol*, with Connie Stevens.

below, left: With Mia Farrow (*Rosemary's Baby*).

below, right: With Marcel Marceau (*Shanks*).

above: Castle playing director in *Day of the Locust.*

below: Ellen, Georgie, Terry, and Bill in the Castle garden.

Ricardo Montalban was wonderful to work with, a fine actor. Formerly a dancer, he was agile and a great athlete. His charm and good looks gave the film an added dimension. He was a perfectionist, and the fast schedule constantly bothered him.

"Bill," he questioned one day on the set, "why do you keep me standing in a corner, talking? I should stride up the great hall, then into the courtyard, then finally back into the great hall and up the staircase. The scene requires great movement—I cannot play it stationary, standing in a corner."

I glanced at my watch, but seeing how unhappy he was, I put my arm around his shoulder. "Ricardo, let's see how you would play it."

His face lit up. "I'll show you." Striding down the great hall, the length of the stage and then back, he then leaped out onto the courtyard, then swept back into the great hall and onto the staircase. At the top, he yelled down, "This is how the scene should be played—you agree, Bill?"

"I agree," I said. "But we'll play it with you standing in the corner."

"But why, amigo?" he said angrily. "You agree with me."

"Time, Ricardo," I sadly said. "I have only fifteen minutes budgeted to get the scene. I agree that your way would be perfect, but it would take me four hours."

To celebrate finishing the picture, Ricardo and his charming wife, Georgiana, invited Ellen and me to join them for dinner.

Sitting in their comfortable living room, Ricardo and Georgiana toasted Ellen, who was pregnant at the time. "When is the baby due?" Georgiana asked.

Ellen smiled. "Any moment, Mrs. Montalban."

"Please call me Georgiana."

"That's a beautiful name. My father's name was George," Ellen said. The candles flickered at the dinner table. The rest of the room was dark, except for the lights of the city sparkling in the distance. Ellen seemed unusually happy. She raised her wineglass. "I would like to propose a toast." We all raised our glasses. "To the Montalbans, a beautiful couple . . . and to the birth of our child." Ellen looked at me and smiled. "If it's a girl, Bill, if it's agreeable to you, I would like to name her Georgiana."

October 2, 1954, 2:00 P.M. I was home waiting.
"I think it's time," Ellen said softly.
Clutching my stomach, I felt a cramp. Ellen drove us to the hospital.
My stomach cramps became more intense as I paced the waiting room at Cedars of Lebanon. By 4:00 P.M. , the pain was unbearable. I continued pacing. The hands on the clock climbed—4:30, 4:40, 4:45—it seemed an eternity. My labor was intense.
At 5:20 P.M. our obstetrician came in. "It's a seven-pound baby girl. Ellen's just fine."
My pain disappeared immediately.
Georgiana was here.

The last time I saw Harry Cohn was in Hawaii. Georgie was two, and Ellen and I decided to take her on her first trip.
It was late afternoon, and the setting sun silhouetted a lone figure on the beach. We suddenly realized it was Harry Cohn. He greeted us warmly and asked if we'd walk with him. No longer bursting with energy, his movements seemed slow and and labored, as if he were unsure of himself. He spoke softly, almost gently. The three of us walked along the beach. Glancing at her watch Ellen politely said we had to get back to the hotel for an early dinner date. Harry Cohn made a simple request. "Please walk with me just a little longer."
Harry Cohn died on February 27, 1958. Memorial services were held inside a huge sound stage at Columbia. The stage was packed with the greats, near-greats, superstars, producers, directors, executives—not only from Columbia but from the entire industry, each alone with his own thoughts. Danny Kaye delivered the eulogy. I started to cry and suddenly realized that for the first time I was crying at a funeral.

130

PART II

Horrors!

Chapter XVIII

Don't Drop Dead

IT all began on a dark and stormy night—thunder, lightning, rain. "Let's go to the movies," I said to Ellen.

"It's pouring," she announced, looking out the window.

"So what?" I returned. "We're going to be inside."

Windshield wipers working overtime, we could barely make out the long line of umbrellas with people underneath—all patiently waiting to see Henri-Georges Clouzot's *Diabolique.*

Word was around that *Diabolique* was doing great business, but I never expected the excitement that surrounded the theatre. Only the very young would venture out on a night like this, or the very crazy—like myself.

A young couple waiting on line in front of me couldn't have been over sixteen years old. The pretty girl and the pimply-faced youth were getting soaked. "How come you're standing in line to see this picture?" I asked.

"My friends told me it really scares the shit out of you."

"That's what I heard, too," the girl agreed excitedly.

It was an amazing phenomenon—hundreds of youngsters waiting patiently to have the "shit scared out of them."

The theatre was packed, sold out. All kids—some of them didn't even seem old enough to read the English subtitles for the French film, but it didn't matter. They wanted thrills and chills, and *Diabolique* delivered in a big way.

I watched transfixed as the movie unfolded its grisly tale

before my eyes. A dead body coming out of a tub; glassy eyes, milky white, being taken from their sockets. There was a roar of shock that rocked the theatre.

"Let's leave," Ellen whispered.

"Not on your life—I'm loving every minute of this." (Ellen still can't stand a horror movie. I can hardly get her to sit through one of mine.)

The collective emotional release of all those screaming kids was exhilarating, incredible! Leaving the theatre, I felt a strange sensation—a reawakening of some sort.

"Let's get some coffee."

"It's still pouring," Ellen said.

"We're not going to have coffee in the rain." Entering a deserted coffee shop next to the theatre, I pulled Ellen over to a table excitedly. "Did you ever see anything like what happened tonight? Those kids wanted to be scared. . . . They loved it! They probably have never seen a real horror film—it's been ten years or more, in fact, since Lorre, Lugosi, or Karloff."

Ellen smiled. "I haven't seen you this excited for months."

"Young audiences are starving for this type of picture, and I want to be the one to satisfy their hunger."

"It's the genre you love." Ellen sipped her coffee.

"I want to scare the pants off America. When that audience gave that final collective scream, I knew that's where I wanted to take them—only I want louder screams, more horror, more excitement."

My enthusiasm was contagious, and Ellen caught it. "Much longer lines—all standing in the rain, for one of *your* horror films," she declared.

"Are you with me?" I asked, clutching her hand.

"Of course I am! You're going to have a lot of fun."

My first step was to find a book more frightening than *Diabolique,* which wasn't as easy as I had thought. Reading novels, stageplays, and original screenplays proved a waste of time. One evening, bringing home a book, *The Marble Forest,* I lucked out. Excitedly I gave it to Ellen to read. We both

134

agreed it was more frightening that *Diabolique* and, if properly done, would really scare the kids.

The plot of *The Marble Forest* concerned the frantic attempt by a small-town doctor to locate his daughter, buried alive in a cemetery by an unknown madman. Suspicion is cast from one seamy character to another as time runs out on the futile subterranean search. In a surprise twist, the doctor himself is revealed to have been the culprit all along, having engineered the grisly goings-on in a successful attempt to shock his weakhearted father-in-law into a heart attack, thereby gaining his riches.

Checking on the rights to the novel, I was astonished to find it was the work of thirteen separate authors—all well-known mystery writers—writing under the pseudonym Theo Durant. They were all members of the San Francisco chapter of the Mystery Writers of America. Each one had written a separate chapter, and an editor had assembled the finished novel, adjusting the different writing styles to make it look like the work of one author.

I was able to purchase *The Marble Forest* at a modest price plus a small percentage of the film. I now had everything but the finances to make the film.

Robb White, a writer with whom I had worked before, wrote the screenplay. "Robb, the title *The Marble Forest* is wrong for the picture."

"Why? It's a good title." Robb took a drag on his pipe.

"It's not box office. We need something that'll pull the customers in."

Robb continued puffing his pipe. "How about *Buried Alive?*" he suggested.

"Not bad," I said, "but I'd prefer a one-word title."

"How about *Ghastly?*"

"No."

"*Gruesome?*"

"What's our picture about, Robb?" I asked. There was a long pause as we both smoked. "It's a dance of death," I volunteered. "Let's call the picture *Macabre.*"

"Who the hell can pronounce it?" Robb stated.

"Who the hell cares?" I said. "It sounds good."

The next step was to make a deal with one of the major studios. Going to Columbia, I approached Sam Briskin, who was now running the studio. "It's a new trend, Sam—the rebirth of the horror film. We'll make a fortune."

"You've never produced a picture," Sam stated flatly.

"What difference does that make?"

"There's a big difference between producing and directing. Columbia will let you direct anytime, but we cannot take a chance on you producing."

"Bullshit!" I muttered under my breath.

Ellen and I dined at an expensive restaurant that evening, and over chocolate soufflé, I took the plunge. "Darling, I've got a wonderful idea. . . ."

"I know," she said sweetly. "You want to mortgage our house and go into business for yourself. It's about time!"

The following morning, I hocked our home and Robb put in his share of the $90,000 needed to make *Macabre*.

Actually, I knew very little about producing a picture, and now that everything was falling together, I started to worry. Calling my longtime friend Howard Koch, one of the best producers in the business, I asked for a meeting.

"Howie, I really don't know my ass from my elbow about producing—you gotta help me." Both Howard Koch and Aubrey Schenck, his partner, became my guardian angels. If it weren't for them, *Macabre* would never have been made.

We went into production on August 15, 1958. The exteriors were shot in Chino, California, with interiors—including an elaborate graveyard set—created on the sound stages in Hollywood. The entire picture was filmed in *nine* days!

"We're getting a masterpiece—another *Diabolique*—only much better," I said enthusiastically to Ellen who was on the set watching us shoot.

The similarities between *Macabre* and *Diabolique* were obvious. Both films centered around a plot to shock to death a person with a heart condition. Both ended with double-twist, surprise climaxes, preceded by their shocking horror—

Diabolique's body rising from the tub, *Macabre*'s unearthly mummy in the coffin.

"There's something wrong with it, Robb. All the ingredients are there, but there's something missing." We were looking at a rough cut of *Macabre* in the projection room.

"Looks good to me, Bill."

"No," I said, shaking my head. "It doesn't have that blood-curdling quality that I tried to get."

"You think we should add some more horror? We could reshoot."

"We're out of money," I stated. "One ingredient's missing, but I can't put my finger on it."

That night, lying in bed, tossing and turning, I tried to sleep. My house was mortgaged to the hilt and I would probably have to sell the goddamn bed. The same nagging thought kept me awake—*something* was missing. But what? Suddenly, sitting bolt upright, I shouted, "Wake up, Ellen—I've got it! An insurance policy!"

"Go back to sleep. . . . We've already got an insurance policy." Ellen rolled over and promptly went back to sleep.

"Not for us," I shouted. "For *everybody*! I'm going to insure the entire world against death by fright during the showing of *Macabre*." It was a crazy scheme, but that's exactly what the movie needed—a sales gimmick.

I had heard that Lloyds of London would insure anything or anybody. Calling an insurance company, I asked the operator to put me in touch with one of the brokers that handled Lloyds of London.

"Good morning," a cultured British voice declared.

"I'd like an insurance policy."

"For yourself, sir?" The voice dripped molasses.

"No. I want to insure everybody in the world."

"Sir, there are approximately two billion people in the world." The voice had chilled.

"I know that," I impatiently replied. "And I want to insure every one of them in case they drop dead." The phone went dead.

Finally managing to get an appointment, I arrived at the

insurance office. Three men were waiting in the walnut-paneled office—two Britishers and an American. The American blew his nose; the Englishmen cleared their throats.

I noticed the outer door to the office was left open and I started to close it. "Please leave it open." Waiting for the reason, I found none forthcoming. Possibly an eccentricity, I thought, or perhaps it was in case I had to be forcibly ejected.

Except for occasional nose blowings and coughs, silence filled the room. They waited for me to begin. "Gentlemen, I know my request sounds strange," I tried to reassure them, "but the policy is merely a sales gimmick for my motion picture."

Glancing at the others, the American wiped his nose, then spoke. "Insuring the entire world is an absolute impossibility."

"Why?" I innocently inquired.

"There's not enough manpower to contact everyone. It would take hundreds of years." The American slowly rose from his desk, crossed the room and closed the door. An instinct told me he was interested. He then addressed his colleagues. "If we were to insure Mr. Castle personally against any claims from the audience, I think it would amount to the same thing." Again, blowing and coughs while I waited for the British to agree.

"Let me completely understand this," I summarized. "If anyone actually should drop dead, I would collect from Lloyds of London and pay *their* beneficiary—is that correct?"

"That is correct," came the reply.

Something completely new in the annals of insurance was taking place.

"It's going to be difficult to arrive at a proper price for the policy. . . . We have nothing written in our tables of insurance," declared the American.

The British contingent took out a pad and produced a pen. "How many people do you think will actually expire during the exhibition of your motion picture, *Macabre*?"

I hesitated before answering, and the American quickly

138

picked up the cue. "Would you say that twenty-five people might drop dead?"

"*Nobody's* going to drop dead," I predicted. "It's just a publicity stunt."

"But somebody *has* to drop dead; otherwise it won't work."

The four of us sat for hours bargaining on people's lives. The British went to twenty, I grudgingly gave them two; the American brought the death rate down to ten. I threw in an extra death, making mine three. We finally arrived at five lucky people who would not live through *Macabre*.

The policy cost $5,000—$1,000 a head. A slight problem presented itself—I didn't have the $5,000 to pay for the policy, but I arranged to pay it off like car payments, over a period of two years.

MACABRE
INSURANCE POLICY

The Producers of the film MACABRE, undertake to pay the sum of ONE THOUSAND DOLLARS in the event of the death by fright of any member of the audience during the performance.

BENEFICIARY AGREEMENT

In the event of my decease by fright during the performance of the motion picture "MACABRE," I hereby instruct the producers to pay ONE THOUSAND DOLLARS ($1,000) Life Benefit to my beneficiary named below.

Beneficiary's name   Relationship

I understand that if I have a known heart or nervous condition the One Thousand Dollars ($1,000) is not payable.

Name

The above agreement is insured by Lloyds of London

Desperately needing a major company to release the film, I contacted Ben Kalmenson, vice-president in charge of distribution at Warner Bros. He agreed to screen the picture and suggested I come to New York the following week.

There were a dozen men present during the showing of *Macabre*. Each one had been given an insurance policy before the picture started. At the end of the film, there was complete silence—twelve dark suits were suddenly struck deaf and dumb.

Trying to break the silence, I plunged into cold waters. "Well, fellas . . . how'd you like the picture? . . . And the insurance policy—isn't that a great gimmick?"

Coughing and nose blowing answered my questions. It seemed everyone was blowing and coughing that season. Ben Kalmenson asked me to come to his office the following morning.

"How much did the picture cost, Bill?"

"Ninety thousand," I answered honestly.

"Warner's is prepared to pick up the picture for forty-five thousand and twenty-five percent of the profits."

"But I paid ninety thousand, sir—I'll be losing money."

"We've decided it's a risk picture. And with our paying for the prints and advertising . . . you must be willing to take the gamble."

"When can I let you know, Mr. Kalmenson?"

"Take your time. . . . Call me tomorrow."

"Mr. Kalmenson, I talked it over with my wife, and unless we can get the full cost of the picture, I'm afraid I'll have to say no."

Warner Bros. wasn't the only company around, and I decided to gamble that other studio reactions would be more financially rewarding. But I had a sinking feeling that Warner Bros. had made the best offer. Perhaps I had acted hastily in turning them down.

Several weeks later, my agent, Nat Goldstone, excitedly called me from San Diego. "There's a Warner Bros. picture that just opened, and they're using your insurance gimmick. You'd better fly down here and see for yourself."

140

I couldn't believe my eyes. There were lines of people around the block, waiting to get into a Warner Bros. picture—and on the theatre marquee, in bold letters: "YOU ARE INSURED AGAINST DEATH BY FRIGHT!" Grabbing one of the policies that were being handed out, I realized it was *mine*—word for word, except Warner Bros. was substituted for Lloyds of London.

"I'll sue the bastards—they stole my gimmick!" I was in the office of the biggest plagiarism lawyer in Southern California.

"It's an open-and-shut case," the attorney declared. "We'll get an injunction against the picture and the use of the policy. It'll cost them a fortune."

"Jack Warner is on the line. He wants to speak to you." We were just finishing dinner the following night.

"Hello," I barked.

A soothing voice came over. "Bill, I'm terribly sorry this happened. I had no idea it was yours. . . . One of our publicity men, some young eager-beaver, came up with the idea, saying it was his own. . . . Please drop your suit, Bill. . . . I've fired the publicity man. You know we would never do anything like this knowingly."

"Mr. Warner . . . I just want to protect my insurance gimmick."

"Tell you what I'll do. . . . We'll buy *Macabre* for the ninety thousand you have in it."

"Hold on just a minute, Mr. Warner." Turning to Ellen, I whispered, "He's offered ninety thousand. . . . Shall I accept? We'll be even."

"Tell him no," Ellen whispered.

"But we'll be safe. . . . We'll get our money out."

"Why did you make the picture in the first place—to break even? Tell him *no!*"

"Sorry, Mr. Warner," I whispered, "but thanks for calling." The suit was dropped, and I've always given Jack Warner, an admirable man, the benefit of the doubt.

* * *

"Who the hell is going to release the picture?" I was talking to Robb White, who also had money at stake on *Macabre.*

"How about showing it to Columbia?" Robb suggested.

"They turned us down originally. Screw 'em!"

"Allied Artists—they need pictures."

"They release cheap low-budget pictures, Robb."

"But they're aggressive."

"They've got to be," I said, "or they'd starve. Oh, well, what have we got to lose—I'll call them."

The lights went up after the showing of *Macabre* in the Allied Artists projection room. Johnny Flynn, in charge of publicity, excitedly waved his insurance policy. "This'll kill 'em," he said.

Steve Broidy, president of Allied Artists, turned to me. "You made a fine picture. With the proper publicity campaign, it'll make a lot of money. . . . What did the picture cost you?" Steve asked.

"Two hundred fifty thousand," I lied, without blinking an eyelash.

"Bullshit!" Broidy snapped.

"No, Steve, it's the truth." (I had my fingers crossed.)

"You're a liar!" He was smiling, but it was a Mexican stand-off. "I'll tell you what I'll do. . . . I'll give you a hundred fifty thousand and seventy-five percent of the profits." Grabbing his hand, I started to shake it before he could change his mind. I was in business!

Chapter XIX

The Skeleton Factory

A CLOCK was projected on the screen, its single large hand stationary on zero. As my voice came over the sound track, the hand began to move slowly, ticking off the seconds . . . 5 . . . 10 . . . 15 . . . 20 . . .

"Ladies and gentlemen . . . when the clock reaches sixty seconds, you will be insured by Lloyds of London for one thousand dollars against death by fright during *Macabre*. Lloyds of London sincerely hopes none of you will collect. . . . . But just in case, isn't it comforting to know that your loved ones are protected? You are now insured against death by fright!"

Suddenly the screen went black and the theatre was in total darkness. The audience, ill-at-ease, tensed themselves and waited to be scared out of their wits. Standing in back of the darkened theatre, I sincerely hoped no one would collect. We had opened in Boston to long lines waiting patiently to get their insurance coverage. Carefully reading the policies, they signed their names at the bottom and, clutching the official paper, secretly hoped that some member of the audience—not themselves—would collect that night. Anything for excitement.

Each theatre that played *Macabre* had lines around the block—bigger than *Diabolique*—more excitement and anticipation. A giant insurance policy hung over the theatre marquee, even bigger than the film's title.

143

"You know, Johnny, they're buying the policy." We were standing outside a theatre in Philadelphia watching the crowds. "They can't imagine what could be so horrifying that it might frighten them to death."

John Flynn smiled and slapped me on the shoulder. "We broke the house record tonight, Bill."

"When we get to Minneapolis on Sunday, I want you to order a black hearse. . . . Also have them bring along a coffin—something large enough to accommodate me."

Sunday night in Minneapolis, I arrived at the theatre in the black hearse. Covered in a dark cape and hidden from the lines of people, I got inside the coffin and closed the lid. It was pitch-black and I had trouble breathing. Crowds watched the attendants lift the coffin from the hearse and set it down in front of the theatre. I felt the bump as the coffin was placed on the sidewalk. Ready to make my grand entrance, I reached up to open the lid. It wouldn't budge. Shit, it was stuck!

"Help," I screamed, "HELP!" The only sounds I heard from my resting place were the scuffling of feet. Then silence. The movie must be starting. "Johnny! Get me outta here—I'm dying." Where the hell was Flynn! Frantically pounding my head against the coffin, I knocked myself out.

Gasping from the smelling salts, I found myself lying on the sidewalk. The coffin and hearse had disappeared.

"I thought it was part of your act," Flynn said, administering the smelling salts.

Lying flat on my back, I looked up at the disappointed crowd which surrounded me. A belligerent customer who had seen an earlier performance, accosted me. "You're the producer of this picture, aren't you, mister? . . . It's not horrific—it's horrible!"

I whispered to Johnny, "For chrissakes, get me outta here quick, before they kill me. I'll be the only one to collect on the policy."

As we traveled across the country, more and more people

flocked to see *Macabre*. Catering to the public's basic need for excitement, I had nurses in uniform in attendance at every theatre and an ambulance waiting outside to carry off the fainthearted.

Macabre, a modest little picture that cost $90,000, grossed $5,000,000 at the box office. I had always recognized the potency of showmanship. Now I had proof that it was pure gold, and I was determined to mine it over and over again.

No one ever collected on the policy.

Allied Artists wanted another picture immediately, and the exhibitors (theatre owners) wanted another Castle gimmick. I decided on a good old-fashioned ghost story, complete with a haunted house. Robb White and I began to write it.

The male lead had to be someone special—elegant, fey, with an offbeat personality—and, of course, there had to be a new gimmick—something original and more daring than the insurance policy.

I lucked out on another rainy evening. Drinking coffee at a small shop near the Samuel Goldwyn studio, I spotted the perfect lead for my new picture—Vincent Price. He was everything the role demanded, and there he was sitting at the next table. We had met years ago backstage at a play, but I doubted that he remembered me.

Approaching the table, I smiled. "Hello, Mr. Price, do you remember me?"

Looking up, he shook his head. "Sorry, I don't."

An embarrassing pause followed. "May I join you for coffee?" I asked.

Price smiled. "Why not?" Another pause. "I'm depressed," Price added. Not wanting to intrude on his depression, I sipped my coffee silently. As if to answer my unasked question, he continued. "I just lost out on an important picture this morning. A part I wanted to play was given to another actor."

Commiserating with Price, I paid the necessary condo-

145

lences, and after a reasonable time went into my pitch. "Mr. Price, fate has brought us together this rainy night." Vincent Price looked up and waited for me to continue. "I'm starting a picture in a few weeks—*The House on Haunted Hill*—it's a ghost story." He seemed interested, so I continued. "A millionaire invites six people to spend the night in a haunted house. He chooses the people carefully and offers to pay a great deal of money to each one if they agree to spend the entire night in the haunted house." Pausing, I watched Price's reaction.

"Sounds interesting," he said. "Go on."

"During the night, many strange ghostly things happen . . . blood dripping from the ceiling . . . walls shaking . . . apparitions appearing. The millionaire—the part I want you to play—has plotted to kill his wife. She plots to kill you. . . . It's a battle of wits."

Price smiled. "Who wins?"

"You do, of course. She tries to throw you into a vat of boiling acid."

Price's eyes gleamed. "How charming!"

"Suddenly you rise slowly from the vat . . . body eaten away. You're just bones—a living *skeleton!*" Vincent Price ordered a piece of pie and hungrily attacked it as I continued. "Your skeleton scares the shit out of your wife and she loses her balance and falls into the vat of acid."

"Delicious. . . . Where the hell am I?" he asked, chewing.

"You're working your phony skeleton, like a puppeteer."

"I think I'll have another piece of pie."

The deal was made on the second piece of pie that same rainy night.

I had always felt that roping off a special section for VIPs at a sneak preview is ridiculous. I prefer sitting with the audience to hear their comments and study their reaction. The night of the sneak preview of *The House on Haunted Hill*, I ignored the roped-off section and sat in the fifth row among my friends—the public. As I watched the film, my stomach was queasy and I was soaking wet with fear and anticipation. I felt we had the wrong audience—there were no young people in the theatre. I looked at the man next to me. An elderly, baldish, bespectacled man, constantly fidgeting in his seat. He made me more nervous. "Stop fidgeting," I whispered.

Turning to me, he whispered back, "The biggest piece of shit I've ever seen." With that, he brushed past me and left the theatre.

Ever since the first preview of *The House on Haunted Hill,* I always sit in the roped off section for VIPs.

The House on Haunted Hill was sneaked with the wrong audience. For the next preview, I made sure there was a young audience present, and the results were just the opposite—the response was wildly enthusiastic and the comments on the preview cards were excellent. We knew we had a hit. Even today, critics feel *House on Haunted Hill* is a classic in its genre.

"Bill, can't you come up with another gimmick as good as the insurance policy on *Macabre*?" We were seated in Steve Broidy's office at Allied Artists. Johnny Flynn, the publicity director, was sitting next to me. "How about some sort of sound effects? Like the wailing of ghosts that we can play in the lobby," Johnny suggested.

"It's a good idea," I said, "but we need something to really get the audiences excited."

"How about dressing the ushers as ghosts?" Steve asked.

"Fellas, what is the most exciting scene in the picture? When the skeleton comes out of the vat—right?" Johnny and Steve were in agreement. I continued. "Suppose—after coming out of the vat—we had the skeleton walk off the screen and go into the audience."

"That's impossible!" Broidy said.

Johnny Flynn smiled. "You're dreaming, Bill."

I paused. My mind was racing with an idea. "We build a separate black box and install it next to the screen. The audience won't be able to see it because it'll blend in with the black surrounding the screen. We build a plastic, twelve-foot skele-

147

ton and put it on a wire running over the audience's heads up to the projection booth. At the point where Vincent Price manipulates the skeleton on the screen, the projectionist pushes a button. The black box at the side opens, the skeleton lights up and moves on the wire, traveling electrically over the audience and up into the balcony. We time it exactly to the movement of the skeleton on the screen, and Price, with his contraption of wires, seems to pull the real skeleton from the balcony back into the screen."

"You're absolutely crazy!" screamed Broidy. Johnny Flynn laughed.

"It'll work," I said. "I'm sure."

"We'll have to manufacture hundreds of twelve-foot skeletons and to install them in the theatre will cost a fortune!" Broidy moaned.

"The theatres will pay for them. . . . I've even got a name for my gimmick," I said. "EMERGO!"

San Francisco was our first play date. The Golden Gate Theatre. Johnny Flynn and I had flown up. The theatre was packed, and Johnny and I stood in the back to watch the unveiling of "Emergo."

"Does the projectionist know when to push the button?" I asked Johnny nervously.

"I've told him three times."

"Maybe I'd better go up and tell him again."

"Relax . . . it'll work."

The image of Vincent Price flashed on the screen. He was manipulating his wire contraption and pulling his skeleton out of the vat. The skeleton onscreen was slowly walking toward the audience. Holding my breath, my gaze was riveted on the black box on the side of the screen. Now—*now*. Nothing happened.

"Oh, my God—it's not working!" My face was tense. Another few seconds passed—still nothing. "Johnny, for chrissake . . . what happened? I'll kill that projectionist! . . . Where's the goddamn skeleton?"

After what seemed like an eternity, the box opened slowly. Looking constipated, the skeleton staggered out, dangled for a few seconds, then bounced back into the box.

"Johnny, the sonofabitch skeleton is supposed to come *out*—not go back in—and the fucking thing doesn't light up."

The audience was howling. Suddenly the box opened again. The skeleton popped out and went halfway up the wire. Something snapped and it fell into the audience. The kids rose from their seats, grabbed the skeleton and, hollering, bounced it up into the air. The theatre was a madhouse!

We finally got "Emergo" working for the third show, and by evening, my skeleton was performing beautifully. The audience loved it.

Saturday I was home in Beverly Hills. Ellen was expecting our second baby any minute. The telephone rang. "It's for you, darling, San Francisco calling."

Picking up the phone, I waited for trouble. Larry Blanchard, the publicity director for the Golden Gate Theatre, informed me audiences were going wild and that I should get up there immediately.

I couldn't believe my eyes. The Golden Gate Theatre was sold out for the entire day. Thousands of kids had been waiting on line for hours for the evening performances. That night the line was six blocks long! Rushing to a telephone booth, I called Steve Broidy at his home. "Steve, we're completely sold out! We've done the biggest gross in the theatre's history!"

December 7—Terry Castle was born—a six-pound baby girl. The following week, I flew up to San Francisco again. This time I brought along hundreds of cigars. Lines of kids still surrounded the theatre, ages eight to sixteen. Marching down the line, I handed each kid a cigar. Terry had brought me luck.

Chapter XX

Scream for Your Life

"WHAT'S a 'Tingler' look like?"

"Sort of like a lobster, but flat, and instead of claws it has long, slimy feelers. That's what I think a 'Tingler' looks like." I was in the art department at Columbia, talking to an artist. After the success of *The House on Haunted Hill,* I was back at Columbia. Only this time, I had my own independent production company and I was completely autonomous.

The artist finished sketching. "How's that?" he said.

"Perfect," I said. "People won't be eating lobster for the next five years."

"Vinnie, you've got to play the doctor in it. You'll be perfect!"

"Bill, I don't want to be typecast." Vincent Price puffed on his long, slender cigar.

"Vinnie, with the success of *Haunted Hill,* I think it'll open up a whole new career for you."

Price hesitated. "Well . . . maybe. Tell me a little more about it."

"The character you play has a theory that the 'Tingler' is in everyone's spine. Usually, people who are frightened scream, and screaming keeps their 'Tingler' from growing. Judith Evelyn will play the part of a deaf-mute who runs a silent movie theatre. Experimenting, you scare the hell out of her. Because she can't utter a sound—is unable to scream— her 'Tingler' grows, crushing her to death. You operate, remove the 'Tingler' from her spine, and keep it in a glass jar in your laboratory. Then it escapes and gets into the silent movie theatre. We'll then make believe that the theatre is where the picture is actually playing. The 'Tingler' will attack the projectionist and then get onto the screen. It'll be a movie within a movie. Audiences seeing it will think it's loose in the theatre they're in. We'll put your voice on the sound track and after the lights go out . . . you announce that the 'Tingler' is loose in the audience and ask them to scream for their lives. . . . All hell will break loose."

"Do you think it'll work?" Vinnie asked.

"I know it will."

But it wasn't enough. I was now becoming known as "The Master of Gimmicks." Exhibitors were inquiring what my gimmick for *The Tingler* would be. After the insurance policy and "Emergo," they wanted something bigger—more exciting.

One night the lamp beside my bed went out as I was reading. Getting a new bulb from the kitchen, I started to replace it. "Shit!" I yelled. "I got a helluva shock. Something's wrong with the wire." Suddenly I had my gimmick for *The Tingler*. I shook Ellen excitedly. "Wake up, wake up!"

"What's it now?" she mumbled.

"I'm going to buzz the asses of everyone in America by installing little motors under the seats of every theatre in the country. When the 'Tingler' appears on the screen, the projectionist will push a button. . . . The audiences will get a shock on their butts—and think the 'Tingler' is loose in the theatre!"

By now Ellen was fully awake. "You're stark raving mad!" she observed.

To get Columbia to go ahead with the idea was a herculean task. It meant the outlay of a fortune to design the equipment and to make the little boxes. Teams of special-effects men would have to be sent all over the country to install the complicated equipment in the theatres at night after closing. A manual was printed giving complete instructions with diagrams, etc.

My other gimmicks had proven so successful and paid off so handsomely at the box office that Columbia went along with me. Teams of experts were dispatched throughout the country to install the equipment. Dona Holloway, who had been Harry Cohn's executive secretary, was now my associate producer. She came up with the name of the gimmick—"PERCEPTO." Dona is a fantastic woman, and my production company couldn't have made it without her help and encouragement.

We were in Boston for the opening of *The Tingler* the following day. A snowstorm had delayed the special-effects crew, and when the theatre closed that night, they hadn't arrived. "Percepto" had to be installed.

Dona and I were under the theatre seats with our manuals. She was studying the manual. "Where does the 'B' wire go?"

"How the hell do I know?" I snapped. "Look in the manual."

"Oh, I see . . . it fits into the relay that goes to the projection booth."

"How many buzzers have you screwed underneath the seats?" I asked.

"About eight rows," Dona replied.

"I've done six. We've got eighteen more to go—oh, and fasten them to the seats tightly so the kids can't get at them."

All over the United States, when *The Tingler* got loose, people screamed for their lives. In one theatre in Philadelphia, one patron, a burly truckdriver, got so angry when the motor under his seat gave him a shock, that he ripped out the entire seat in a rage, and threw it at the screen. Five ushers had to control him.

A week before *The Tingler* opened in Boston, *The Nun's Story*, starring Audrey Hepburn, was playing. During a matinee filled with women, the bored projectionist decided to test the "Tingler" equipment. He pushed the switch during a scene where Hepburn and the nuns were praying. The proper Bostonian ladies got the shock of their lives.

In the final count, I think we must have buzzed 20,000,000 behinds.

How can you transform a beautiful woman into a virile, masculine man? You can go to Sweden and have an operation, but my next bold experiment had to be done immediately, and without surgery.

Homicidal was the story of a transvestite. At first I had thought of casting an actor in the two roles. Interviewing many beautiful young men, most of them gay, I finally decided a man was wrong. So, scouring the theatrical offices in Hollywood, I looked for the right girl. For weeks, I searched, but to no avail. I was ready to leave for New York to continue the search.

The telephone rang just as I was leaving the office. "Hello, this is Jerry Lauren. I think I've found the perfect girl for *Homicidal.*" To get him off the phone, I agreed to see his client at 9:00 the following morning.

At noon, I walked into my office, having completely forgotten about my appointment. Jerry and his client had been waiting patiently for me for three hours.

Mumbling apologies, I looked at the young lady. She was strikingly beautiful and had a strange, different quality about her.

"Mr. Castle, I'd like you to meet Joan Marshall."

We shook hands. Her grip was firm. "It's a very difficult part to cast, Miss Marshall. A known face would be easily recognizable to the audience, and the whole success of the picture depends on making audiences believe there are two people—a man and a woman."

"Will you let me read the script, Mr. Castle?" Her voice was low-pitched and husky. Intrigued, I gave her the script of *Homicidal.* While she was reading, I called Ben Lane, head of makeup at Columbia. "Ben, you gotta do me a favor. I know it's short notice, but I'm going to send a beautiful young lady down to you. I want you to make her look like a man."

"That's a tall order, Bill, even for you, but I'll do my best."

Calling wardrobe, I ordered men's clothing sent to my office right away.

Joan Marshall had just finished reading the script. "Mr. Castle," she said, "I know I can play both parts and do a wonderful job. Please give me the chance."

"Joan, go down to makeup. Ask for Ben Lane. I'm going to try an experiment."

Two hours later, Joan Marshall came back to my office. My secretary, not recognizing her, asked the man his name. The transformation was indeed astonishing. I canceled my trip to New York.

The first stop was Drucker's Hairstyling for Men in Beverly Hills, after closing. "Mr. Drucker, I want you to give this lovely lady a man's haircut." An hour later, her beautiful blond hair was shorn. "Now I want it dyed black," I told Drucker.

The following morning we were at the studio of one of Hollywood's greatest makeup and mask specialists. "Ernie, can you turn this beautiful face into a man's?"

Ernie studied Joan. "We'll have to change the nose and make an appliance for the mouth to make it bigger. . . . Change the structure of the face to look more masculine." All this was said while he was measuring Joan's face. "We'll have to change her blue eyes—contact lenses to make them brown. . . . I'll make plastic impressions of her hands to change them."

"Do you think it'll work, Ernie?"

"Don't worry—when I finish with her, she'll be a man!"

The next thing I did was to change the name of Joan Marshall to Jean Arless. It was a neutral name; it could have been either male or female.

Finally we started production on *Homicidal*. The first part of the film concentrated on the male role. The transformation was amazing. Coming on the set dressed in men's clothing and speaking in a deep voice, she fooled everyone, even the crew. All her lovely femininity had vanished—she was a man.

154

The second half of shooting concentrated on the female role. Wearing dresses and a wig matching her own lovely blond hair, she suddenly became feminine, and the reaction of the crew was bewildering.

Alfred Hitchcock's *Psycho* was the biggest box-office hit that year. I waited in New York with Dona Holloway to see the film. Mr. Hitchcock had used his own very unusual gimmick for *Psycho*—no one was allowed into the theatre once the picture began. Hitchcock's idea worked. Audiences stood patiently in line waited for two hours for the film to end.

"Mr. Hitchcock's gimmick is working beautifully," Dona observed. "Audiences will wait for hours if a picture is exciting enough."

Psycho ended, and the crowds coming out looked white and shaken.

"Dona, I wish I had a gimmick for *Homicidal* that is better than *Psycho*'s. But how can I top Alfred Hitchcock?"

CHAPTER XXI

Cowards' Corner

"YOU'RE absolutely nuts—it'll never work." I was sitting in the office of Columbia Pictures in New York. Having been through the same routine before, I was quite prepared.

"You thought I was crazy when I insured an audience against death by fright. I was crazier still when I put skeletons in every theatre. And you were ready to put me in a straitjacket when I put buzzers under every theatre seat."

"But your new idea will absolutely not work. . . . Impossible!"

"I tell you it will." I paused as I paced the room. "Look, we'll call my new gimmick 'The Fright Break.' *Homicidal* runs for an hour and forty minutes. My suggestion is that during the last two minutes of the picture—the part where the girl goes toward the house—I'll stop the picture. Then my voice will go over the sound track. I'll say something like, 'Ladies and gentlemen, if you're too frightened to see the last two minutes of *Homicidal,* please go to the box office and get your full admission price refunded. You must leave immediately. You have only sixty seconds to get your money back.'"

There was a groan. "Look, Bill, it's tough enough to get money at the box office these days. . . . Now you're suggesting that we give it back."

Theatre owners were appalled at the idea of giving money away, but I kept on insisting. To shut me up, they decided to throw me a bone. They agreed to have one test engagement to try out my new gimmick. The unlikely city picked for the one engagement was Youngstown, Ohio—far enough off the beaten path so no one would ever hear of my folly.

Opening day in Youngstown, Ohio, the newspapers carried big ads telling the public about the "Fright Break." Radio spots carried the same news to the public. Arriving at the theatre for the first performance, I was amazed to see the 3,000-seat house completely sold out. There was a huge sign in front with bold black letters reading: "MONEY-BACK GUARANTEE." We had agreed that the first show would not be a fair test, that curiosity might overcome the temptation to collect a refund. The audience for a second performance, presumably cued by the first group, would demonstrate whether thrills could overcome natural greed.

Elated, I went across the street, had dinner, and arrived back at the theatre just in time for the second show, which was to start at 8:30. Entering the theatre, I was delighted to find that the second show was equally packed; every seat was filled.

Standing in the back, in their blue suits, were top brass from Columbia and exhibitors from RKO, who had flown in especially to see what would happen.

Homicidal played beautifully. The screams came just at the right places. The audience was glued to its seats. It was about five minutes before the "Fright Break." One of the vice-presidents from RKO turned to me, "Well, Bill, we shall soon see."

I remained silent—nervous. Again, the time clock was playing an important part of my life as I waited for the minutes to tick by. Finally, two minutes before the end, the movie stopped. I held my breath as I heard my recorded voice make the announcement:

This is the "Fright Break!" You hear that sound? The sound of a heartbeat! Is it beating faster than your heart? Or slower? This heart is going to beat for another sixty-five seconds to allow anyone to leave this theatre who is too frightened to see the end of the picture, and get your *FULL ADMISSION REFUNDED.* Ten seconds more and we go into the house. It's now or never! Five! Four! You're a brave audience! Two! One!

There was a pause which seemed endless—and then—the audience raced up the aisles trying to get to the box office. The theatre was now almost empty—thousands of people on line getting their money back.

The blue suits turned their backs on me. The head man from Columbia punched me in the arm muttering, "Jerk!" I was left completely alone.

The manager of the theatre, a little man in a worn tuxedo, stood in a corner, puzzled. He hesitated and then walked over to me. "Mr. Castle, something is wrong."

"I know goddamn well something is wrong," I snapped.

The manager again hesitated, then spoke softly. "The show opened at six-thirty—the house was full. When the picture ended at eight-fifteen, just a few came out. As a matter of fact, I had to turn away lots of people who were waiting to get in."

Suddenly it hit me. "Oh, my God." I yelled. The audience stayed to see the picture twice so they could get their original admission price refunded. Calling my blue-suited friends, I explained that larceny had set in.

The following day, cards were printed in five different colors, each color designating a different performance. The 2:00 performance, red; 4:00, green; 8:00, black; and 10:00, orange. As a customer bought a ticket, he was given the color of his show, and God help him if he couldn't show the right color for the performance. The "Fright Break" now worked beautifully.

Time and *Life* did articles with pictures showing what happened in Youngstown, Ohio.

Every theatre now used the "Fright Break." Of all the films I had made, *Homicidal* was the most fun. When we finally got the kinks out of the money-back guarantee, less than one percent of the audiences asked for a refund. Apparently a girl would sometimes ask her boyfriend or husband to get a single admission refunded and she would tell him what he had missed. But most of the time the boyfriend refused to go and the girl stayed right with him. A few of the curious wanted to see if they were actually paid back in real money.

Then we really got going and began to heighten the fun and publicity with additional stunts. Yellow stripes appeared on sidewalks near the curb, leading past the theatres—and stenciled on the stripe: "Cowards, keep walking." Inside, large yellow footsteps were stenciled on the floor from the seats back to the box office—and over the box office there hung a sign: "Cowards' Corner." A blood-pressure outfit sat on a table nearby, attended by a nurse who offered free tests to cowards. A yellow light bathed Cowards' Corner, and a recorded message kept repeating, "These cowards are too frightened to see the end of *Homicidal*! Watch them shiver in the Cowards' Corner. Coward . . . coward . . . coward. . . ."

As a final touch, we required anyone demanding a refund to sign a yellow card which read "I am a bona fide coward."

The stares and jests of people waiting to buy their tickets provided the ultimate deterrent.

At the end of *Homicidal*, I used a split screen to show Jean Arless as both the man and the woman. Both Jean Arlesses bowed to the audience, as if taking a curtain call. Bewildered audiences placed bets in the lobby on whether it was a man playing a woman or a woman playing a man. I never did tell.

Homicidal got great reviews. I consider it one of the most original of my motion pictures. *Time* magazine chose it as one of the ten best pictures of the year, liking it better than Alfred Hitchcock's *Psycho*.

William Castle fan clubs were now forming throughout America, almost in every city, 250,000 strong. Four full-time secretaries at Columbia answered the fan-club mail, sent out cards, souvenirs, autographed pictures, etc. Every time I visited a city, hundreds of kids met me at the airport. I was becoming a star. My name was now above the title on every marquee.

Alfred Hitchcock is in every one of his films, and audiences have fun trying to spot him on screen. I decided that the same idea would work for me, and with apologies to the great man, I now became part of the main title. For *Homicidal,* I appeared in the main title, sitting in a chair with a frame in front of me and beginning to embroider the word "Homicidal" as I spoke to the audience. I reminded them of *The House on Haunted Hill, The Tingler,* and now, the most frightening of them all—*Homicidal.* When I finished my embroidery, I stuck myself with a needle, sucked blood from my finger, and showed my handiwork to the audience—*Homicidal.* The public loved it, and as a result we became good friends. Kids would stop me on the street, calling me by name, and ask for my autograph. I had become the Pied Piper of the young.

In order to insure *Homicidal's* success in Europe, Columbia decided to send me on tour. My itinerary—England, Germany, France, Holland, Belgium, Spain. The plan in each major city called for my appearance on stage, watching myself embroider the main title and talking to my image on screen. Germany was the first country and arriving in Düsseldorf via the autobahn, Ellen, Eric Mueller, who was sales representative for Columbia in Germany, and I saw posters for *Homicidal* everywhere.

Opening night we played to a full house. I waited in the wings as the house lights darkened and the main title began. Walking on stage, I studied my image onscreen doing the embroidery. Suddenly my image began to speak in perfect German. In awe, I yelled with delight, "Jesus, I speak German!" This brought the house down. My surprise was so spontaneous that we kept it in every performance throughout Europe. I hadn't realized my voice had been dubbed in many languages—French, Italian, Spanish, Dutch. I wondered what I would sound like in Japanese.

It was in France that I got an idea for a gimmick for my next picture. While driving through the countryside, I noticed a house, isolated and boarded up, looking foreboding in the night. Stopping the car, Ellen and I walked toward it.

"Ellen, I wonder if this house is for sale. I'd like to buy it."

160

Ellen, used to my crazy schemes, didn't bother to answer, but instead suggested we continue our journey. I insisted on buying it. The house looked haunted.

Ellen smiled. "What could you possibly do with a haunted house?"

"Have twenty million keys made—all but one with the same number. That one key fits the lock on this door. Keys will be passed out in theatres all over the world during the picture, and the lucky person with the right key owns this haunted house. What a gimmick! Think of the publicity the picture will get. . . ."

"What picture? Haven't you put the cart before the horse?"

"I haven't got one yet . . . but I'll think of something."

A day later, I had purchased one haunted house.

After a successful tour, I was back in my office at Columbia working on my next picture, *13 Ghosts.* An average family—father, mother, older daughter, younger brother—inherit a house from an eccentric uncle and move in. The weird uncle had been experimenting with the "other world" before mysteriously dying. The father finds a strange pair of goggles, puts them on, and witnesses 13 hideous apparitions. When he removes the goggles, the 13 ghosts disappear.

Planning to give away my haunted house in France with my key gag, I settled down to make the film. We had a lot of fun creating the 13 ghosts:

CAST OF GHOSTS:
1. The clutching hands.
2. The floating head.
3. Flaming skeleton.
4. Screaming woman.
5. Emilio with cleaver in his hand.
6. His unfaithful wife.
7. Her lover.
8. Executioner and decapitated head.
9. Hanging woman.
10. Lion.

11. Lion tamer without head.
12. Dr. Zorba.
13. ?

I began to have constant headaches while filming *13 Ghosts,* and Ellen insisted I go to an ophthalmologist and have my eyes checked. The only time available for me was on a Saturday when I wasn't shooting, and the doctor agreed to see me.

Wearing the heavy metal frames and looking through the assorted lenses, I felt I was in a strange, distorted world. With each new lens the doctor inserted, my vision became more blurred. Finally the right lens was inserted and everything suddenly cleared. I needed glasses, but I had the right gimmick for *13 Ghosts.* My haunted house and key would have to wait. I now had "ILLUSION-O."

Audiences would be given cardboard glasses—I would call them "ghost viewers." When the actor onscreen put on the goggles, the audience would put theirs on and see the ghosts. When the actor took off his goggles, the audience would remove theirs—and *voilà!*—the ghosts would disappear. However, it was easier said than done.

Many months and thousands of dollars were spent trying to make ghosts appear and disappear. Forty tests were made, each one failing. I started to regret the waste of time and had about decided to shelve the entire idea when we finally succeeded—a simple pair of green and blue plastic lenses of just the right density made the ghosts appear miraculously. Hundreds of thousands of "ghost viewers" were manufactured.

With the advertising slogans, kids all over the world flocked into the theatres clutching their ghost viewers, waiting for the unknown.

"See Ghosts in ECTOPLASMIC COLOR."
"13 Times the Thrills!"
"13 Times the Fun!"
"13 Times the Screams!"
"You'll believe in ghosts too when you see them through the new 'ghost viewer.' Free to everyone who sees this movie."

162

Besieged with the same question from theatre owners and audiences—"What's your next idea?"—and now being crowned "King of the Gimmicks," I decided it was time to try to abdicate my throne.

The abdication was short. In Hawaii with Ellen and the girls, I was sunning myself poolside at the Kahala Hilton, reading a story in *Playboy* magazine. It was a macabre tale of a man named Sardonicus who becomes so terrified while robbing his father's grave that his face becomes permanently frozen in a wide, frenzied grin. He dies a horrible death, grinning to the bitter end.

Rushing to the nearest telephone, I purchased the film rights to "Sardonicus" and hired Ray Russell, the author, to write the gruesome screenplay for my next picture.

Using a British cast, I managed to re-create England on Columbia's sound stages in Hollywood. We built a graveyard where Sardonicus, opening his father's grave, steals a winning lottery ticket from his father's body. The spooky moors were built on another stage where dried ice, sprayed with a heavy smoke, kept the fog low. Sardonicus's castle was a Gothic re-creation, and this, too, was shrouded in fog.

Creating the grinning face was a problem. In order for the mask to appear realistic, Guy Rolfe, playing Mr. Sardonicus, was fitted five times. His mask had to conform to the contours of his mouth, yet appear three times the normal size. Rolfe also had to be able to speak with it on. Finally we achieved the perfect grin—not humorous, but horrible. Hours were lost in shooting because Rolfe could not tolerate wearing the mask for more than an hour at a time.

Another little goodie was the leeches. One of Sardonicus's victims, while being tortured, had to be covered with the dreadful little monsters. Always one for reality, I got a bottle filled with the real thing—long, slimy creatures. The day the scene was shot, the victim refused to have the leeches put on his body. Demonstrating their harmlessness, I put several leeches on my own chest. "See, it's nothing," I told the actor. "They're perfectly harmless." When they started to suck my

163

blood and I couldn't pull them off, I quickly changed my mind. They weren't as much fun as I thought. I postponed the scene until artificial leeches could be made.

The sheer joy of making *Mr. Sardonicus* made it one of my favorite films. But the exploitation and selling of it was another matter.

Columbia had seen the final cut of the picture and demanded that I reshoot the final scene, which they cautioned would be unacceptable to audiences. In the scene in question, Sardonicus, unable to eat or drink because of his frozen grin, goes insane as he slowly and agonizingly dies. Columbia wanted a more palatable ending and insisted I let Mr. Sardonicus live. I refused adamantly, and just as adamantly they demanded another ending.

During the stalemate, I suddenly realized that Columbia had unknowingly given me the gimmick for the picture. I would have two endings—Columbia's and mine—and let the audience decide for themselves the fate of Mr. Sardonicus.

My new gimmick was the Punishment Poll and a special gadget, the Activator Booth. Arriving at the theatre, patrons were given a card with a hand imprinted—four fingers closed into a fist, the thumb pointing upward. "Mercy" was printed atop the raised thumb. When the card was turned upside-down, the thumb now pointing downward, the printing now read, "No Mercy." By exposing the card to the Activator Booth set up in the theatre lobbies, the luminous thumb glowed in the dark.

Just before the final scene, the picture stopped and my image came onscreen, asking the audience how they felt about the fate of Mr. Sardonicus. Should he be punished—or not? Thumbs down meant death; thumbs up, life. My image onscreen then began to count the voting. (The theatre managers actually did the count.) Invariably, the audience's verdict was thumbs down. It's always amazed me how bloodthirsty audiences are. Contrary to some opinions (just in case the audience voted for mercy), we had the other ending. But it rarely, if ever, was used.

Luring the patrons into the theatre were loudspeakers blasting:

> Have you ever envied the thrill-hungry Roman crowds in the Circus Maximus who, with a wave of the thumb, could make life or death decisions that sealed the fate of many a gladiator?

> The fate of that ghoulish character Sardonicus is in your tender little hands.

> You have the opportunity of literally deciding the monstrous fiend's fate.

The leopard never changes its spots—and never have I. From the very beginning I craved recognition and applause. Constantly needing to prove myself to someone—anyone. I had now achieved all that and more, but still I was hungry. Having to create a new, fresh gimmick for each picture was becoming tiresome. Critics were now starting to attack, claiming the only reason my films were successful was the gimmicks, and I was unable to make an important thriller without one. Never having had the luxury of a big star for my films, I had been forced to build my little empire on ingenious showmanship. Hollywood was a snobbish town, and important stars refused to associate themselves with my modest-budget exploitation pictures. So, after many years, I still had to prove myself, this time getting an important star—anyone.

Robert Bloch, author of *Psycho*, wrote the screenplay for my new film, *Strait-Jacket*. Submitting the final script to Columbia, I advised them that I intended not to use a gimmick on this one. I immediately encountered resistance. They firmly stated that exhibitors wouldn't book the film without a Castle gimmick. Frustrated, I told them the script was strong enough to stand on its own.

We were still in a stalemate when I got an urgent call from Leo Jaffe, Columbia's executive vice-president, to fly to New York immediately. There was trouble ahead. I hoped I'd be up to it.

Chapter XXII

A Sob, a Scream . . . a Bloody Ax!

"BILL, she loves the script. . . . If our meeting with her today is successful, she'll star in *Strait-Jacket*."

Bob Bloch and I were seated in Leo Jaffe's plush office at Columbia's headquarters in New York. Glancing at my watch, I saw it was 11:00 A.M. and inquired, "What time is the meeting?"

"At noon," Jaffe said. "We're invited for lunch." Opening his desk drawer, he pulled out a report. "Joan Crawford's last picture with Bette Davis, *Whatever Happened to Baby Jane?*, killed them at the box office." Leo stretched and gazed out his window overlooking Fifth Avenue. "You win, Bill. No gimmicks. We feel we don't need it with Joan Crawford."

"Thank God!" I muttered, relieved.

Strait-Jacket was the story of Lucy Harbin, an ax murderess found guilty of the slaying of her husband and his mistress. Pronounced insane, she was sent to a mental hospital. Twenty years later, she was released and allowed to live on a farm with her brother and his wife and her own lovely daughter. A series of shocking and brutal ax murders occurs, shattering the quiet surroundings.

Promptly at noon, we arrived at Joan Crawford's apartment. Just before Leo rang the bell, he turned to me. "Don't bullshit Crawford, she's smart. . . . Watch every word you say. . . . And be sure you know what you're talking about."

The great star herself opened the door. I was amazed to see that she didn't look as tall in person as she did onscreen. She was dressed very simply and wore an apron. Kissing Leo Jaffe, she warmly greeted Bob Bloch and me. "I hope you like what I've cooked for lunch."

The three of us entered the foyer and started to proceed to her living room. Suddenly a sharp command: "Take off your shoes, all of you." We took off our shoes, as instructed, as Joan explained. "Everybody takes off their shoes. I have new white carpets."

Crawford was one of the most dynamic women I'd ever met. A mind like a steel trap. She knew what she wanted and always got it.

"Gentlemen, I like the script of *Strait-Jacket*," Joan announced as she was serving our luncheon. The quiche lorraine was delicious, and I was ready for a second helping. She continued. "*Strait-Jacket* will have to be completely rewritten as a vehicle for me, or I will not accept the role."

Suddenly I lost my appetite. Bob Bloch and I looked at each other. Leo's face was impassive. No one was eating. Crawford, all business, continued. "Now, here's what I want done to the script. . . ."

Two hours later, completely baffled, we agreed we'd do the rewrite. It meant starting practically from scratch, but getting Joan Crawford was worth it. She had complete approval of cast and cameraman, and—thank goodness—Joan approved me to produce and direct.

That night Bob Bloch and I restructured the entire story as Crawford had requested. The following day, we met with her again and told her our ideas. She liked them and agreed to star in *Strait-Jacket*.

During the ensuing weeks of preparation, I found her demands excessive. Crawford is a perfectionist and usually is right, and I was starting to worry about directing her. Would she be difficult on a set? Stories had been floating around Hollywood that she could be hell on wheels—that she and Bette Davis had feuded on *Whatever Happened to Baby Jane?* I

167

became more and more troubled. Was Joan Crawford more than I could handle?

Dona Holloway buzzed me on the intercom. "Darling, can I see you for a moment?"

"Trouble?" I asked.

"No, I'll be right in. Joan is worried about her wardrobe. She wants it done in New York."

"Oh, Christ!" I said.

"Now, don't get your blood pressure up," Dona said soothingly. "Joan just asked me to come back to New York and help her shop. You think I should go?"

I knew my blood pressure was up because my head started to throb. "How soon can you leave?" I asked Dona.

Dona telephoned from New York. "Don't worry, Bill . . . Joan's a pussycat. . . . We went shopping this afternoon—everything's fine. Oh—and Bill—Joan asked me when you plan to start rehearsals."

"Rehearsals?" I screamed. "Who in the hell said anything about rehearsals? I just want to start shooting. . . . No goddamn rehearsals. . . . I never have rehearsals before I shoot. . . ."

"Good-bye, darling." Dona hung up.

Joan Crawford arrived in Hollywood and we began rehearsals. Using a bare stage with folding chairs, we started to block the motion picture that I would eventually shoot. Leif Erickson was cast as Crawford's brother. Rochelle Hudson played his wife, and a relatively unknown actress was set to play Joan's daughter.

The first day of rehearsal, I was filled with trepidation. Joan Crawford is a dedicated actress. She has no patience with incompetence and is a stickler for perfection. The actress playing her daughter was nervous. Completely in awe of the great lady, she was speechless and it showed in her performance.

Crawford tried patiently to work with her. "Speak up, darling, I can't hear you." The girl tried harder. "Darling . . . if I can't understand what you're saying, how will an audience?

168

Let's try the scene again, and please . . . use more voice and be forceful." The girl was trembling. Joan again took her aside and tried to make her feel at ease.

"Let's try the scene again," I said.

"Darling, I'm getting nothing from you," Joan said to the actress.

During lunch, Crawford asked me to come to her dressing room. "The girl's sweet, Bill, but she can't play the part. She hasn't had the experience."

"But, Joan, we've already signed her for the picture. She was just nervous this morning. . . . Meeting you. . . . Give her more time."

Joan was firm. "No, Bill . . . start looking for somebody else."

"Please . . . work with her for a few more days, and then . . ."

Joan cut me off. "She'll be the same. She's absolutely wrong for the part. I insist we recast."

I tried to get Crawford to change her mind, but she was adamant, and deep down I knew she was right. It was difficult breaking the news to the young actress, but I think she was relieved. Diane Baker was my choice for the replacement, and the rehearsal the following day had electricity. Not afraid of Crawford, Diane Baker met her on an eye-to-eye level, and although she respected Joan, she gave her no quarter. Crawford sensed this, and together they made the words in the script come to life.

Rehearsals over, we were ready to begin shooting the following Monday. The telephone rang in my office and my secretary said it was Rock Hudson. "This is Rock, Bill," the familiar voice came through. "I need a favor. . . . A young actor I know is starting out. He's never done a picture, but I think he's star material. Do you have a one-line bit open?"

I remembered giving Rock Hudson his one-line bit in an earlier picture of mine. Smiling, I said, "Of course, Rock. Bring him in."

Lee Majors ("The Six-Million-Dollar Man") played the

one-line bit. He died onscreen after his one line when Joan Crawford found him in bed with a younger woman and, using an ax, chopped off their heads.

I had to find someone to play Diane Baker as a child of six . . . someone that resembled her. I asked Diane to bring in all her baby pictures. We were sitting in Crawford's dressing room, looking over the photographs. Suddenly Joan looked up and handed me a picture. "Bill, who does this photo of Diane, age six, look like?" Looking at the picture, I was stunned. It was the image of my own daughter Terry, now six. Joan continued. "Do you think Ellen would consider letting Terry play my daughter?"

"I don't know," I answered. "I'll ask her."

That night rehearsals started at home. Every evening after coming home from work, Terry and I would play the game. She would lie on the couch, pretend she was sleeping and, waking up, would rub her eyes and look at me with fear in her eyes. She was supposed to see her mother kill her father and another woman with an ax.

Ellen became increasingly worried. "Bill, what happens if Terry becomes frightened on the set? Don't forget—there are at least sixty people watching. And I forbid you to tell her what she's supposed to actually see."

"Can't I even tell her it's a *small* ax?"

Ellen finally persuaded me to take Terry on the set the day before she was supposed to work to let her rehearse the scene on the real set, with Joan Crawford, not at home as she had been doing. Terry arrived, and I asked her to lie on the bed in the corner of the room we were using in the scene. She was frightened, shy and withdrawn. What had previously been a game was now for real.

"Darling . . . now pretend you're sleeping. . . . Wake up and look at the nice lady with a baseball bat." (I had given Crawford a baseball bat for rehearsals instead of an ax.)

"No, Daddy . . . I wanna go home."

"Please, Terry. . . . Just once. . . . For Daddy?"

170

"Daddy, Daddy . . . I wanna go home." Tears streamed down her face.

"Darling, don't you want to be in Daddy's picture?"

"No, Daddy, please. I don't want to be in any picture."

"Mommy," I said, "take Terry home. . . . Her career in motion pictures has abruptly ended."

When a head is chopped off with an ax, what does it sound like? Not ever having heard the sound of a head being chopped, I had no idea. I asked the special-effects man.

"Maybe a block of wood."

"It'll sound like a block of wood," I said.

"How about using a wet telephone book?"

"Let's try it." It sounded just like a wet telephone book being cut with an ax.

The following day I brought a large watermelon that I had stolen from Ellen's refrigerator. Wielding an ax, the prop man cut it in half. The squish was perfect. It sounded exactly like a head being lopped off.

"Get me the Gillette Razor Blade Company," I told my secretary.

"Whom shall I ask for, sir?"

"Anybody," I barked. "Try to get the president."

Shortly afterward, a Mr. Barker came on the line. "Yes, Mr. Castle, this is Gillette Razor Company. What can we do for you?"

"I'm shooting a picture in Hollywood with Joan Crawford . . . *Strait-Jacket,*" I announced. "I'd like to have a tie-in with Gillette. . . ." There was a pause as Mr. Barker waited for me to continue. "Some slogan, Mr. Barker, like . . . 'Go see *Strait-Jacket* and then cut your head off with a Gillette.'" Mr. Barker hung up. I just couldn't break the gimmick habit.

"Paul, I've just spoken to Joan Crawford, and she's agreed to go out on tour with *Strait-Jacket.* She's even said she'll appear onstage all over the country. But it's going to have to be

171

the biggest, most dazzling extravaganza that I've ever had." I was speaking to Paul Lazarus, vice-president of advertising.

"It's going to cost a small fortune, Bill. Joan Crawford travels in style." Paul sounded hesitant.

"But, Paul, it'll be worth it. She'll sell out every theatre where she appears. Word of mouth will snowball." Again a long pause. "Paul, are you listening?"

"Just thinking, Bill. Tell you what—give me until tomorrow, and I'll try to figure this out."

Thanks to Paul Lazarus, Columbia not only agreed to the tour, but opened their purse strings—a tour fit for a queen. Paul Lazarus, a brilliant man in his field, made it possible to achieve the box-office success that we had, by his guidance and belief in us.

"We need a large bus—can we rent one of New York City's? I want it fitted with an icebox for food . . . a portable bar for cold drinks. . . . I want a detailed map of every theatre we open in, the exact time Crawford will appear onstage. . . . We must have a trial run on the day before to see if we can make the theatres on time. . . . Ads—big ads—in every paper. . . . Radio, TV spots announcing the big event. . . . I must have room for the men from Loews. . . . We will be carrying important press and all of Columbia's publicity people—oh, yes, and police—we must have cordons of police outside every theatre to control the mob . . . and security people riding the bus." I had been in New York a week planning and mapping out the logistics with Richard Kahn, Columbia's exploitation director. Manhattan—Brooklyn—Bronx—Queens—Staten Island— Three theatres a night for seven days. If the tour went well, we would do the same thing in other parts of the country. It couldn't fail. Somebody of importance had to introduce Joan Crawford on stage and Dorothy Kilgallen, a well-known columnist, agreed.

"For chrissakes, Dona, we're supposed to pick up Crawford at five. Where the hell's the bus? I told that sonofabitch driver. . . ."

172

"Relax, it's only three-thirty. Everything's been arranged."

"But, Dona, the bus isn't here. . . ." Promptly at five o'clock the bus rolled in, filled with theatre men, police, and press. Our first stop—Joan Crawford's apartment to pick her up. Dorothy Kilgallen was to meet us there.

Our next stop—Loews in the Bronx. It was like New Year's Eve on the bus—eating, drinking, noise making—the excitement was contagious, for everyone but me. I was so nervous I couldn't eat or drink, and I didn't feel like breathing. Two blocks away from the theatre I could see the beams from the klieg lights traveling across the sky—and then I saw the people. Mob would be a better word. Hundreds of people surrounded the theatre. Police were trying to hold them back. As the bus pulled up in front of the theatre and Joan Crawford, magnificently dressed, stepped down, there was a roar. The crowd went wild. Police had used ropes to keep them back, but the mob started to break through. A row of policemen, their arms locked, formed a cordon to keep them back.

Joan threw kisses to the crowd, thanked them for coming, and then disappeared backstage. The theatre was sold out for the six o'clock show. People unable to get tickets had waited outside for a glimpse of Joan Crawford.

"Ladies and gentlemen, Miss Dorothy Kilgallen." Dorothy approached the microphone. "Thank you for coming," she said. "I have the honor and privilege tonight to bring to you one of the great ladies of the screen—Miss Joan Crawford."

There was a pause as the spotlight followed Joan's entrance. Two thousand people stood on their feet and cheered. It was five minutes before Joan could speak.

Sweating, I looked at my watch. "We've got to get Joan in and out of here fast. We have another theatre at eight o'clock."

Dorothy Kilgallen asked Joan questions. Then the audience was invited to question Joan onstage. We were running late. I signaled to Crawford onstage to wind it up. Graciously she concluded the performance, and we were on to our eight o'clock show. Bigger crowds—more police—every theatre we played. Joan Crawford was a superstar, and the public worshiped her. Her ability to relate almost on a personal level with the masses, and the feeling that she cared about them, were the main reasons.

In one theatre Crawford actually invited the audience to join her for hamburgers at a little restaurant next door. Taking her seriously, they mobbed the restaurant. Hamburgers were sold out—as a matter of fact, everything in the whole place was sold. A little restaurant in Brooklyn was now famous because Joan Crawford had eaten there.

All the rumors I had heard about Joan Crawford being difficult were false. She is truly a great artist. Directing her was one of the greatest experiences of my life.

P.S. At the theatres, I gave out cardboard axes streaked with simulated blood—I just couldn't resist a gimmick.

CHAPTER XXIII

Girls of the World

Whenever the light bulb flashes in my brain and won't go off, it's crazy time. Loss of appetite, insomnia and constant pacing are telltale signs.

Strait-Jacket had been a dazzling success at the box office, and a star name over the marquee had completely spoiled me. I was not yet in the big time, but damn well knew that I wanted to be. I longed to play someday at Radio City Music Hall. Critics around the country had grudgingly admitted that I could make a picture without a gimmick, and while the reviews on *Strait-Jacket* were mostly favorable, they considered it another horror exploitation picture.

I fantasized that someday I would hear the phrase "The envelope, please," and win the coveted Oscar. "Ladies and gentlemen, thank you for bestowing this great honor upon me. . . . I will now put my legs behind my neck and balance the Academy Award on my head. . . ." Someday, but when?

Unable to eat my luncheon at "21" in New York, I was telling Paul Lazarus my new idea. "Not one star, Paul, but thirteen . . . all beautiful girls, of different nationalities, from almost every country in the world."

Lazarus patiently tried to explain that what I was suggesting was impossible. The logistics, coordination, and language barrier would be insurmountable.

I continued selling. "Paul, it'll be an international smash.

175

Each girl will be the star of the picture in her own country. Her name will go on the marquee. For example, in Germany we'll star the German girl, France the French girl, in Japan the Japanese girl, and so on. Think of the publicity we'll get around the world. I'll contact the leading magazine or newspaper in each country, talk them into running a talent search for the perfect teen-ager to represent them. There'll be international judges selected to choose the winners."

"But the costs will be exorbitant."

"I'll get everything for free. The magazines will be delighted with a Hollywood tie-in—it'll build their circulation—and the airlines will give free transportation for the publicity they'll get."

Paul's head shook doubtfully in my direction. "Bill, it's the first time I've had to turn you down. It's just not feasible."

"I'll prove it'll work. Let me go around the world and try to set it up. What have you got to lose?"

Paul sighed.

"You'll never take no for an answer, will you, Bill?"

Around the world in twenty days, I was out of breath but successful. The magazines and newspapers enthusiastically agreed to sponsor us, and the airlines accepted for the publicity.

The worldwide contest ran over a period of eight weeks, attracting thousands of entries from beautiful teen-age girls all vying for the glamour prizes:

> A guaranteed film role in the William Castle Production of *The Candy Web*. Accommodations provided for the winner and chaperone during filming. $300 in spending money plus all expenses paid. First-class air transportation to Hollywood and return for two persons. A complete wardrobe from the leading fashion house in each country.

As the planes arrived carrying the "girls of the world," television cameras recorded my meeting each one and welcoming her to Hollywood. The teen-agers and their chaperones were then taken to Hollywood's Montecito Hotel. Giving the

176

girls several days to relax and visit various Hollywood land-marks, I prepared for shooting the following Monday.

The most difficult task was teaching the girls the rudiments of acting and how to get used to the camera. Compounding the confusion, the bilingual interpreters were going crazy trying to keep up with the teen-agers' demands for equal rights. It was like the United Nations in session. Each girl who couldn't speak English, I taught by rote. The girl would mimic each line I spoke. A crash course in English.

The idea for *The Candy Web* (in America retitled *13 Fright-ened Girls*) was created by Otis L. Guernsey, Jr., film critic for New York's *Herald Tribune.* The story took place in an exclusive boarding school in Switzerland, which we shot at a hotel in Arrowhead, California. Diplomats working in London for their respective embassies sent their daughters to the posh boarding school. During holidays, the teen-agers would pick up bits of high-level secret negotiations from their fathers and, returning to school, would then trade bits of information. The teenagers decide to try their hand at espionage, al-most messing up the balance of world power.

The first day turned into complete bedlam as I assigned the roles according to talent. Each girl, screaming in her na-tive tongue, insisted she should have the bigger part. Finally the storm passed, the sun came out and Arrowhead became Switzerland. *The Candy Web* began.

The temperaments of the various nationalities showed up more and more as we progressed. One morning shooting had to be halted because of a hair-pulling contest between Argentina and Italy. But gradually the girls settled down and, working diligently, began to act as though they'd been in front of the camera all their lives.

A bus that drove the girls from boarding school to the air-port was used for the beginning of the picture. The same scene was shot thirteen times, exactly the same way, with one important exception: each time there was a different girl driving the bus, creating the effect that each girl was narrat-ing the opening in her own language:

177

Well, I suppose there is one thing special about us—our *fathers*. You see, they help run the world. My father is a diplomat and all that means is that he and a lot of other diplomats get together and talk about world problems.

These are my friends. They come from just about every place. This is me (actual name of girl), and today I'm the luckiest girl in the world . . . I've won first prize in Latin. First prize means I can drive this bus to the airport. It's such a wonderful day, we're all going home . . . Well, not home exactly, but to our embassies. I guess in a way, we're ambassadors, too.

This opening enabled us to use different versions to play in different countries, exploiting the girl from each of these countries to aid in audience identification.

When the picture was released, it was planned so that I could personally attend the premiere in each city, escorting the teen-ager and introducing her on stage. International press coverage was tremendous. Each girl, her name on the marquee as the star, was treated like a queen—parades, floats, bands, klieg lights. Sold-out houses everywhere. *The Candy Web* became an international holiday.

In the attic of my home, I rummaged through an old trunk filled with books and finally found it—*Zotz*, written in 1946. I had always thought it would make a good motion picture, and rereading it that evening, I found it still to be refreshingly delightful.

The story of a college professor who finds a magic coin that gives him power over everything and everybody. Simply by holding the coin in one hand, pointing with the other and saying the word "Zotz," the professor could do anything—drop a moth in flight, make a racing car seem slow, even fly. The War Department uses the professor as a human military weapon to sink ships, stop guns, slow down tanks.

My main concern was that fans would not accept my departure from horror into comedy, and only after deliberating for many days did I finally decide to take the risk.

After obtaining the rights to the novel, I received a call

from Walt Disney inquiring whether I would be interested in selling *Zotz* at a big profit. He felt it would make a wonderful Disney film and politely told me it was not my style. I declined his offer as graciously as possible, but wondered if I had made the right decision. Comedy was a new world for me.

Tom Poston played the professor. Julia Meade, Cecil Kellaway, Jim Backus and the famous Margaret Dumont, of Marx Brothers fame, rounded out the cast. The change of pace was therapeutic for me, and I found myself just as much at home creating laughs as I did getting screams.

When the picture was just about to be released, I took out extra success insurance. Millions of golden plastic "Zotz coins" were manufactured and sent to theatres all over the world. Huge billboards, put up weeks in advance of our openings, had just the word "Zotz" printed on them. Car bumper stickers and "Zotz buttons" by the thousands went out, and the magic "Zotz coins" were distributed in cities weeks before opening. I wanted the kids to get used to saying, "Zotz, Zotz, Zotz."

My worries about doing a comedy completely disappeared when the picture opened. Thousands of kids flocked to the theatres to learn how their magic "Zotz coins" worked. The aftermath was a joy to behold. The kids of America were "Zotzing" each other and everybody else. Imagination is a marvelous thing. I've often wondered how Walt Disney would have made the picture.

The telephone was the star of my next film, and the telephone companies around the country were my main target—unknowingly, they were soon to be in real trouble. I had bought a suspense novel by Ursula Curtiss—the story of two pretty teen-agers making crank phone calls and telling strangers, "I saw what you did, I know who you are." Then one of the strangers, who has just murdered his wife, gets the call, finds out who they are and where they live, and plans to kill again.

For the teen-agers, I cast two girls who were still in high

school—Andi Garrett and Sarah Lane—neither of whom had ever acted before. Universal-International agreed to my using two unknown girls, but insisted I try to get a star for a cameo role. Calling Joan Crawford, I explained the situation and asked if she'd play a small role as a favor to me. She graciously agreed to help me out. John Ireland was cast to play the murderer, and Leif Erickson the father of the teen-agers.

In the days of the silent films, to get the cast in the mood before a scene, directors used music—a violinist or pianist would select music to match the mood of the given scene. Using the same principle, I played a record each morning before shooting—a little jingle I had written.

> Don't laugh little girl,
> Better run for your life,
> The man you just talked to
> Has murdered his wife.

Just to keep the girls in practice, I allowed them to actually make several crank calls a day from numbers picked at random out of the phone book. To experience the actual results, they improvised the calls, getting a sense of reality which they would later translate to the screen.

Picking a Mr. William Harrison from the phone book, Andi would sexily purr into the phone, "Hello, is Bill there? This is Alice. I've been waiting for him about an hour. He promised to meet me. . . . Oh, is this his wife? Sorry, I must have the wrong number."

Sarah would dial a number and imitate a child pleading, "Mommy . . . Mommy? Is this Mommy? But I told Mommy I'd call her so she'd pick me up at the movie theatre, but this is the wrong number and I spent my last dime. Would you call my Mommy for me, please, and tell her to come get me?"

"Is this Mr. John Hamburger? That's fine. Would you send over six you-know-whats with pickles and onions?"

I began to plan the campaign for the release of *I Saw What You Did*. Tying up with telephone companies around the country and having huge plastic phones in front of each theatre advertising the picture seemed good showmanship at the time. But the gimmick backfired and the wrath of the phone company descended upon me full blast. A phone number placed in the newspapers around the country asked people to call for a special message. Upon dialing, a girl's voice answered and whispered sexily, "I saw what you did, and I know who you are," and then made a date to meet the potential customer at whatever local theatre was showing the picture.

The whole gimmick would have worked beautifully, except the teen-agers of America took the "phone game" seriously. While I had expected some reaction, I wasn't prepared for what happened, and neither was the phone company. It seemed that almost every teen-ager in the country was on the phone, making crank calls by the thousands, jamming the phone lines.

In retaliation, the telephone company would not allow us to advertise any further phone numbers and also took away the huge plastic phones in front of the theatres. They even threatened to disconnect my home telephone, and when I tried to apologize, they hung up on me.

To guarantee safety for the patrons of *I Saw What You Did,* I devised still another promotional gimmick—a special shock section in the theatres, where audiences could avail themselves of seat belts, much like those in airplanes, so they would stay in their seats during shocks.

By 1964 I had built a mini company within a major studio. A staff of twenty, under contract, did nothing but work exclusively on my films, sometimes around the clock. A lucrative sideline was a merchandising company headed by Sidney Balkin, an expert in the field. His department ran as a separate entity, licensing my name and logo for many products— horror greeting cards, masks, sweatshirts, T-shirts, games, plastic assembly kits, toys, Halloween masks, and so on.

Television was now becoming a formidable enemy of the movies. Business was off in theatres everywhere, and the sharp decline was starting to hurt me badly. In order to gain more revenue, movie companies had made the mistake of selling their almost current movies to television. As a result, people stayed home to watch free movies.

I felt the declining box office on my next picture, *The Night Walker,* costarring Robert Taylor and Barbara Stanwyck, both big stars that I felt would be strong enough to pull customers in. The picture played to almost empty theatres.

At Paramount I tried my hand at comedy again, starring Sid Caesar in *The Spirit Is Willing,* a comedy-ghost story. Again the results were disappointing. TV was winning out.

I tried again with Sid Caesar, in a gangster spoof called *The Busy Body.* This time I surrounded him with a cast filled with comedy stars—Jan Murray, George Jessel, Kay Medford, Dom DeLuise, Bill Dana, Ben Blue, Richard Pryor, Godfrey Cambridge, Marty Ingels, Arlene Golonka, Robert Ryan, Anne Baxter, John Astin, John McGiver. Even Sonny and Cher played bit parts. Again we failed at the box office. My small empire was beginning to collapse, and by 1967 I was ready to throw in the towel. I had tried everything, from insurance policies, flying skeletons, and buzzing the audience, to money-back guarantees, bloody cardboard axes, big stars, and big telephones. I still had my French haunted house, but that would have to wait. It was hard to believe that the low-budget exploitation picture was at an end. Perhaps someday they would make a comeback, but I couldn't wait.

Desperately I started to search for the miracle that would save my career. I had to find something—*anything*—or I'd be out of business.

Then, from Heaven, the miracle appeared. Or was it Hell?

PART III

Rosemary: A Trilogy

Chapter XXIV

Heaven

3 Rosemary's Baby Levin 11–14–23 elec cr l&l
1–722–1131
RACK K–12

Galley no. 5

Unrevised proofs. Confidential. Please do not quote for publication until verified with finished book.

ROSEMARY'S BABY a novel by IRA LEVIN
RANDOM HOUSE New York

First Printing

"Who the hell put these galley proofs on my desk?" I asked Lisa, my secretary. Little did I know at the time that the word "hell" was most appropriate.

Lisa came into the office. "Marvin Birdt came in while you

were in the cutting room." (Birdt was a literary agent.) "He was in a hurry, left the galleys, and said he'd call you later."

Again glancing at the title, *Rosemary's Baby,* I spoke with indifference. "It's probably some story about an unwed mother . . . cheap exploitation. Who in *hell* wants to make a picture like that?" (Again *the word.*)

Lisa buzzed and said Marvin Birdt was on the line. "Marvin, *Rosemary's Baby* is not for me. . . . You know the bottom has fallen out of the horror films."

"Bill, read the galleys. . . . They'll knock you on your ass."

"I'm busy . . . maybe next week."

Marvin's voice became confidential. "You must read the galleys immediately."

"I can't," I protested.

"Call me tomorrow morning . . . early," he said. "And start reading now!"

"Agent talk," I said to Lisa.

I had read so many books and manuscripts in the last weeks, each one worse than the other, that I wasn't about to waste an evening reading more junk. As I left the office, Lisa called after me, "You're forgetting the galleys." Rushing down to my car, she handed me the envelope.

"Thanks for remembering, Lisa," I said sarcastically. "Oh, well, I'll start the damn book. What have I got to lose?"

CHAPTER I

Rosemary and Guy Woodhouse had signed a lease on a five-room apartment in a geometric white house on First Avenue when they received word from a woman named Mrs. Cortez that a four-room apartment in the Bramford had become available. The Bramford, old, black and elephantine, is a warren of high-ceilinged apartments prized for their fireplaces and Victorian detail. Rosemary and Guy had been on its waiting list since their marriage, but had finally given up.

Three hours later, I was on the last page. My face was bathed in sweat and I was shaking. "Ellen, this is one of the most powerful books I've ever read—what a motion picture it'll make." I was trembling with excitement. "Please read it . . . even if you have to stay up all night."

Dawn was just breaking when Ellen finished the book.

"Well," I said, "what do you think?"

"It's disturbing . . . frightening and brilliant." Ellen was as excited as I was. "But you're going to have trouble with the Church."

"Even if they ban it," I said, "Catholics will go."

"Marvin, a quarter of a million dollars—that's impossible! I don't have that kind of money." Marvin Birdt was in my office. I had my coat off, sleeves rolled up, a pad and pencil in front of me. The agent sat cool and collected. He knew he had something big. "Jesus, Marvin, give me a break, or I'll be out of business."

"I gave you a break, Bill, when I let you read the galleys. You were the second one I gave the book to."

"Who was the first?"

"You know I can't tell you," he said. (Later, I found out it was Alfred Hitchcock.)

My shirt was now soaking wet. I tried not to show my anxiety, but I was failing miserably. "How about a six-month option for ten thousand to be applied against the purchase price of fifty thousand and a small percentage of the picture?"

The agent yawned. "Don't be ridiculous."

I went to the closet and changed shirts. "Marvin, you're my friend . . . my buddy."

Marvin agreed, then flatly stated, "A quarter of a million dollars!"

"Oh, God!" I moaned. I was slowly losing *Rosemary's Baby.* "Can you give me a week to think it over?"

"My advice is to act now, Bill. Otherwise someone else will buy it." He lowered his voice. "Confidentially, another studio is interested in it."

"Who? Where?" I asked.

"You know I can't tell you that."

187

Christ, he was exasperating! Was it just agent talk? Somehow I felt he was telling the truth. "Will you submit an offer of one hundred thousand cash, an additional fifty thousand if the book becomes a best seller, and five percent of one hundred percent of the net profits?"

Marvin stretched. At least he didn't yawn. "I'll submit the offer," he said, "But I doubt if they'll accept it."

The next twenty-four hours were the longest I'd ever spent—the minutes seemed like hours. Both Dona and Ellen tried to calm me down, to no avail. Every time the telephone rang, my heart pounded. "Why doesn't Marvin Birdt return my calls?" I asked Dona. "Do you think he's really out, or has he sold *Rosemary* to someone else? You call and tell his secretary you're somebody else. . . . Tell him it's Alfred Hitchcock's office . . . anything. I know he's playing games."

It was Saturday morning, and against my protests, Ellen insisted we go for a drive along the ocean—anything to make me relax. We pulled into a gas station at Malibu, and I called home to see if there were any messages. My daughter Georgie told me Marvin Birdt had called.

"Did he leave a number where I could reach him?"

"No, Daddy, he said he was going out."

"What else did he say?" I begged.

"Nothing, Daddy . . . except that he would call you later."

"For chrissakes, Ellen, let's drive home quickly. He may call back any minute. Please hurry."

That night at 8:00, the agent called. "Bill . . ." he began. My heart stopped. The pause seemed like an eternity. "Congratulations . . . you've just bought *Rosemary's Baby*."

I collapsed in a chair and started to laugh. I couldn't stop. Then I started to worry. . . . What if I was wrong and couldn't raise the money to make the picture?

Lisa said Robert Evans (in charge of worldwide production for Paramount) was on the line. "Hello, Bill, this is Bob," his cultured, modulated voice came through.

"Hi, Bob, how are you?" my nonchalant voice returned.

"Just fine, Bill. And how are you?"

"Just great," I assured him.

"I hear you've just bought *Rosemary's Baby*—is that correct?" he inquired.

"That's correct," I stated.

"I haven't read it yet, but I hear it's great." There was a long pause as we each waited for the other to speak.

"Hello, Bob?"

"I'm still on. Any plans for it?"

"No plans," I answered.

"I hope we'll be able to make it together. . . . Don't forget, you're one of the family."

"I know that, Bob," I said with a tear in my voice. (Sixth cousin, twice removed on the lower left, I thought to myself.)

"Let's meet soon and talk about *Rosemary*."

"Anytime," I answered.

"Anytime" was three mornings later. Bernard Donnenfeld, Robert Evans's partner in charge of business affairs, was on the phone. "Hello, William." His voice was saccharine.

"Hello, Bernie, how are you?" I inquired.

"Fine, just fine. And you?" He went one step further than Evans. "And how's Ellen?"

"Just fine, Bernie."

"And the girls?"

"Fine, Bernie, fine."

After discussing family life, he got down to business. "Charles Bluhdorn has just flown in from New York and is at the studio." Donnenfeld made this announcement with reverence as if the Red Sea had just parted. (Charles Bluhdorn, the head of Gulf & Western Industries, had recently acquired Paramount and now owned it lock, stock, and barrel.) I waited patiently for Donnenfeld to continue. "Mr. Bluhdorn would personally like to meet you this afternoon at four." These words were uttered as if I were about to be knighted. Again a pause. "Are you still there, William?" He probably thought I had fainted from joy.

"Shall I bring my lawyer along me with me, Bernie?"

189

"That's not necessary, it's just a social meeting."

Promptly at 4:00, I was in Donnenfeld's outer office. His secretary said, "Go right in—you're expected."

Donnenfeld was nowhere in sight, but seated behind his desk was Charles Bluhdorn himself—medium height, dark hair, steel-rimmed eyeglasses, conservatively dressed, with a pleasant, open face. He could have been the corner grocer, except for his eyes, the most penetrating I had ever seen. Without a word being spoken, I felt I was in the presence of a human magnet. I experienced a slight shiver as the magnetic force before me involuntarily pulled me toward him. He spoke softly, with a slight Austrian accent. "Hello, Mr. Castle, I'm Charles Bluhdorn. Please sit down." His eyes locked into mine and I felt he saw right through me. "I have big plans for Paramount," he said softly, "and they include you." I nodded my head in total agreement, completely mesmerized. Rising, Bluhdorn walked to the center of the office. "Can I get you some refreshments—a drink, perhaps?"

"No, thank you, sir," I said.

"Well, then, to business. . . . Bob Evans tells me you have a great book—*Rosemary's Baby*." I sat silently. Bluhdorn returned to the desk and sat down. "Would you like to make the picture for us?"

"Yes, sir, I would," I said.

Bluhdorn smiled, but his eyes never left mine. "Good . . . then the rest will be easy." Again I waited. "Your services as producer . . . how much would you want?"

"Producer and *director*," I corrected.

Bluhdorn nodded silently. A brief pause, and then he smiled again. "You haven't answered my question . . . how much?"

"Mr. Bluhdorn, sir," I stammered, "I think my attorney, Mr. Baerwitz, should negotiate for me."

His eyes clouded over and he now spoke in a flat tone. "For *Rosemary's Baby* I will not negotiate with lawyers. If this is what you desire, your attorney will have to meet with Mr. Donnenfeld. Then Mr. Donnenfeld will have to come to me." Again a pause. "It's up to you, Mr. Castle. Your lawyer and Donnenfeld, or . . . you and me."

His eyes again locked into mine. I made a quick decision. Negotiating with one of the great minds in the financial world was a challenge. I had heard stories of his genius, and some perverseness in my ego decided to take him on. "Mr. Bluhdorn, I'm ready to negotiate with you."

"Call me Charlie," he said disarmingly.

I knew I was on dangerous ground, and calling him Charlie didn't make it any easier. "May I ask you a question, Mr.— Charlie?" I said.

"Of course."

"Have you read *Rosemary's Baby?*"

"No, I haven't," he admitted. A small victory for me. Bluhdorn didn't really know what he was buying. Smiling, he leaned back in the chair. "Why is it so difficult for you to answer my question? How much do you want?"

Taking a deep breath, I took the plunge. "For my services as producer/director—four hundred thousand and sixty percent of the profits."

At this point Charles Bluhdorn started to laugh—a loud, harsh laugh, without amusement. "You are a clown," he roared, "a big, ridiculous clown. Come down, Pinocchio," he continued after he stopped laughing, "I'll offer you one hundred fifty thousand and thirty percent of the profits."

"No deal," I said.

Again a pause as he took off his glasses and rubbed his eyes. "I have another appointment soon; let's close for two hundred thousand and forty percent of the profits."

The warning signs were up. The terms he offered were more than I had hoped for. One thing stopped me from saying yes—I knew what I had—he didn't. "Well, Castle"—he dropped the Mister—"yes—or no." He started to walk toward the door, then suddenly turned. "If I walk through that door, *Rosemary's Baby* is finished at Paramount. No one—and I mean no one—will renegotiate!"

My mind was racing. I tried to remain composed, but he

191

read right through me, his penetrating eyes searching. "Make it two hundred fifty thousand, Mr. Bluhdorn, and fifty percent of the profits."

"It's a deal," he answered without hesitation, and for the first time shook my hand. Walking behind the desk, he again sat down. "How old are you, Castle?"

"Fifty-three," I answered, surprised at the question.

"Have you ever heard of Roman Polanski?"

"Of course," I answered, tightening up.

"You've seen his pictures?" he asked.

"*Repulsion* and *Knife in the Water*," I answered.

"And?"

"He's quite a talent."

"A genius," Bluhdorn stated. "And thirty-two years old. Wouldn't it be wonderful," he continued, "if Polanski, with his youth, directed *Rosemary's Baby* and you, with your experience, produced? You could teach each other so much."

"No deal," I flared. Bluhdorn looked at me silently. "Look, Mr. Bluhdorn, the reason I bought *Rosemary's Baby* with my own money was to direct the film. . . . It's going to be an important motion picture, and I'm not going to miss the opportunity of directing."

Bluhdorn spoke gently. "I did not say you would not direct *Rosemary's Baby*; I just ask you to keep an open mind. The money will remain the same if you just produce . . . or produce and direct. So that cannot be a consideration."

I stood up furious. "I direct *Rosemary's Baby*, Mr. Bluhdorn, or no deal!"

"Look, at least do me one favor. See Polanski. . . . Talk to him. I'll fly him from London, and with your permission send him the galleys of *Rosemary's Baby*. If, after you meet, you call me and say, 'I don't want Polanski' . . ."

"Then you'll let me direct?" I asked.

"You have the word of Charles Bluhdorn."

Some people have called Charles Bluhdorn eccentric. But in the dealings I've had with him, I've found him to be an honorable man. A tough negotiator, but a fair one, and his handshake is worth more than most written contracts.

On my first meeting with Roman Polanski, I took an instant dislike to him. A short, stocky man, dressed in the Carnaby Street fashion of the time, he seemed cocky and vain, continually glancing into the mirror in my office. I had made up my mind that he would not direct *Rosemary's Baby*. I asked him to sit down, which he declined. He insolently faced me, legs spread apart. It was useless trying to make small conversation with him, so I decided to make the meeting brief and get rid of him.

"You've read *Rosemary's Baby?*" I asked.

He nodded, as if the use of words would be completely wasted on me. My dislike grew. "What did you think of it?" I asked coldly.

For the first time he spoke, his accented voice jarring me. "I like it very much. . . . It will make a great picture." Again he glanced at his own image in the mirror.

"You would like to direct *Rosemary?*" I asked.

"That's why I'm here. Nobody will be able to direct it as well as Roman Polanski."

I had prepared three loaded questions for him, and I felt like a matador, sword raised, the bull in front of me. I was ready for the kill.

Question number one: "Mr. Polanski, obviously you will want to make many changes in translating the novel to the screen." (Ira Levin's novel was perfect for the screen, and I wanted absolutely no changes.)

Suddenly Polanski became intense. "The book is perfect . . . no changes must be made."

"No changes?" I asked with surprise.

"It's one of the few books I have read that must be translated faithfully to the cinema."

Point one for Polanski.

Second question: "The camera must move around a lot and the use of strange, weird shots to tell the story . . . don't you agree, Mr. Polanski?"

"No, I don't, Mr. Castle. Actors tell story . . . like peeping through keyhole of life. I do not like crazy tricks with camera . . . must be honest."

Point two for Polanski. That was exactly the way I felt the film should be made.

Polanski's face now stretched into a grin. "Why call me Mr. Polanski? . . . My name is Roman."

In spite of myself, I started to like him. I said grudgingly, "Please call me Bill."

He dropped into a chair. "Bill, we can make a wonderful picture together. I have been looking for a long time for a *Rosemary's Baby*. To work with you would be my privilege."

Somehow he seemed a different person now—warm, friendly, and enthusiastic. Suddenly I found *myself* glancing into the mirror and the image there I didn't like. "Roman, if you had the choice of anybody in the world to write the screenplay, who would you pick?"

Without hesitation he answered my question. "Me, of course."

"Why you?" I asked.

"Because I stick right to book."

Point three for Polanski.

The next two hours were spent in discussing plans for *Rosemary's Baby*. I found Roman Polanski fascinating, brilliant, and wonderfully receptive. When he left the office, I picked up the phone and called Charles Bluhdorn. "Charlie," I said, "you were right. Roman Polanski is the only one who can direct *Rosemary's Baby*."

Polanski went back to London to write the screenplay. When he had finished, he sent me his first draft. He had kept his word. Although it was overly long, he had followed the book very closely and did an excellent job. Calling from London, he told me he was going to arrive the following week and would appreciate it if I would find a house for him— somewhere near the ocean. His fiancée, Sharon Tate, would contact me.

On Sunday morning, the doorbell rang at our home on Alpine Drive in Beverly Hills. I saw a strikingly beautiful woman. "I'm Sharon Tate." Her voice was soft and musical.

Introducing her to Ellen and the girls, I found they were delighted with her unaffected simplicity.

194

"I think I've found a house for you and Roman," I said. "Right on the beach. The owner, Brian Aherne, is going to Europe and wants to lease."

Sharon loved the house and felt that it would be just right. Later that afternoon, Sharon Tate, barefoot, stood on the beach gazing at the ocean. Sunlight filtering through her honey-colored hair; her eyes danced with excitement. "It's perfect . . . Roman and I will be so happy here."

"I'd like to get Richard Sylbert to do the sets." Sylbert, one of the top production designers in the business, had been working with Mike Nichols, and had just completed designing the sets for *The Graduate.*

"He's expensive, Roman," I said. We were at my home having lunch. Polanski had just arrived from London.

"He'll be worth it," Roman said. "He's brilliant."

"We'll have to watch the costs on the picture," I cautioned.

"Don't worry, Bill. *Rosemary's Baby* will not be an expensive picture to make," he assured me.

"Do you have any actress in mind to play Rosemary?" I inquired.

"Tuesday Weld could play the part. What do you think?"

"She's a fine actress," I said, "but . . ." My voice trailed off.

"Do you have a better suggestion?" he snapped.

"I think the role was written for Mia Farrow," I said.

Polanski thought for a moment. "I don't agree. Tuesday Weld would be better."

"How about Guy Woodhouse?" I asked. We both agreed that Robert Redford would be perfect.

"How about Minnie and Roman Castevet?"

"Alfred Lunt and Lynn Fontanne?" Roman suggested.

"I hear Alfred Lunt is ill and Lynn Fontanne won't leave him."

"Fredric March could do it, or Melvyn Douglas," Roman suggested, then paused. "Let's have an artist draw the characters the way I think they should look and dress." A top Paramount artist created the drawings to the last detail, under Polanski's guidance. It was amazing; the characters in *Rosemary's Baby* seemed to come to life.

"I think Paramount is suing Robert Redford." We were in Bob Evans's office discussing our ideas for casting.

"I know Bob Redford well," Roman said. "Let me give him the script, off the record."

Evans nodded approval. "Have you boys made a decision on Rosemary?"

"Roman likes Tuesday Weld. I like Mia Farrow."

"I don't think Mia's available," Evans said. "She's scheduled to do a George Cukor picture, but I'll check it out with Richard Zanuck at Fox. Meanwhile, why don't you set a meeting with Tuesday Weld?"

"Why won't you at least meet her, Roman?" I patiently asked.

"Because Ruth Gordon is all wrong for the part," Roman flatly stated. "I saw her last picture, *Inside Daisy Clover,* and hated it. Besides, I don't like meeting actors. They make me nervous."

I tried another tack. "Look, Roman, her husband, Garson Kanin, is an old friend. I promised him we'd have lunch with Ruth. You've got to do me a favor."

"And have lunch with her," Polanski finished the sentence for me.

"Please, Roman," I pleaded.

"Okay," he muttered. "Just for you—but a short lunch."

The following day I conveniently forgot about the luncheon. At 12:30 I was nowhere near the commissary. I kept my fingers crossed and waited for the explosion. At 3:00 Roman tracked me down. "Where the hell were you?"

"I thought the luncheon with Ruth was tomorrow," I apologized.

"You knew goddamn well it was today." There was a pause.

"Well," I said, "what'd you think?"

"She's perfect for the part of Minnie Castevet. Sign her."

196

* * *

Every actress in Hollywood felt she was right for the part
of Rosemary, but Roman was adamant about Tuesday Weld,
and I still hoped we could get Mia Farrow. The telephone
rang in my office and Lisa said Richard Zanuck was on the
line.

"Hello, Dick."

"Bill, the Cukor film just fell through. Mia's available."

I sent a script to Mia and arranged a luncheon meeting
with Roman, Mia, and myself. (It seems that every meeting in
Hollywood must be over lunch.) Mia Farrow, fragile, vulnerable and slightly fey, completely captivated Roman, who
finally agreed to let her play Rosemary.

Given the legal problems with Robert Redford, our next
big problem was in finding the actor to play Guy Woodhouse, Rosemary's husband.

"How about Richard Chamberlain?" I suggested.

"No."

"Robert Wagner?"

"No."

"Alan Bates or James Fox?"

"They're too British."

"Tony Curtis?"

"Too old."

"Steve McQueen?"

"Wrong."

"Paul Newman?"

"He's busy."

"Well, who in the hell is going to play the part!"

"Robert Redford." Roman assured me. "I've spoken to
him and he's agreed to meet me tomorrow for lunch. Our
meeting must be an absolute secret because of Paramount's
pending lawsuit against him."

Only four of us knew about the secret meeting—Polanski,
Redford, Bob Evans, and myself. I was in Bob Evans's office
when the shit hit the fan. Polanski was on the verge of getting
Redford to agree to play opposite Mia when a young, eager
Paramount lawyer, not knowing the purpose of the secret

meeting, spotted Redford and, rushing over to the table, served him with a subpoena. The damage was done, and no amount of persuasion on Polanski's part could convince Robert Redford to come near Paramount again.

I was in my office looking through the casting directory when Lisa announced that Sidney Blackmer wanted to say hello. I hadn't seen him in many years. When I was a kid in New York, he had been a matinee idol. Sidney had aged well—he must have been in his seventies. "You look just great," I said.

"I'm in Hollywood a few days . . . I live in South Carolina now."

"Sidney, is that a toupee you're wearing?"

Blackmer smiled. "Why do you ask? Does it look that bad?"

"No," I said, starting to get excited. "Would you mind taking it off for a moment?"

"Not at all." He did as I requested.

"Now, turn it around, and put it on backward." Puzzled by my strange request, he did as I asked. "Perfect!" I yelled. Jumping up, I hurriedly dialed Polanski. "I've found Ruth Gordon's husband. . . . I'm sending him right down. . . . He's perfect!"

Everyone agreed that Maurice Evans would be great for the role of Edward Hutchins, "Hutch," so I signed him.

Dr. Sapirstein gave us more trouble. I was in Polanski's office, and he was studying the picture the artist had drawn of Dr. Sapirstein, the obstetrician.

"How about Luther Adler?" I volunteered.

"He doesn't look like the sketch."

"Raymond Massey?"

Roman shook his head in disagreement. We were both looking at the sketch of Dr. Abraham Sapirstein mounted on the wall—a tall, gaunt, bearded man, with shaggy hair, dressed in baggy clothes.

"Who does he remind you of?" Roman asked me.

I shook my head, puzzled. "Fred Astaire?"

"Look again," Roman insisted. "Without the beard."

198

"You're not thinking of—oh, no!"

Roman smiled. "You'd be perfect for the part, Bill."

"Roman, for chrissake—I can't play Sapirstein; I'm no actor."

"You started as one," he insisted. "I read your studio biography."

"But that was a long time ago. I stopped acting because I was lousy."

"I'll make you great. Please . . . you have to play the part."

"Bill, this is Bob [Evans]. Roman wants you to play Sapirstein. . . . I think it's a great idea."

"No way, Bob. It's going to be tough enough producing the film, keeping Polanski on schedule, without having to sit on the set all day as an actor."

Polanski was furious and wouldn't speak to me, but I was adamant in my refusal.

Calling an old friend, Ralph Bellamy, I asked him to come to the studio. "Ralph, you'd be perfect for the part of Dr. Sapirstein. . . . There's only one problem."

"What's that?" Ralph asked.

"You have competition."

"Who?"

"Me." I smiled. "But I think you'll win by default."

Polanski reluctantly agreed to Bellamy, but insisted that he go to Frank Hoffer, my tailor in Beverly Hills, for a wardrobe exactly like mine.

For the part of Laura-Louise, one of the witches living in The Bramford, Roman came up with the wonderful idea of using the comedienne Patsy Kelly.

We were still no closer to our male lead.

Walking across the Paramount lot, I heard my name being called and, turning around, saw John Cassavetes, a talented actor, run toward me. "Bill, have you found anybody to play the male lead?"

"Not yet, John," I answered.

199

"Well, what about me? I could play the devil out of the part—no pun intended."

"I don't know, John; let me talk to Roman."

Polanski was excited with the idea of using Cassavetes as Guy Woodhouse, but Robert Evans wasn't quite sure. "Don't you think Cassavetes is too dark and brooding? It's on-the-nose casting—audiences would suspect him immediately. We need someone more romantic, more of a conventional leading man. . . ."

"Somebody like Robert Redford?" Polanski muttered disgustedly.

We were scheduled to start filming in three days. At the last moment, Bob Evans agreed to let John Cassavetes play the dark, brooding father of *Rosemary's Baby*. We were ready to begin.

CHAPTER XXV

Purgatory

A CAMERA was mounted on the rooftop ledge across the street from The Dakota. Location—Seventy-second and Central Park West. The Dakota, foreboding and fortresslike, housed some of New York's elite. Almost a century old, it had fallen into bad times during the twenties, and only recently had become the "in" place to live.

Scene 1—EXTERIOR BRAMFORD—DAY
The panoramic of New York from a high building, finishing on The Bramford. [The Dakota was The Bramford in Ira Levin's novel.]

Polanski, perched like an eagle on the rooftop, looked through the camera. "A rehearsal, please." The assistant director, speaking through a walkie-talkie, signaled to Mia and John waiting on the corner.

Scene 2—EXTERIOR STREET
GUY and ROSEMARY WOODHOUSE walk down the street and enter the main gate of The Bramford.

Dissatisfied with the rehearsal, Polanski turned to the cameraman, William Fraker. "The camera is not placed right. We move it to the end of ledge . . . better vantage point."

It was the first day of shooting on *Rosemary's Baby* in New York. Looking at my watch, I saw it was almost lunchtime.

The company had been on the rooftop since 7:00 that morning. "Roman, we've been here for six hours and haven't gotten a shot."

Roman reassured me with his boyish grin. "You worry too much, Bill."

"That's the job of a producer," I said, taking a cigar from my pocket and nervously starting to light it.

"You smoke too much . . . that's the eighth one this morning." Pulling the cigar from my mouth, he stepped on it. "Not until after lunch will I allow you to smoke another cigar." Roman seemed more concerned with my health than with getting the first shot.

Scene 24—EXTERIOR STREET—NIGHT

Rosemary and Guy walk along approaching The Bramford. The night is mild and balmy. As they get nearer, they see a group of about 20 PEOPLE gathered in a semicircle at the side of a parked car. Two police cars are double-parked, roof lights spinning red. Rosemary and Guy walk faster, hand in hand, straining to get a better view. Cars on the street slow questioningly; windows scrape open in The Bramford and heads look out beside gargoyle's heads. The roof of a Volkswagen is crumpled to the side; the windshield is crazed with a million fractures.

ONLOOKER

Dead.

SECOND ONLOOKER

Gee, did you hear that crash. Wow.

Rosemary and Guy stand on tiptoes, craning over people's shoulders.

POLICEMAN

Get back now, will you?

The shoulders separate. On the sidewalk lies Terry, watching the sky with one eye, half of

202

her face gone to red pulp. A blanket flips over her, settles, and red blotches soak through in one place, then another. Rosemary wheels, eyes shut, her right hand making an automatic cross. Her mouth is tightly closed.

GUY
Oh, Jesus. Oh my God.

Midnight—in front of The Dakota—humid, hot—a nightmare. The Dakota, with its gargoyles, seemed restless and angry. Crowds of gawkers, held back by ropes, strained to get a better look at Mia, who had recently married Frank Sinatra. New York's finest, assigned to the company, did their best, but shooting in Manhattan, especially at night, is next to impossible.

Polanski, completely oblivious to the crowds, was on his knees scrutinizing the dead girl. "Blood—bring me the blood." The makeup artist brought the bottle of blood. Grabbing it, Roman held it up. "Blood is phony . . . does not look real. . . . Make new blood."

The onlookers, not used to motion-picture jargon, gasped at Polanski's bizarre request. A young man, one of the onlookers, tugged at my arm. "Hey, mister—for fifty bucks, the director can have a pint of mine." I didn't tell Polanski because he would have used it.

I was amazed at Roman's eye for detail. A perfectionist, he refused to compromise. If I had been directing the picture, I could have finished the scene in several hours. Polanski was taking several nights.

Pacing and agitated while waiting for the new blood, I noticed Elia Kazan watching me intently. "You seem frustrated." Kazan must have been reading my mind.

"What are you doing here, Gadge?"

"I live just across the street," he replied. "Thought I'd watch Polanski at work. He's slow, isn't he?"

"Roman will pick up speed once he gets going."

"How does it feel, letting someone else direct your picture?" Kazan pointedly inquired.

203

"I don't mind one damn bit!" I said the words, but I didn't mean them.

It was dawn when the assistant director called, "It's a wrap for tonight. Tomorrow, six P.M., same place, same scene."

The gargoyles of The Dakota seemed to yawn. They, too, were exhausted. Polanski, the perfectionist, was slow and tedious, but the two scenes he had gotten that night were brilliant. Could Paramount afford it?

The fourth night. We were still at it.

Scene 24—EXTERIOR BRAMFORD—NIGHT

> An old couple is coming along the street. MRS. CASTEVET is wrapped in light blue, with snow-white dabs of gloves, purse, shoes and hat. Nurselike, she supports her husband's forearm. He is dazzling, in an every-color seersucker jacket, *red* slacks, a pink bow tie, and a grey fedora with a pink band. He is 75 or older; she is 68 or 69. They come closer with expressions of young alertness, with friendly quizzical smiles.

SECOND POLICEMAN
Are you the folks, the Castevets on the seventh floor?

MR. CASTEVET
We are. (A dry voice that has to be listened for.)

SECOND POLICEMAN
You have a young woman named Theresa Gionoffrio living with you?

MR. CASTEVET
We do. What's wrong? Has there been an accident?

SECOND POLICEMAN
You'd better brace yourself for some bad news. (He waits, looks at each of

204

them in turn.) She's dead. She killed
herself . . . Jumped out of a window
on the top floor.

Boris Karloff had an apartment on the top floor of The
Dakota. He grew orchids.

The gawkers were ever-present. "Cut!" Polanski's voice
stopped the scene. "Where's Anthea?" he demanded. Anthea
Sylbert, our talented costume designer, rushed in. "Sidney's
jacket is too rumpled. Press it!"

"But it's summer and his clothes would be rumpled from
the heat."

"Not Mr. Castevet—he's different. Get it pressed," Polanski ordered.

"At two in the morning? Where?" Anthea asked.

"That's your problem—do it!" Polanski turned away.

"Would you like a drink?" a husky voice inquired. I was
standing on the sidewalk, miserable, consulting my watch.
"You look as if you could use one," the husky voice continued.

Looking up, I spotted the voice. It was Lauren Bacall, who
lived at The Dakota with her husband Jason Robards. "I sure
could use one," I gratefully answered. "But I shouldn't leave
the company."

"Nothing's going to happen for a while," she said.

Sitting on the couch in Lauren Bacall's spacious living
room, I glanced around. Several pictures of her former husband, Humphrey Bogart, were apparent.

"You seem uptight, Bill. Relax, you'll last longer."

"He's so damn slow. We should have been out of here days
ago."

"You're going to have a great picture, that's all that matters, isn't it? Do you know *Rosemary's Baby* is number two on
the best-seller list? The film can't miss."

Scene 6—Exterior 7th Avenue—A Beautiful Summer
    Day
    Guy and Rosemary are shopping.

205

It was pouring.

"Bernie," I screamed long distance to Bernard Donnenfeld in Hollywood. "It's raining. What in the goddamn hell can *I* do about the rain? I know we're behind schedule, but we can't shoot in the rain when the script calls for a beautiful day. . . . No, we can't change the script. . . . Bernie, how can you blame the rain on Polanski? That's ridiculous. Yes, Bernie. . . . Yes, I guarantee the sun will shine tomorrow." (My lips to God's ears).

Scene   65—EXTERIOR   STREET   OUTSIDE   HUTCH'S
APARTMENT—DAY
Rosemary and Hutch walking along.

The traffic was impossible and Maurice Evans couldn't remember his lines.

"Hello, Bernie . . ." I yelled long distance. "I don't *know* when we'll get out of here. . . . We're going as fast as we can. . . . Yes . . . yes, Bernie, I know we're behind schedule. I'm pushing Polanski as much as I can. . . . I know I'm the producer. . . ." (I should be the director, I thought to myself.) "Bernie, I just can't make him go any faster. Have you seen the rushes? They're great, aren't they? Please, don't worry, Bernie . . . I'm not. I assure you, *I'm not worried*. . . ." (Jesus, I was worried sick.)

Scene 108—EXTERIOR MADISON AVENUE—DAY
Rosemary absentmindedly walks along the
Avenue. She crosses the street. A car
HONKS and swerves to avoid her.

DRIVER
For god's sake, lady!

Rosemary pulls the charm out from under
her dress, undoes the chain and drops it
in the sewer grating.

ROSEMARY
So much for tannis root.

206

Take 20—The goddamn tannis root wouldn't fall through
the sewer grating and traffic had jammed.

"Hey, mister," I screamed at a truckdriver who had pulled
up to watch. "Will you please move your truck? You're blocking my sewer. Shit, I know it's a *city* sewer, but we're trying to
make a movie, *Rosemary's Baby* . . . You read the book? . . .
How'd you like it? . . . Fuck you too, mister!"

We were dropping even farther behind schedule, and my
daily arguments with Paramount were frazzling my nerves.
If only I was directing, we'd have been out of here days ago.
Why did I hire Polanski? The answer was simple—he was
brilliant; but to watch him work had become exquisite pain.

"Roman, trying to shoot on Fifth Avenue during the lunch
hour is absolutely crazy."

"I want realism, Bill; it can be done."

"But how are you going to get Mia into a telephone booth
without being mobbed? How?" I asked, exasperated.

"Bernie, I can't talk to you now—we're shooting on Fifth
Avenue in the middle of lunch hour. . . . For God's sake,
Bernie, it's the most important shot in the picture. No, we
can't shoot it in Hollywood—the studio isn't the same as Fifth
Avenue."

I rushed breathlessly back to the telephone booth. Roman
was setting up for the scene, and the crowds were impossible.
Fighting my way through, I pulled Roman aside. "That was
the studio. I promised Donnenfeld we'd be back on Monday.
I know you're trying to rehearse. . . . Yes, Roman, I know
it's tough, but you're the one who picked Fifth Avenue—and
during the lunch hour. What? I should go back to the hotel
and put on my brown suit? What's wrong with the one I've
got on? . . . You don't like it because it's blue? Roman,
you're absolutely mad!"

Rushing back to the hotel, I got into my brown suit. Anything to make Polanski happy—to get him to go faster.

Completely out of breath, I rushed back to the phone
booth. Polanski was still rehearsing. The crowd had grown,
and Mia was still waiting for Dr. Hill to call her back.

"Roman, I'm wearing my brown suit. Now will you speed it up?" Looking around, I noticed Ralph Bellamy dressed in the same brown suit, standing next to me. We looked like a twin act.

Scene 116—Interior Phone Booth—5th Avenue

> ROSEMARY
> I beg you, I beg you.
> (silence)
> I can't stay here.
>
> DR. HILL (off scene)
> My office at eight o'clock.
>
> ROSEMARY
> Yes, thank you.
>
> DR. HILL (O.S.)
> All right.
>
> ROSEMARY
> Dr. Hill, my husband may call
> you and ask . . .
>
> DR. HILL (O.S.)
> I'm not going to speak to anyone.
> I'm going to take a nap.
>
> ROSEMARY
> Thank you, Dr. Hill.

She replaces the receiver, breathing deeply in relief. She notices that somebody is standing outside the door. It is a man looking like Dr. Sapirstein.

Ralph Bellamy, back to camera, was standing outside the phone booth.

Scene 116—Interior Phone Booth—
> Rosemary, who has been bending to pick up

> her suitcase, is unable to move as she sees Dr.
> Sapirstein. She remains in this position for sev-
> eral seconds until the man walks a few steps
> away.

As Bellamy walked the few steps out of camera range, I walked in, timing my movements exactly with his. Wearing the brown suit, I stood with my back to the phone booth for several seconds. Then I turned and Rosemary, with relief, exited the phone booth. It was only me—nice, gentle, gray-haired, and chomping on my perennial cigar. I said my one line—"Excuse me"—and, entering the telephone booth, inserted a dime and began dialing. Polanski had the last word. I played part of Sapirstein—a very *small* part.

"Roman, do we ever let the audience see the 'Baby'?" We were back in Hollywood on the stages at Paramount. Richard Sylbert had created the interior of The Dakota to perfection. We were shooting in Guy and Rosemary's apartment, and while the crew was preparing for the next sequence, which was a difficult lighting job, Roman and I sprawled on Rosemary's bed. I read aloud from Levin's book.

> Asleep and sweet, so small and rosy-faced, Andy lay wrapped in a snug black blanket with little black mitts, ribbon-tied around his wrists. Orange-red hair he had, a surprising amount of it silky-clean, and brushed. His lips pouted and he opened his eyes and looked at her. His eyes were golden-yellow, all golden-yellow, with neither whites nor irises; all golden-yellow, with vertical black-slit pupils.

"How the devil do we get that effect?" I asked Roman.
"We could use a cat's eyes."
"You mean photograph a cat?" I asked.
"Just his eyes . . . might be interesting."
"What about his hands? His feet?"
Roman smiled. "And his tail? What'll we use for a tail?"
"And the buds of his horns?" I countered.
Roman joked. "The kid looks exactly like his father."
There was a pause as we both wrestled with the problem of

photographing the "baby." "You want me to order a cat?" I volunteered, "Maybe a Siamese?" Again a pause as we both stared at the wall in Rosemary's room, each trying to visualize his own concept of the "baby." "Do you think the audience will be expecting to see it?" I asked.

"Of course," Polanski answered. "But I don't think we should ever let them."

"They'll feel cheated," I said.

"On the contrary, Bill. Everyone will have his own personal image. If we show our version—no matter what we do—it'll spoil that illusion."

"I think we should at least photograph the cat's eyes," I suggested.

"I disagree," Roman said. "If I do my job right, people will actually believe they've seen the 'baby.'"

Polanski was right. Many people leaving the theatre believed they had seen Him. Imagination plays strange tricks. When *Rosemary* was shown on TV, columnists reported that "due to censorship," ABC had cut the scenes where the 'baby' was shown." Rosemary's "baby" was never photographed.

"Shit," I said. "How are we going to get by using the word 'shit' on the screen? I tell you, Roman, they'll make us cut it out."

"Ridiculous, there's a 'new wave' coming in. Pictures are growing up—and words more verbal than 'shit' will soon be acceptable."

"Impossible," I said.

"If the camera records truth, then sound must record *everything* people say."

"Not gutter language," I protested.

"You're naïve, Bill . . . grow up."

"Yeah . . . I know you're trying to protect Paramount, Bernie, but Polanski *insists* the witches in the dream sequence be bare-assed." I was sitting in Donnenfeld's office at the studio, trying to drink the coffee that he had offered me. "Bernie, for chrissake, the witches can't wear skintight suits—they'll look ridiculous." (I remembered the Indians with the

210

bathing caps.) "All of them naked, Bernie . . . not just top-less witches, but bottomless, too."

Rising, I poured myself another cup of coffee. I knew Donnenfeld was justified in being concerned. The MPAA (Motion Picture Association of America) could give Paramount trouble and insist the sequence be eliminated from the film. I tried to reassure Donnenfeld, and my voice took on a note of encouragement that I didn't feel. "Look, Bernie, the witches are old bags, and the warlocks aren't too appetizing-looking either, but we're going to photograph them in semidarkness. . . . Look, I'll tell you what—I'll insist that Polanski protect us by getting head shots—you know, eyes, close shots on the faces, then we can cut away if we're in trouble."

The company was shooting in the Castevets' apartment. Polanski was falling further behind schedule and was becoming impatient because he was unable to get what he wanted out of the scene.

"Please, Roman, I promised Donnenfeld you'd take it easy with the witches in the dream sequence. . . . I know you're trying to get realism, but bare-assed witches and warlocks is going too far. . . . Jesus, Roman, that 'new wave' of yours is going to submerge Paramount."

Between Polanski, Bob Evans, and Bernie Donnenfeld, I felt like a ventriloquist's dummy. Donnenfeld was constantly worried about the increasing costs; Evans, with his famous "nose for box office," saw the potential of the picture, and encouraged us; Polanski ignored everybody. I was constantly in the middle, trying to keep my finger in the dike. Frankly admiring Polanski's daring, and his visions of a "new Hollywood," I held my breath and prayed daily that Paramount would let us finish *Rosemary's Baby*.

"Roman, we're days behind schedule and the costs are mounting." We were again both sprawled on Rosemary's bed waiting for Bill Fraker to light the next setup. "Yesterday we were supposed to do four pages; you did a half page. It's four o'clock and you haven't gotten one shot."

Roman grinned. "You shouldn't smoke in bed."

"Goddammit, Roman, you're not my wife. Do you realize that if Paramount closes us down, it's the end of both our careers!"

Polanski looked up at the set's ceiling, his impish face suddenly serious. "*Rosemary* will be a blockbuster, but I will not compromise. You understand, don't you?"

Trying to be patient, I puffed nervously on my cigar. "You and I know it, but Paramount doesn't have our crystal ball. You're going to have to go faster to get them off my back."

Realizing we were both lying in ridiculous positions, I started to get up, but Polanski pulled me back. "Calm down . . . trust me. Tomorrow I promise you, I'll take them off your back."

Polanski kept his word. The eight-page sequence in which Guy and Rosemary have dinner for the first time with the Castevets—a tough sequence to shoot—was completed in one day. Paramount relaxed—at least for the time being.

Scene 19—INTERIOR BASEMENT LAUNDRY ROOM—DAY

Polanski was trying to do the entire five-page sequence in one complicated setup. He was having trouble and was on Take 55. Bob Evans had just left the stage. He had congratulated Polanski on the brilliant film he was getting. Puffing on my tenth cigar, I had been tempted to suggest that Evans not praise Polanski. It would make him overconfident and he would slow down still further.

Standing in the background, I pulled out my eleventh cigar and started to light it. "Bill," a voice whispered. Turning around, I noticed Bernie Donnenfeld. "I'd like to talk to you," he said, motioning me to leave the stage. I followed him outside. "When do you think Mia will be finished in the picture?" Donnenfeld calmly asked.

"Another five weeks," I answered. "She's in almost every shot."

"No possible way of finishing with her earlier?"

"If we work on Saturdays we could knock a week off," I said.

"You may have to."

"Why?" I asked. "Polanski's getting a great film; it's a little late to rush it."

"It isn't Polanski—it's Frank Sinatra."

"Sinatra? What's he got to do with it?"

"He's shooting a film in New York and Mia's in it. She's supposed to report for work next week."

"No way," I said.

"He just phoned. I wouldn't take the call. Will you speak to Roman and tell him the problem?"

"You don't know Polanski," I said.

"You don't know Sinatra."

He called when I was in the projection room. The Paramount operator announced, "Mr. Sinatra calling for Mr. Castle." I had known Sinatra since we first started at Columbia, but I hadn't spoken with him in several years. He had always been warm, friendly and direct—a no-nonsense guy that I admired.

"Hi, Frank," I said.

"Hello, Bill, how are things with you?"

"Great, Frank—and you?"

He came right to the point. "When is Polanski finishing with my wife? I can't get a straight answer from anybody. Level with me, Bill."

"We're behind schedule, Frank, but I guess you already know that."

"Mia's supposed to start in my picture on Monday. Will she be finished by then?"

"No, Frank, I'm afraid that's impossible. Even by working Saturdays, she'll be at least three weeks."

There was a long pause.

"Then I'm pulling her off your picture tomorrow."

"That'll mean shutting us down, Frank."

"Sorry to have to do that to you, Bill, but there's no other choice."

"That means that Paramount will shut your picture down—and nothing will be gained."

"At least I'll have my wife with me," he snapped.

"Frank, please reconsider."

I had alerted Polanski about the chance of our being shut down indefinitely, and we both agreed there was nothing to do but wait.

The next day we learned that Mia decided she wanted to finish the picture. She wasn't leaving for New York.

"Roman, I think we'd better wrap for the rest of the day. Mia's in no condition to continue. We'll start fresh tomorrow, for the climax of the picture."

Scene 131—INTERIOR CASTEVET APARTMENT—NIGHT

Rosemary watches them until she is by the bassinet which is angled in their direction. With her free hand, she catches the black-covered handle and swings the bassinet slowly, gently, around to face her. Taffeta rustles, the black wheels squeal. She looks in. Smiling gently, she slowly reaches her left arm to take the baby. The smile fades on her face and changes into an expression of horror. She backs slowly away and freezes with her eyes wide open.

ROSEMARY
What have you done to it?
What have you done to its
eyes?

They stir and look to Mr. Castevet.

Mr. CASTEVET
He has His Father's eyes.

Rosemary looks at him, looks at Guy—whose eyes are hidden behind a hand—looks at Mr. Castevet again.

ROSEMARY
What are you *talking* about?
Guy's eyes are *normal!* What
have you *done* to him, you
maniacs?

214

She moves from the bassinet, ready to kill him.

> MR. CASTEVET
> Satan is His Father, not Guy. He
> came up from Hell and begat a
> Son of mortal woman!

> MR. WEES
> Hail Satan.

Mr. Castevet cries, his voice growing louder and prouder, his bearing more strong and forceful.

> MR. CASTEVET
> *Satan* is His Father and His Name
> is Adrian! He shall overthrow the
> mighty and lay waste their temples!
> He shall redeem the despised and
> wreak vengeance in the name of the
> burned and the tortured! Hail, Adrian!

> MRS. CASTEVET
> He chose *you* out of all the world,
> Rosemary. Out of all the women
> in the whole world, He chose *you*.
> He arranged everything 'cause He
> wanted *you* to be the mother of
> His only living Son.

The thought suddenly crossed my mind that Mia was reacting to the emotional strain of her disagreement with Sinatra. I was stunned by her performance as the vulnerable Rosemary seeing her baby for the first time. She was overwhelming. Cast and crew applauded her brilliance.

We were back in New York again for the winter exteriors. It was several weeks before Christmas and the city was alive with shoppers. I was half-dead, but still screaming at Donnenfeld long-distance.

"Bernie . . . we'll definitely be out of here before Christmas. That's a promise. Have I ever broken my word to you? . . . That wasn't my fault, Mia was sick. . . . Bernie . . . I swear to you . . . the troops will be home for Christmas. . . . No, Bernie, we're not waiting for the snow. . . . But we can't shoot in the rain. . . ." My words seemed hollow: I had heard them before. I promised we'd be finished by Christmas, but I didn't say what year.

Scene 84—EXTERIOR PARK AVENUE—DAY

> With its center line of Christmas trees—sunny, clear, cold day. Rosemary walks slowly, carrying her pain inside her. Her coat is slightly snug over her stomach.

> Rosemary passes Salvation Army Santa Clauses shaking their bells, stores with their Christmas windows. She reaches the Time-Life Building and walks around looking for Hutch. It's five-to-eleven on her wristwatch. She sits down on the low wall at the side of the forecourt. She lifts her face to the sun, and listens to the noises of the busy street. With her eyes closed, she speaks to herself.

> ROSEMARY
> Pain, begone! I will have
> no more of thee!

Mia sat shivering, huddled in a corner. The icy wind seemed to rip right through her—frightened, pregnant and alone. Deep lines circled her feverish eyes, her face pale and ravished.

A camera was mounted on the rooftop ledge across the street from The Dakota. Location—Seventy-second and Central Park West. The Dakota, foreboding and fortresslike, housed some of New York's elite. Almost a century old, it

216

had fallen into bad times during the Twenties, and only recently had become the "in" place to live. . . .

We had come full circle. The last shot of *Rosemary's Baby* was the first shot in the picture. Roman Polanski wasn't satisfied with the original shot and decided to do it again. It seemed as if we were starting the goddamn picture all over again!

CHAPTER XXVI

Hell

"DONA," I yelled, "Come into my office. Sit down and make yourself comfortable. I want to read you some of my 'fan mail.' 'William Castle,'" I read aloud.

> You have unleashed evil on the world. You will not live long enough to reap your rewards.
>
> Unsigned.

Tossing the letter into the wastepaper basket, I read another:

> *Rosemary's Baby* is filth and YOU will die as a result. Lover of Satan, Purveyor of Evil, you have sold your soul. *Die. Die. Die.*

Into the basket. I continued reading aloud:

> Bastard! Believer in Witchcraft. Worshiper at the Shrine of Satanism. My prediction is you will slowly rot during a long and painful illness which you have brought upon yourself.
>
> Your immortal soul will forever burn in the pits of hell where you belong. . . . I am your mortal enemy and will see that you are destroyed. You have unleashed evil upon the world.

"Shall I read more of them?" I asked Dona, glancing at the fifty unopened envelopes on my desk.

"No, please, no." Dona's eyes teared up. "Those people are sick. . . . I think you should notify the police."

After the critical acclaim and the box-office bonanza which was more than any of us hoped for, the poison-pen letters had slowly started to trickle in, increasing until I was receiving an average of fifty letters a day, most of them unsigned.

"How can people be so vitriolic?" Dona asked.

"There are a lot of nuts around," I answered. "I've received crank letters on my other pictures, but none like these."

"What are you going to do about them?"

"Nothing," I said, tossing the remaining letters into the basket. "Absolutely nothing."

More and more people saw *Rosemary's Baby* and more and more poison letters came in. First, I was amused, then angry, and finally frightened at the hatred that poured forth. Most of my mail now remained unopened.

Excited by the unbelievable success of *Rosemary's Baby,* Bob Evans asked me to come to his office. "Our *Baby* is breaking theatre records everywhere. Here—look at some of these figures."

"I knew the film would be successful, Bob, but in my fondest dreams, I never expected anything like this."

Evans smiled. "How does it feel to be so successful, Bill? Everyone's talking about the picture."

"Yeah—I know," I admitted. (But we weren't talking about the same thing.)

Evans pulled a script from his desk drawer. "How would you like to produce the next Neil Simon picture?" he asked. Stretching, Evans continued, "Paramount has a deal with Simon . . ." I noticed the title on the script's cover: *The Out-of-Towners,* and waited for Evans to continue. "I just spoke to Neil Simon. We both felt that you would be the ideal producer."

"But Simon is a comedy writer; I make shockers."

"Why not a change of pace, Bill? Read the screenplay. And if you decide you want to produce, call him in New York.

219

He's anxious to hear from you." Scribbling on a piece of paper, he handed me Neil Simon's number.

It was "All Hallows Eve," Halloween. Witches, pumpkins, and goblins, trick-or-treat, things that go bump in the night! I had gone home early to read the screenplay, but Ellen wanted me to go trick-or-treating around the neighborhood with the girls.

"Join us. We won't be gone more than a couple of hours . . . and it'll be fun for you."

"I'm tired, darling. Besides, I have to read this script."

Cold cuts were on the table. Ellen and the girls had eaten earlier, and the girls, in costumes, had now left. I made a sandwich and tried to eat, but I wasn't hungry. A wave of nausea passed over me, then disappeared.

"Page One, Scene One," How often had I read those words. The script was hilarious, dialogue that only Neil Simon could write, and I read it straight through without a pause.

A change of pace might be good for me for more reasons than one.

Picking up the phone, I quickly reached Neil Simon in New York. "Doc, the screenplay is marvelous. I couldn't stop laughing."

"Glad you like it, Bill. I would love to have you produce it. . . . Be great fun working with you."

"How soon would you want me to come to New York?"

"As soon as possible. We're planning to shoot the entire picture in New York. There's a lot of work to be done."

"Is tomorrow soon enough?" I laughed. Suddenly I felt a pain in my groin that broke my laughter. "Sorry, Doc, it's indigestion." I had broken out in a cold sweat.

"Get here as soon as you can, Bill. . . . I need you."

"I'll be there on Monday. And thanks for your confidence." Hanging up, I had a strange premonition that I wouldn't get to New York.

Another wave of nausea hit me. The room started to spin. I tried to stand but couldn't. Another sharp pain. Then blackness.

Ellen and the girls found me on the floor when they returned that fateful All Hallows Eve—the girls clutching bags of goodies and followed by their little friends, all laughing, dressed as witches, devils and goblins.

When I awakened, I was in bed and my good friend and physician, Dr. Robert Woods, was at my side. Ellen tried to hide her worry.

"I can't leave you alone for a single moment," she said.

"I'm just tired . . . occupational hazard being a producer." I tried to make light of it.

Dr. Woods probed. "Does it hurt there?" he questioned.

The pain had passed and I was beginning to feel better. I tried to get up, swayed, and Dr. Woods eased me back into bed. "Take it easy, Bill."

"I read the funniest script, Ellen, by Neil Simon. . . . I've decided to produce it. We're leaving next week for New York. . . ."

"You won't be able to produce anything if you don't take care of yourself. Now shut up and try to get some sleep."

I tried to sleep, but couldn't. Shrouded letters filled with hate took on weird and frightening shapes. Starting to shiver, I felt the sharp pain again in my groin.

Ellen was bending over me. "Try to sleep, darling."

I was burning up and then shivering. I wanted to tell Ellen how hilarious the script was, but somehow I couldn't laugh. The pain was too intense.

"Rest, darling."

The night never seemed to end. I swallowed sleeping pills that Dr. Woods had left, but they didn't work. The sharp pain had subsided, leaving just a dull, throbbing ache.

In the morning, I tried to urinate but couldn't. "Ellen, I'm all right. . . . I have to get to the studio."

Ellen was on the phone calling Dr. Richard Peterfy, an old friend and urologist. "Have Bill drink as much liquid as he can—water, juices, anything. The more the better. I'll stop by later."

Pitchers of water—drinking, drinking, drinking. I tried desperately to urinate. Nothing.

The following night they rushed me to the hospital with uremic poisoning. I felt and looked like a Macy's Thanksgiving Day balloon.

"Ellen, I'm sleepy. . . . Please let me sleep. . . . I just want to sleep. . . . Float away high up in the sky. . . ."

"Get him up. . . . Keep him walking. . . ." I heard voices from a distance and suddenly found myself on my feet, being supported and walked up and down the room, up and down, up and down.

> Your immortal soul will forever burn in the pits of hell where you belong. . . . You will slowly rot. . . . You have unleashed evil upon the world. . . .

The lower part of my body was gone. Oh, my God, what happened to my legs? Who took my legs? Voices coming from a tin can blasted my ears. Indistinguishable at first, they now formed words. "Take it easy. . . . You'll be all right. . . . Try not to move." *Who the hell could?* "You'll be fine. . . ."

I was in surgery. They had given me a spinal. Silence, and then, "Thank God it's not the kidneys." I heard Dr. Woods's voice and then Dr. Peterfy's, "The water's coming out, Bill . . . quarts of it. There was a blockage." The Macy's Thanksgiving balloon was starting to deflate.

After six days in the hospital, they said I could go home.

"You're not going to New York. You're going to take a rest. The studio will still be there."

"But, Ellen, I feel fine—I peed three times today," I boasted proudly.

"Get on the phone and call Neil Simon. Tell him you're ill and can't do the picture."

"But, Ellen," I protested.

"Get on that phone," she ordered.

Saturday morning, Robert Petkin, a friend, called. "Bill, would you and Ellen like to join us for *Plaza Suite* at the Huntington Hartford? Neil Simon wrote it and he's great."

"Yeah, I know," I replied despondently. "Wait a minute— I'll ask Ellen.

"For chrissakes, Ellen, I'm not an invalid. We're going to see *Plaza Suite* with the Petkins."

By evening I felt lousy. The dull pain had returned, but I wasn't about to give in to it.

Plaza Suite was a funny play—laughter all around me, but I couldn't join in. After the performance, I had trouble walking back to the car.

Rosemary's Baby is filth and you will die as a result. . . . You have sold your soul. *Die. Die. Die.*

The same thing was happening again. The damn blockage. I couldn't urinate. This time Ellen didn't wait. On the telephone to Dr. Peterfy, arrangements made for me to go directly to the hospital. This time, surgery.

I was badly frightened. I had never had surgery. The following morning I was on the table. Everything went black— except for the witches.

It was several days before I learned what had happened in the recovery room. Coming out of anesthesia, a patient's first question is usually, "Will I live?" "Is it cancer?" I had cried out, "Rosemary, for *God's* sake, drop that knife!"

Ellen held a glass jar. "Look at your two babies, Bill." Two brownish kidney stones, the size of small rocks.

"Oh, God!" I said. "Did they come out of me?"

"Take it easy, darling, and get well. You'll be home in two weeks."

Bastard! Believer in witchcraft . . . Lover of Satan . . . I will see that you are destroyed.

Home again. Living like a vegetable. Then *again*, the stoppage. *Again*, the hospital. *More* surgery, *more* stones. They couldn't locate the one stone still inside of me—*the devil that was killing me.*

Your immortal soul will forever burn in the pits of hell. *Die. Die. Die.*

I heard the night nurse whisper to an orderly, "The composer of *Rosemary's Baby* is still in a coma."

Composer? "Nurse," I yelled, "what are you talking about?"

"Nothing, Mr. Castle. . . . Go back to sleep."

"Please, for chrissakes, nurse, tell me." I was frantic.

"Christopher Komeda suddenly fell while skiing. . . . Blood clot in the brain. . . . He's in a coma."

"Where is he?"

"Third floor."

"Oh, my God!"

Scene 24—Interior Time-Life Building—Day
> A stainless steel phone booth. A Negro girl is in it. She finishes soon and comes out with a friendly smile. Rosemary slips in and dials. On the first ring a woman's voice answers.

GRACE CARDIFF (O.S.)
Yes, who is this, please?

ROSEMARY
My name is Rosemary Woodhouse.
I have an appointment with Mr.
Hutchins. . . . Is he there?
(silence)

Hello?

GRACE CARDIFF (O.S.)
He was taken ill this morning.

ROSEMARY
Taken ill?

GRACE CARDIFF (O.S.)
Yes. . . . He's in a deep coma at
St. Vincent's Hospital.

224

Christopher Komeda, the talented Polish composer, passed away.

The story of *Rosemary's Baby* was happening in life. Witches, all of them, were casting their spell, and I was becoming one of the principal players.

"Ellen, please . . . not surgery again." I was at home in bed, so weak I could barely talk. "Please . . . no more cutting. . . . I can't take it." I was living in a constant nightmare, in a maze from which I couldn't escape. "Please, Rosemary, for God's sake, drop that knife!"

Staring at our bedroom ceiling, I realized I had lost track of time. Day blended into night as I watched the patches of sunlight on the ceiling slowly fade. Voices from the next room filtered through. Straining, I heard Dona talking to my wife. "One of the finest urologists in the country is at UCLA. If I can arrange an appointment for him to see Bill . . ."

Ellen's voice lowered. "He can't go through surgery again, Dona, he won't make it."

My sickness had taken its toll. Now, barely able to stand without Ellen's help, I managed to pull myself together. One more journey into the unknown—with a small spark of hope, the UCLA urologist, *someone, something,* that could possibly save me.

"Mr. Castle, here is the stone that is causing the obstruction." The distinguished urologist was pointing to my X ray. Ellen was at my side. "You have two alternatives—surgery . . ." his voice trailed off.

"What's the other alternative?" I whispered.

"Sodium bicarbonate injections may dissolve the stone. It's a calculated risk." The urologist paused. "It'll take extreme willpower on your part."

Looking at Ellen, I spoke softly, "Anything to keep from going through surgery again."

The doctor switched off the light that illuminated the X ray. "Surgery would be quicker. I'm certain we can remove the stone. Sodium injections are experimental. They will have to be given twice a day, every day, for months. You will suffer, run high fevers, and it may not work."

"Please," I pleaded, "I'll do anything but I won't be cut again . . . by Rosemary's knife."

"I beg your pardon?" the urologist said.

"Nothing . . ." I said. "Nothing." I turned my head away as the tears rolled down my face.

Scene 127—INTERIOR GUY AND ROSEMARY'S APARTMENT BEDROOM—NIGHT

> Guy is in the doorway with Mr. Fountain. Behind them, Dr. Sapirstein with a loaded hypodermic, the needle up and dripping, his thumb at the plunger. Other people appear behind them: Mrs. Gilmore, Mrs. Fountain, Dr. Shand.

MRS. GILMORE
We're your friends.

MRS. FOUNTAIN
There's nothing to be afraid of, Rosemary; honest and truly there isn't.

DR. SAPIRSTEIN
This is nothing but a mild sedative to calm you down.

> Rosemary is between the bed and the wall. They come toward her.

GUY
You know I wouldn't let anyone hurt you, Ro?

> Rosemary picks up the phone and strikes with the receiver at Guy's head. He catches her wrist. Mr. Fountain catches her other arm and the phone falls as he pulls her around with startling strength.

226

ROSEMARY
(Screaming)
Help me, somebody!

> A handkerchief is jammed into her mouth and
> held there by a small, strong hand. They drag
> her away from the bed so Dr. Sapirstein can
> come in front of her with the hypodermic and
> a dab of cotton.

The hypodermic with the sodium bicarbonate was plunged into my side. I felt the liquid surging through me. My face was hot, the fever burning.

"Another injection this afternoon. Be here at four."

Days passed into weeks, weeks into months. Ellen and I went nowhere, saw no one. I merely lived for the next injection, and my darling Ellen lived through it with me.

"Today we will take X rays and see if the stone is smaller."

I held my breath as the infernal machine photographed my insides.

"I'm afraid the injections haven't worked. . . . The stone is still present. I recommend surgery." Dr. Peterfy took out his appointment book. "Shall we schedule it for next Monday?"

"Please, Dr. Peterfy, give it more time."

"We're running out of time, Bill."

"Please, give me one more week."

An impatient sigh, "One more week, Bill. . . . And then I insist."

Please God, let the stone dissolve. Take the devil out of me. Please help me, I prayed.

I noticed a hummingbird outside the doctor's window. I heard the faint whirring, humming sound of its wings. I had read somewhere that the wings move sixty times a second—why was I remembering that piece of trivia now? The week had passed. Again I was ready for the infernal machine that saw right through me.

"Wait in my office." There was excitement in the doctor's voice.

"Please tell me."

"Not yet, Bill. I want to be certain."

We waited in the doctor's office, Ellen and I. Each of us silent, afraid to talk. An eternity passed.

"The stone has completely vanished! Dissolved . . . the treatments worked!"

I thanked God silently, then kissed Ellen. We were still unable to speak. Hugging Dr. Peterfy, I danced round and round. I remembered I had danced with a man once before in my life—in Greenwich Village, the man in the Black Derby Hat.

"Do you think I could drive Bill to San Francisco with the girls?" Ellen was talking to Dr. Woods.

"Of course. Bill's been through a traumatic experience, but I think the trip will do him good. Just see he gets plenty of rest and doesn't overdo it."

Each day that passed, I was feeling more like myself and although I was still weak, I was gaining strength rapidly.

It was a beautiful day and the Golden Gate Bridge was flooded with sunlight. San Francisco was alive and I felt good to be part of it. We stopped for gas and I got out of the car to bask in the warm sunshine. The headlines hit me like an earthquake:

RITUALISTIC SLAYING

SHARON TATE AND 4 OTHERS MURDERED!

Film star Sharon Tate, another woman, and three men were slain Saturday, their bodies scattered around the Benedict Canyon estate, in what police said resembled a ritualistic mass murder.

The victims were shot, stabbed, and throttled. On the front door of the home was written the word PIG. . . .

228

"I have to go back."

"No," Ellen cried. "You can't."

"I must. Roman Polanski needs me." Again life was imitating the picture. When would it stop?

Polanski was incommunicado at Paramount Studios, hidden from the ugly glare of publicity. He was living in an office. No one was allowed to see him. Security guards surrounded the studio.

Dona met me at the gate, and took me to him. Alone and stunned, Roman stared at me. Handing me a piece of paper, he spoke in a monotone. "Print 'PIG.' "

Confused, I looked at him. "Why, Roman!"

"Do as I ask . . . please!" I printed the word. "Again . . . please, Bill, again!" Pausing, I looked at him. Then his eyes welled with tears. "Sharon, my poor Sharon. . . . And our baby."

"Pray for Rosemary's Baby."

Ironically, all my life I had yearned for the applause, approval and recognition from my peers; and when the awards were being passed out, I no longer cared. I was at home, very frightened of *Rosemary's Baby,* and still very ill.

Awards and Nominations for "Rosemary's Baby"

Academy Award, Best Supporting Actress—Ruth Gordon.

Nomination, Academy Award, Best Screenplay—Roman Polanski.

Golden Globe Award (Foreign Press).

Nomination, Producers Guild, Producer of the Year—William Castle.

Photoplay Award—William Castle.

Excerpts from an interview with Roman Polanski, the New York *Times,* September 23, 1973:

229

POLANSKI: ROSEMARY'S BABY AND AFTER

by Charles Higham

"When I made *Rosemary's Baby,* I was severely attacked by Catholic groups and individuals. Never by witches, as some people said. Witches told me they liked the film!"

What about the claim by William Castle, the producer of *Rosemary's Baby,* that during the shooting of the film witchcraft caused him to become severely ill? And that while he was recuperating in the hospital, Christopher Komeda, the film's composer, was fatally injured in a fall?

"Ridiculous! If anything caused Bill Castle's illness, it was having too much success with the picture." Polanski gets up, paces impatiently around the living room. . . .

PART IV

And Now, Ladies and Gentlemen . . .

Chapter XXVII

Look, Ma, He's Talking!

EXCERPTS from an interview with Marcel Marceau, the New York *Times,* Sunday, November 25, 1973:

MARCEL MARCEAU—LOOK, MA, HE'S TALKING
by Aljean Harmetz, Los Angeles

Sweating slightly in the sunlight—his white shirt half-buttoned, his plate full of sausage and fruit Jello—Marcel Marceau could be any middle-aged business man relaxing by the Pacific on a Sunday afternoon.

A thin, fragile-looking Frenchman of 48, the world's greatest pantomime artist is not working at his trade today. Motionless in his webbed beach chair, he plunges into anecdote after anecdote, shaping his past and future without once using his hands—relying instead on what he has called "the deceitful phrases that raise barriers against comprehension between men."

Marcel Marceau and his brother/manager Alain were at our beach house in Malibu overlooking the Pacific. Aljean Harmitz had chosen the ideal setting to capture the great Marceau in the simplistic surroundings of sun, sand, and water.

Aljean's husband, Richard, Dr. Harold Karpman, an eminent cardiologist, Ellen, Georgie, and Terry sat basking in the warm September sun, and listened in silence. Aljean aptly put on paper our mood that Sunday afternoon.

233

There is at first meeting a certain wonderment that he can speak at all. For so long he has addressed himself to describing man's fate wordlessly—pitting himself as Everyman against strong winds, and recalcitrant ladders and the invisible cages in which life traps us all. One listens to the words pouring fluently from his mouth in two languages rather as one watches a chimpanzee in ruffled panties riding a unicycle, or a poodle in a sequined jacket walking hesitantly across the circus ring on its hind legs.

A top photographer was clicking away, trying to record Marceau's every expression. I wondered if perhaps I had done this great artist—creator of illusions, a man who fills his stage with invisible folk—a disservice by inviting him to enter the frightening world of my horror films.

Marcel stood up restlessly. Shaking the sand from his black velvet pants, he gazed out toward the ocean. "You will excuse me . . . I would like to walk along the water's edge." His words were tinged heavily with a touch of his native French.

When he stands, his body seems boneless, his neck flowing like water into his shoulders, his shoulders to his chest, his chest to his thighs. It is something beyond agility, beyond grace. Each separate finger and toe, each separate muscle, is an instrument, a working tool. For 25 years he has used this instrument to bewilder and amaze.

"Bill, please walk with me. . . . We have much to discuss before I return to Paris." Excusing myself, I followed him. "We have worked together, my friend, for many weeks. . . . Please be honest with me. . . . Have we accomplished what we tried to do?"

I thought for a moment before I answered. "I don't know, Marcel. I honestly don't know. You were brilliant. I'm sure of that. As for myself, I feel I might have failed. Your art of mime—is it compatible with my horror?"

"Not horror, my friend; 'fantastique' is the better word."

We continued to walk in silence. I smiled—a more unlikely

234

pair of creative collaborators would be hard to imagine; a producer of terror and the mime Marcel Marceau.

Paule Mason, the writer, had arranged my first backstage meeting with Marcel, and had accompanied me to his performance.

Slowly the theatre darkened. A pinpoint of light picked him up center stage—his face, in clown white, his lips etched in bright red, charcoal accenting his eyebrows and two dots that seemed like permanent tears. "The art of mime," Marceau had been quoted as saying, "is the portrayal of the human being in its most secret yearnings. By identifying itself with the elements that surround us, the art of mime makes visible the invisible, and concrete the abstract."

Spellbound, I watched the silent vignettes. His magic moved from a butterfly to a fish, to a human battling the elements, buffeted by invisible winds. He was climbing nonexistent stairs, tugging at invisible ropes. I whispered to Paule, "He's magnificent! What kind of a man is he?"

Paule whispered back, "I'll tell you later. . . . His 'Youth, Maturity, Old Age, and Death' sequence is next. . . . He accomplishes in less than three minutes what many novelists have failed to do in volumes."

The theatre rocked with applause as the curtain came down for the intermission.

Standing in the lobby with Paule, I glanced around. "It's amazing how young his audience is—I thought they would be my age."

"I don't think anybody here is over thirty," Paule remarked.

"What's Marcel like?" I asked.

"Warm, friendly, almost childlike in his enthusiasm," she answered. The buzzer summoned us for the second act.

When the performance was over, the youthful audience cheered wildly and gave Marceau a standing ovation. Flowers were thrown onstage. There were sixteen curtain calls. I had never seen anything like it.

235

Backstage, a huge crowd of people waited patiently to shake his hand and have him autograph their programs with his trademark, a flower, and the name "Bip." A chunky, expansive man stood nearby. Seeing us, he approached. "You are Monsieur Castle," he said in accented tones. "My name is Alain Mangel. I am Marceau's manager and brother. Marcel is expecting you." Ushering us into an anteroom, he advised "You must be patient until he is finished."

"Does he see this many people every night?" I inquired.

"Marcel loves to greet the people."

An hour later, the man in clown white finally greeted us. I tried unsuccessfully not to show my awe. "Mr. Marceau, your performance was brilliant."

He had obviously heard the same compliment many times. "I am a lover of the *'fantastique.'* That is what we call your pictures in France. I have seen them all. *Rosemary's Baby* is my favorite." Marceau had done his homework well, and as he continued to rattle off my credits, I sank onto the couch in amazement.

"Give me a few minutes to take off my makeup and change, and then we shall dine."

"Mr. Marceau. . . ."

"My friends call me Marcel, and you, I feel, are my friend."

I told him of my idea—the story of a deaf-mute puppeteer and an eccentric old man.

"I will play both parts," Marceau interrupted.

"Exactly! The old man, a scientist, is experimenting . . . making dead animals live. The deaf-mute, Malcolm, is his assistant. Finally the old man dies, and . . ."

"And . . . Malcolm brings him back to life," Marcel again interrupted. "It's like my 'Youth, Maturity, Old Age, and Death.'"

"Exactly!" I said again. "Malcolm has an ugly stepsister who is married to the town drunk. They beat Malcolm . . ."

"Like Cinderella," Marcel suggested.

"They are killed and . . ." I began.

236

"Malcolm brings them back to life," Marcel said. "It's almost a *grim* fairy tale, isn't it?"

"Exactly!" I agreed once more. We were in instant accord.

"Tell me the end—what happens in the end?"

"I haven't told you the middle yet, Marcel."

"The middle makes very little difference, my friend. If a story has a good beginning and a great end, the middle can be fixed." Marceau stood up, and bending, touched his toes. "We will not make a horror picture . . . this you must promise."

"I don't know, Marcel—I can't promise."

"Fantasy, yes, but horror, no," he declared.

"But my audience *expects* a horror film from me," I stated.

"My audience *doesn't*," Marcel snapped.

We were in Marcel's Beverly Hills Hotel suite. Lawyers had worked around the clock preparing the contract so that Marceau and his brother could leave for Paris that afternoon. Several unopened bottles of Dom Perignon were sitting about, ready for the toasts when the contract was signed. Alain had finished packing and was urging Marceau to sign. Pen poised, Marcel looked at me and then at his lawyer. Motioning to the attorney, he excused himself and went into the bedroom. Alain screamed in French, "Hurry, Marcel, or we will miss the plane."

In mournful tones, the lawyer announced that Monsieur Marceau wished to have one new clause inserted into the contract.

"What's that?" I impatiently asked.

"That he has complete autonomy."

"What the hell does that mean?" I asked angrily.

"Simply that he has final approval on cast, director, writer, score . . . anything creative."

"Bullshit!" I yelled. "He probably wants to approve me. . . . I'll give him no approvals."

"We will miss the plane." Alain screamed.

"Be still." Marcel screamed back.

"Goddammit, we have no deal!" I screamed louder and started to walk out the door. Giving creative autonomy to any artist—no matter how great—was tantamount to giving away the picture. A producer must retain the right of all approvals in order to protect his film, and I wasn't about to sign them away, even if it meant blowing the deal.

"Bill, can we talk privately?" Marcel took me into the bathroom. His brother was now on the telephone in the bedroom, and his lawyer was arguing with my lawyer in the living room.

"Please don't be angry with me, my friend."

"I'm furious, my *friend*," I answered.

"I am merely trying to protect myself. . . . It is my first starring film role, and I want to be certain."

"Of what?" I said coldly. "If you don't trust my judgment, forget it."

"It isn't that," he said sadly. "I am worried about who will direct me." There was a pause as we looked at each other. I realized he had a point.

"Who would you like to direct?" I asked.

"Roman Polanski. He did a great job on *Rosemary's Baby.*"

"He's unavailable," I said. "He's preparing Robert Evans's picture *Chinatown.* Besides, he's too expensive."

Alain's voice filtered through the bathroom door. "Please—hurry, Marcel."

"Who will direct me?" he asked.

"I have the perfect director—talented, sensitive, and experienced." I mentioned the director's name and found that Marcel had never heard of him.

"What happens if the director and I don't agree? Who will arbitrate?"

"I will."

"Who will you side with?"

"I will always side with the director."

"Even if he is wrong?"

"He is the captain of the ship."

"But if he is wrong," Marcel persisted.

"Then I'll tell him privately . . . not in front of you. I will not deball him."

"You are certain of this director, Bill?"

"Certain, Marcel. You will love him."

Pausing, he studied my face. "I trust you, Bill . . . with my career. I will now sign the contract."

The following night, 4:00 A.M. Paris time, the telephone rang. The operator announced it was Marcel Marceau calling.

"The director you spoke of—I cannot sleep, thinking about him."

Trouble already, and we hadn't even started the picture! "Go to sleep, Marcel. We will talk tomorrow."

"Now," he persisted. "We must talk *now.* . . . I want you to direct."

I was stunned. I hadn't directed since turning over the helm of *Rosemary* to Polanski. "I can't, Marcel . . . I won't."

"Please think about it. I'll call you back in one hour." Before I could say more, he hung up. I knew I had no choice. Marceau was unsure of himself in the medium of film and had always worked by himself onstage. It would be a challenge to direct a genius.

Again we were on the phone. "Marcel, if I decide to direct, who's the boss?"

"You are, Bill. I am at your feet—you will find me disciplined."

"I may seem soft and gentle on the surface, but inside I'm tough, Marcel. It's going to be *my* way."

"I understand perfectly, my friend. That's the way it should be."

When I announced we were leaving for Paris in three days, Ellen said it was impossible. There was shopping to be done and the girls had another week of school. I assured her they could shop in Paris and that the girls could miss the last week of school.

I had arranged conferences with Marceau and Ranald

239

Graham, the writer of the screenplay. Marceau had found two French mime actors that he thought would be perfect for the parts of the sister-in-law and her husband. He also wanted his own Paris costumer to design the wardrobe, and his wigmaker to make his wigs.

Paris in the spring is unlike any other city in the world, except when it's raining—which it was. In spite of the downpour, the City of Light was alive. Still on jet lag, we were whisked to Marcel's home about sixty miles outside Paris. Cobblestone streets glistening in the rain led the way to Marcel's two-hundred-year-old restored farmhouse in a magnificent setting surrounded by beautiful trees.

Marceau greeted us dressed as a gentleman farmer and bid us enter his private domain. Photographs of the world's "greats," all autographed, adorned the walls. A fire was roaring in the giant hearth. Georgie and Terry were particularly delighted with one room, filled with hundreds of dolls dressed in the costumes of all the countries Marcel had visited. I was fascinated with the hundreds of Palikh lacquered boxes, decorated with fantastic birds and beasts. "Each time I have toured Russia I have collected these," Marceau explained.

Marceau was a marvelous host, and after a magnificent dinner he insisted on acting out every part in the motion picture, which we now called *Shanks*.

The following day I met with Philippe Clay and Tsilla Chelton, who indeed were perfect for the parts of Marcel's in-laws in the film. I tried to negotiate with their French agents. I had always found American agents difficult, but French agents are impossible. What could have been agreed on in twenty minutes, took two days. The language barrier didn't make things any easier. Thank God, I knew how to say yes and no in French.

"Alain, the costumes should be designed in Hollywood and not in Paris. We'll save time and money. The prices here are prohibitive." Alain Mangel was to be my production associate on *Shanks*.

"But Marcel insists."

240

"Talk to him, Alain."

"I have, Bill. He is stubborn."

"What about the wigs? We certainly can find wigs in Hollywood."

"Marceau has used Bertrand, the finest wigmaker in Paris, for years."

"Alain, you're my assistant . . . and we must make this film inexpensively."

"*Oui*, Bill, I understand perfectly. I am your associate, but also Marcel's brother."

"What the hell difference does that make? The solution is very simple—just tell him no!"

"It's not so simple, Bill—why don't you try it?"

Ten days passed swiftly. Paris, one of the most expensive cities in the world, had welcomed me with open arms. Why not?—I was a Hollywood "pigeon" and my wings were being clipped in the name of Art.

On our last evening, Marcel hosted us at a charming bistro in Montmartre. "My friends," he said, "A toast to another *Rosemary's Baby.*" As our wineglasses clinked, I thought to myself, "That's all I need!"

At two in the morning, we emerged from the restaurant and Marcel, in an expansive mood, decided to give a final performance. On a deserted street, with Montmartre as a backdrop and a full moon lighting the stage, Charlie Chaplin, Buster Keaton, Stan Laurel, Harpo Marx suddenly came to life. Two gendarmes keeping vigil in the silent night joined in the festivities. Marcel's performance ended to spontaneous applause. Bowing, he held up his hand.

"And now, my friends, for an encore—I will do one more. See if you can guess who it is." The impersonation looked familiar. I knew the gestures, even the walk—and then an invisible cigar was smoked. Marcel Marceau knew me . . . much too well.

"*Merde!* My costumes are all wrong and the wigs do not fit my head." We were all in Hollywood at Paramount. Steven North called my office, informing me that Marcel was unhappy. North was a young producer I had chosen to work with.

"For chrissake, Marcel, you were the one that wanted the wigs and costumes made in Paris."

"They are unacceptable. I look ridiculous in the wig, and the costumer did not follow my instructions."

"Marcel, be reasonable. We start shooting one week from today."

Standing in the background, Alain voiced his opinion. "Marcel, the wigs fit fine, and the costumes look right."

"You shut up and stay out of this." Then the volley of French that seemed angry and endless. "Bill, my friend, we must create my wardrobe here and get new wigs."

"But, Marcel," I protested, "we are on a tight budget, and we don't have time."

Marceau smiled, and with the great charm which I was beginning to recognize, sweetly said, "Time is of no great importance. . . . Everything must be perfect. Together we are going to make a brilliant picture. . . . And if more money is needed, I am sure you can get it from Paramount."

"*Merde.* That's what you think," I said under my breath.

"My makeup is terrible . . . The entire concept is wrong. . . . As the old man, I must look aristocratic. Instead I look like the Indian on your American nickel."

Weeks had been spent in creating the makeup. "He looks great, doesn't he, Alain?"

"Perfect, Marcel," Alain agreed. "I didn't recognize it was you."

"You stay out of this. You know nothing." Again the outburst in French. "Bill, be honest with me. . . . Tell me the truth. I don't look like an aristocrat, do I? My nose is too big and I have too many wrinkles."

"You're supposed to be eighty, Marcel. . . . You'd have wrinkles."

"But not ugly ones, Bill. And look at my nose. It's too crooked. . . . Can we not straighten it?"

"We don't have the time, Marcel," I insisted. Again the charm. "You will find time, Bill. . . . *You* can do anything."

242

"Shall I wear a kerchief around my neck for Malcolm?"

"It'll be too cluttered, Marcel. You're better off without it."

"I would like to wear it—don't you agree?"

"No, Marcel, I don't."

"Yes, Bill, you do."

In all fairness to Marcel, his ideas were usually brilliant. In all fairness to me, I had a schedule to meet and a very low budget—something that Marcel didn't understand or really care about. Accustomed to giving his own commands and to being alone onstage, he found it difficult to take direction. He was insecure in a new medium and was constantly on guard.

"Marcel, you are like an artist who wants his canvas finished before he starts." We were on the stage and I was trying to block a scene. Marcel was impatient.

"Bill, last night I rehearsed the scene myself, in my living room. . . . I have it all worked out."

"Please, Marcel, give me a chance to stage it my way."

"Why won't you allow me to show you the way I have planned it?"

"Because I'm the director, Marcel."

"My way is better," Marcel stated flatly.

Marceau's scene was far more imaginative than the one I had planned. Grudgingly I admitted that his version was superior. The invisible tug-of-war that he usually performed was becoming more and more visible on the set of *Shanks*. Both of us were now on guard.

"You wish me to walk like this?" Marcel slouched and proceeded to walk like "Everyman." "Anybody can walk this way . . . it means nothing. I must walk my own way, or not at all."

Grudgingly I agreed that Marcel's special walk was superior.

"Cut!" The camera stopped rolling. "I think you're overacting, Marcel. Your facial expressions are too exaggerated."

"But, Bill, Malcolm's loss of speech and sound would make

243

him express with his face and hands. . . . All his frustrations must be told in silence."

Now starting to doubt myself, I decided that perhaps I should let this great artist have his own way. He was a dedicated man, a perfectionist, and he was spending all his waking hours on the two characters he was portraying. His boundless energy and perseverance made Malcolm and Old Walker a joy to behold.

"I was not good in that scene." We were watching the rushes. "Please, Bill . . . I would like to reshoot it. I can be better."

"Marcel, you look just wonderful onscreen."

"I am not satisfied. Let me reshoot. Charlie Chaplin once told me that when he wasn't satisfied, he would reshoot an entire week's work. Please—all I ask is one scene."

"Marcel, we don't have the time or the money."

"Cut! Print!"

"Let me try it again, please. . . . I can do better."

Every day the stage was filled with spectators—Paramount personnel, visitors from other studios, producers, directors, actors—all coming to watch the great Marceau work.

"You are positive I am good. I think perhaps I can be better. Please tell me the truth, Bill."

"You're brilliant, Marcel. We're getting a good picture."

"Just good?"

"Great, Marcel."

"Are you certain?"

"Positive."

The old man walked toward me haltingly, his every step filled with the pain of arthritis. A trembling hand was placed on my shoulder. The voice that spoke was cracked and enfeebled by the years. "Castle, I must have a word with you . . . alone." Then a gentle pat on the cheek with his gnarled hands. "You know that the starring role in *Shanks* is played by me."

"I know that, Marcel." We were in a corner of the stage.

"Then, why do you give all the close-ups to that young up-start, Malcolm, if you agree that Old Walker is the more important of the two?"

"But, Marcel, you're playing both . . ."

"Don't interrupt me, young man. I will not have fewer close-ups than Malcolm. . . . I am the star of *Shanks.*"

Starting to laugh, I hoped that Marceau was putting me on.

Fifty years younger and remarkably handsome, he greeted me with a warm, firm handshake, the following morning. "It's a beautiful day, isn't it, Bill?"

"Beautiful," I agreed.

"Has that old fart, Walker, been bothering you?"

"A bit." I grinned.

"Don't listen to him, Bill. . . . He's getting senile, and besides, you are the director."

"Sometimes I wonder," I muttered.

"I noticed that you're giving him too many close-ups, Bill. Remember, Malcolm is the star of the picture." Conspiratorially, he drew closer and lowered his voice. "Don't you see what the old man is trying to do?"

"No, Marcel—what?"

"He's trying to steal the picture away from me. But I won't let him—and don't you." Marcel Marceau was jealous of himself.

Was he *only* putting me on? I never was certain.

We had turned from our walk along the beach and were slowly heading back toward the house.

"Be truthful with me, Bill. Do you think that *Shanks* will be better than *Rosemary's Baby?*"

"I doubt it, Marcel."

"We tried very hard together. Didn't we?"

"That we did, Marcel."

"We have made a great picture. A classic. It'll play forever."

"I don't know, Marcel. You were great, but I think I might

245

have failed you. Your world of mime and my world of horror may not mix. Only the audience will tell us."

We continued to walk in silence. Soft waves lapped against the hard sand. A gull with black-tipped wings soared gracefully overhead—perfection in movement. Marcel Marceau. A harsh screech from the gull pierced the quiet—a scream of terror. My world.

CHAPTER XXVIII

Nobody Loves a Cockroach

PUBLIC tastes are fickle, and it is impossible to predict with any accuracy, a year in advance, what an audience will line up for. Most of the studios were gearing themselves for a year of disaster, terror and fear. *The Exorcist* had broken box-office records and proved anew that the public would line up and pay money to have the wits scared out of them.

I felt 1975 would be a big year for me if I could find the right material for a film. Universal Pictures had announced *Earthquake,* with a gimmick called "Sensurround," which gave audiences the feeling of being part of the film. Fox was preparing *The Towering Inferno,* and Zanuck/Brown had bought the rights to Peter Benchley's *Jaws.* It was going to be one helluva frightening year, and I wanted to be part of it.

In searching for an idea, something to really make audiences cringe, I again began delving into the human psyche to find the answer. At a dinner party I attended, a well-known psychiatrist, knowing I had made a career of frightening people, suggested that I was trying to get rid of my own fears by passing them into audiences throughout the world. Lying deep in my unconscious, he suggested, was some terrifying incident that happened when I was very young.

I assured him I had no deeply hidden fears. But I knew otherwise. My life had been built on fear. I probably would never really find out why audiences liked to be frightened; I

247

doubted that anyone actually knew. But I did know what scared them: something they could relate to, something *real*.

In the novel *The Hephaestus Plague* by Thomas Page, I found the possibilities of a truly horrifying premise. As usual, I had very little money to work with, and I knew I would be in competition with the multimillion-dollar disaster films the other studios were preparing. *The Hephaestus Plague* had a common denominator that everyone in the world could relate to, something which evoked universal repulsion—*the cockroach.*

Everyone at some time or another has encountered these unwelcome creatures. *The Hephaestus Plague* added extra elements to the roaches by magnifying their already revolting presence. During an earthquake, they surfaced from the bowels of the earth. They looked like rocks—had no eyes, ate ashes, traveled in car exhaust pipes, made fire. They were superintelligent, ate meat—and *killed!*

A title for a motion picture should have impact, should create a verbal image of what the picture is about, and should be easy to remember. Personally, I like one-word titles. *Jaws. Exorcist. Earthquake. The Hephaestus Plague* proved a problem title from the start.

Hephaestus, the Greek god of fire, was almost impossible to pronounce, much less to remember. When it was announced I was casting the picture, anxious actors would call to ask about the "Hepatitis Plague" or the "Hibiscus Plague." The title would have to go. Searching for a new one was not an easy task. Perhaps I was trying too hard. One evening my daughter Terry, annoyed with her sister, snapped, "Don't bug me," and suddenly I had the title—*Bug.* One word, easy to remember, and telling exactly what the picture was about.

The next hurdle was to cast the bugs themselves. Today's audiences were too sophisticated for the mechanical creatures of the fifties, the era of the supersized, studio-made tarantulas, spiders, crabs, scorpions, etc. I knew I had to find the real thing—*huge, live, ominous-looking bugs.*

I finished the script and signed the director—Jeannot

248

Szwarc, a young, talented Frenchman. The cast was picked: Bradford Dillman, Joanna Miles, Patty McCormack, Richard Gilliland and Jamie Smith Jackson. We had even chosen the cameraman, Michele Hugo. Everything was ready for production—except the bugs.

Marge Pinns, my executive assistant (Dona Holloway retired after marrying Louis Lichtenfield, a successful artist), announced that a lady from the MPAA, the organization that rates films, was on the phone.

"Good afternoon, Mr. Castle," a soft, cultured voice purred. "I'd like to discuss the scene in the film where the bugs set fire to Sylvia and then start to eat her face. . . ."

"What's wrong with that scene?" I parried, "I think it's beautiful."

"And the part where they chew off her head and it rolls on the kitchen floor—don't you think that's a little much?"

"The audiences will love it! Every kid in America will be up all night."

"That's what we're afraid of, Mr. Castle. . . ."

"Marge," I screamed, "everything's ready to go except the bugs. We'll need hundreds of them . . . maybe thousands. . . . Where in the hell am I going to find them?"

"I think I know the one man who can help you."

"Who?" I demanded.

"Ken Middleham. When I worked on *Hellstrom Chronicle* at Wolper Productions, Ken did the insect photography. He's a genius."

"Get him on the phone."

Ken Middleham, director of photography at the University of California in Riverside, was soon on the phone. "Mr. Middleham, I'm making a picture about ten-inch bugs that surface after an earthquake. Each cockroach is capable of belching fire from his behind. They eat carbon and travel in car exhausts. . . . Their swarm is relentless and unstoppable. . . . Scientists struggle to destroy them and unless they are successful in finding a deterrent, America will be burned to the ground. For God's sake, Mr. Middleham, can you help me?"

"No sweat," he replied calmly. I had found my man.

"Oh, and Mr. Middleham . . . before you hang up . . . the roaches are also blind and can't breed. Also, they eat raw meat."

"Still no sweat. When can we meet?"

Hundreds of large incendiary bugs were on the march, and I was their leader. Certainly not the most popular man in Riverside, California, but certainly the most dangerous one, I was now called "King of the Bugs."

Mr. Ken Middleham
University of Calif. Riverside
Riverside, Calif.

Dear Ken,

Thank you for the demonstration. "Ripley would never have believed it." And they actually make fire. My congratulations.

Regards,
Bill Castle

P.S. I question only one thing in your itemized bill—25 pounds of meat! How much meat can the cockroaches eat? We're on a tight budget.

"They're only six inches." I was sitting in Ken's lab in Riverside. "Is there any way of getting them to grow?"

"Stretch 'em." Ken laughed.

"I'm serious. They've got to be ten inches."

"I'll see what I can do, Bill. . . . Maybe feed them more raw meat."

Memo to: Legal Dept. Paramount Pictures
    From: Bill Castle

250

Gene, do we really have to take out fire insurance because of those cockroaches?

"Bill, I have a problem."

"What problem?" *As if I didn't know.* I was sitting on the set
talking to Jeannot Szwarc, the director.

"Joanna Miles is deathly afraid of cockroaches. She doesn't
want them crawling on her. What'll we do?"

"For chrissake, didn't we put in her contract that they
would set fire to her?" I barked.

"She hasn't signed her contract . . . yet. You'd better talk
to her, Bill."

"Joanna," I said sweetly, "the cockroaches are perfectly
harmless. . . . Watch, I'll show you." Picking up one of the
monsters, I placed it on my arm. "Joanna, darling . . .
they're perfectly harmless. . . . Watch how gently it
crawls. . . . Jesus, the sonofabitch bit me! . . .

"Brad, they crawl out of the box, move across the room,
then get onto your bare chest. You're sleeping, see, and you
don't feel them crawling over you. Brad, I promise we'll use
artificial blood. No, Brad, I guarantee it won't be yours. . . .

"Jamie, so the goddamn cockroach gets into your ear—
what's the big deal about that? It's not going to really burn
your ear. . . . What do you mean, if we can't get it out? . . .
That's why we have a doctor on the set. . . .

"Ken, fifty roaches write the name 'Parmiter' on the wall
with their bodies. Also, 'X, Y, and Z,' and the words 'We
Live.' Ken, it's *not impossible.* We never use that word in the
picture business. You'll think of something."

"Fellas, I've used a gimmick in all my pictures and *Bug* is
no exception." We were in a publicity meeting with Bob
Goodfried, vice-president in charge of studio and West Coast
publicity. Impatiently pacing the office, I suddenly turned
and excitedly walked over to Goodfried. Kneeling down, I
started slowly to move my fingers gently across his legs.
"What does that feel like, Bob? Tell me . . . what am I?"

251

"Homosexual?" Bob politely suggested.

"No, no, Bob. I'm a cockroach . . . ten inches . . . and I'm crawling over your legs. Close your eyes and I'll try again. . . . What does it feel like?"

"Certainly not a cockroach," Bob stammered, turning red. "And please cut it out!"

"Fellas, I have a brilliant idea. If we can manufacture thousands of tiny windshield wipers . . . you know, the kind used in cars, but much smaller . . . and install them underneath theatre seats . . . at high points of *Bug*, when the roaches are loose, the projectionist will push a button and the tiny windshield wipers will brush across the legs of the audience. It'll scare them half to death," I announced proudly.

TIME MAGAZINE
July 1974

Show Business: "A PREVIEW OF COMING
AFFLICTIONS"

The Hephaestus Plague, (Bug), a double whammy in which another earthquake disgorges thousands of carbon-munching giant cockroaches from the bowels of the earth.

"We are breeding and training real South American bugs," says Producer William Castle. Reminded, perhaps of the "feelies" of Huxley's *Brave New World*—in which audiences were electronically tuned in to experience the physical impact of every love scene and head-bonking shown on the screen—Castle is planning a floor-mounted windshield wiper device that will softly brush across moviegoers' feet and ankles at crucial moments.

(My idea for the windshield wipers would never actually be used. Exhibitors felt the picture was terrifying enough and feared that audiences might panic if they felt anything brush across their legs. I didn't argue the point because I knew that

252

in some of the older theatres across America, the real things would crawl across the patrons' legs at no cost.)

Fascinated, I watched Ken put his roaches through their tricks. He was indeed a genius. They had actually grown in size.

"Bill, we have a problem." Ken sounded dejected. "It just won't work." He retreated into glum silence.

"What won't work?" I asked. "You've done a fantastic job."

"The script calls for the third generation to be fourteen-inch flying roaches with a wingspan of twenty-four inches . . . and they have to be bright red!"

"We can change their color," I said, trying to be helpful.

"That's the least of my worries. There's no insect that size alive *anywhere* that can fly."

"We could paint bats red," I suggested.

"Impossible—they'd look like bats. You can't change their shape . . . besides, they wouldn't fly if we painted them red."

"How about a thousand red balloons filled with helium?" I suggested.

"They'd look like red balloons. It looks like you're going to have to write the flying bugs out of the script, Bill."

"No way," I said. "They're the climax of the picture. You'll come up with something, Ken, I know you will. Please try."

Several days later, Ken called me on the set. "I've been doing some experimenting," he reported. "I think I may be onto something."

"What?" I eagerly asked.

"Flies—regular household flies."

"But they're going to look just like flies."

"Not when I finish photographing them. I've made some tests."

We looked at the tests in Ken's small projection room. The ordinary flies looked enormous.

"Jesus, they look fourteen inches long. And look at those wings! They're huge! . . . but they're black, Ken. Can we paint them red?"

"I tried that," Ken said sadly, "but they died."

"How about red talcum powder?"

"I doubt if it's light enough . . . insects can't fly with anything on them."

"Try it, Ken. What have you got to lose?"

One week later, Ken called with the news. "I got some phosphorescent powder and sprinkled it on the flies."

"And?" I asked.

"I got *red* flies. . . . Hold on for a second—I want to try something. . . ." Coming back on the line a minute later, "Congratulations, Bill, they're flying."

"Promise me, Ken, that you'll never tell *anybody* how you achieved this miracle. Audiences must not find out they're only flies with red powder."

(When *Bug* opened I would announce that the huge, red-winged creatures were live monsters, captured at great personal risk and brought over from the dense Amazon jungles.)

"Ken, can you get some blue and green phosphorescent powder?"

"Why . . . what for? Is there a new generation coming up?"

"I think I could pull a great publicity stunt. . . . Now here's what I want you to do. . . ."

During the lunch hour in downtown Riverside, Ken and I, in keeping with the Christmas spirit, let loose hundreds of gaily powdered red, blue, and green flies.

The telephone lines in Riverside were tied up for hours with reports to the police of red, blue and green flying objects that looked like flies . . . but weren't; of flying creatures from outer space. . . .

"Bob, I want to take out an insurance policy for Hercules." I was talking to Bob Yeager, the unit publicist on the picture.

"You must be kidding," he laughed.

"I'm serious. A one-million-dollar life-insurance policy. Find me an insurance broker that will insure a cockroach!"

Insured: Hercules Bug   Age: 1 year
Owner: William Castle

Policy No: 746648

Face Amount: $1,000,000
Date of Issue: December 24, 1974

Beneficiary: Any proceeds payable because of the death of the Insured will be paid to the Beneficiary. Unless changed as provided in this Policy, the Beneficiary shall be as designated in the application for this Policy. And additional benefit is provided by rider and is subject to the provisions of the rider.

Initial Premium: $5,000

SUPER BUG . . . Producer William Castle insures his star performer, "Hercules," with Hollywood's first million-dollar cockroach policy, issued by Los Angeles insurance broker Joel Nelson. The policy, insuring the acting bug's life, covers the one-month period when Castle and Hercules leave on a nationwide promotion tour to plug the producer's science-fiction shocker. It is valid only if the cockroach dies a natural death during the trip. It excludes any unnatural or violent demise. Like being squashed under an unfriendly heel, or perishing from food poisoning, expiring on a plane because of the altitude, etc. If, by any chance, Hercules does go to the big kitchen sink in the sky, a group of entomology scientists will be called in to determine the cause of death. Incidentally, Hercules is one year old, and the normal life span of such a cockroach is five years—that is, if it doesn't embark on any promotion tours for Hollywood movies.

Once again, I was going on tour to exploit a motion picture. I was back in my element. Hercules and I, bags packed, were ready to hit the road for personal appearances.

L-a-d-i-e-s and G-e-n-t-l-e-m-e-n . . .

STEP RIGHT UP . . . Meet the Mighty Hercules . . . *Gigantic! Stupendous! Extraordinary!* You will see him on the screen in feats that are mind-boggling. He will be the leader of fifty giant cockroaches who, with their bodies, will write on the wall the alphabet and then form the words, "We Live." This is not a trick, folks—this is *real!* You will also witness the crawly creatures, led by Hercules, eat human flesh and miraculously belch fire from their rear ends. . . . But, before you go on the inside and see the picture . . . Step a little closer, folks. For absolutely free, Hercules will now demonstrate the art of how he makes fire! Watch his rear end, folks—those tiny exhaust pipes. They're now starting to spark . . . starting to burn.

Buy your tickets at the box office now, ladies and gentlemen . . .

I'm gonna' scare the pants off America. . . .